3/43

HANDBOOK OF COMPUTER MANAGEMENT

Handbook of Computer Management

R.B.YEARSLEY and G.M.R.GRAHAM

Gower Press

First published in Great Britain by Gower Press Limited
Epping, Essex
1973

ISBN 0 7161 0095 9

Computerised origination by Autoset, Brentwood, Essex
Printed in Great Britain by
Redwood Press Limited
Trowbridge, Wiltshire

Contents

Management and organisation
Planning
Project planning
Controlling
Budgeting, charging and recovery of costs

Illustrations

Notes on Contributors

Ronald Yearsley is a Director of Brandon Applied Systems Limited. He has worked with computers for over nine years. He was concerned with the early development of computer applications in the education and social services field. He has been involved with consultancy for over four years specialising in the personnel, training and organisational problems of the computer industry. His other positions include being an Editor and joint owner of *Management Decision*, Visiting Lecturer at the Bradford University Business School, and editor of several widely acclaimed books on computers and management subjects. He is also a director of Business Intelligence Services Limited (BIS).

Roger Graham is Managing Director of Brandon Applied Systems Limited and a director of Business Intelligence Services Limited (BIS). His involvement with computers and data processing has spread over ten years. He has planned and implemented large-scale information system feasibility studies, organisation planning, preparation of equipment specifications and selection of equipment assignments. He has also held responsibility for the design and implementation of data processing applications. Working in the United States as well as Britain, he has had experience of most types of industrial and commercial environment including manufacturing and distribution companies, finance and government departments. Writing and lecturing on data processing subjects figure prominently amongst his activities.

Bill Brooks is Computer Manager of the Guided Weapons Division of British Aircraft Corporation. A graduate of New York University in industrial engineering with twenty-five years' business experience, he has lectured throughout North America and Mexico on work measurement and method study for the American Management Association by whom he was awarded a silver medal for making 'an outstanding contribution to management education'. He is currently managing a large computer installation on a bureau basis and has been concerned with creating and implementing computer operating standards.

Martin Christopher (Computers in marketing) is a Lecturer in Quantitative Aspects of Marketing at the University of Bradford Management Centre. He has lectured and written widely on the application of quantitative methods in marketing analysis and planning in addition to which he acts as consultant to a number of UK companies. Mr Christopher is European Editor of the *International Journal of Physical Distribution.* His book, *Total Distribution,* was published by Gower Press in 1971.

Alan H Duncan (Benchmark testing) started programming on the ICT HEC2 in 1958 at the Boscombe Down aircraft test establishment. He was responsible for the analysis of test data, including work on the TSR2 and a real-time on-line system. In 1965, he joined Barclays Bank in charge of computer planning, systems and programming, where he installed the Barclaycard system. At present, he is Head of Planning and Research.

Roy Fabian (Computers in finance and accounting) is a management consultant and a director of Cooper Brothers & Company Ltd. He did his early training in the profession and subsequently spent five years in industry and commerce, where he became involved in data processing from the accountant's point of view. He then managed a data processing service bureau for two years before joining his present company of which he was appointed a director in 1958. In this latter capacity he has controlled assignments of various types, such as on organisation, management accounting, clerical work management and computers, while he has been in charge of the EDP function in the company with responsibility for a large staff of computer specialists.

Basil de Ferranti is on the board of Ferranti Limited. After leaving Cambridge he took a graduate apprenticeship course and in 1954 he joined Ferranti Limited, where he became Manager of Domestic Appliances in Manchester. He was appointed a director of Ferranti Limited in 1957 and from then until 1962 held the appointment of Director of Overseas Operations. In September 1963, at the time of the merger of the Computer Department of Ferranti Limited with ICT, he was appointed Deputy Managing Director of International Computers &

Tabulators Limited. He was appointed Managing Director from 1 December 1964 and in February was made responsible for all strategic issues, and a director of International Computers Limited until 1972. Mr de Ferranti sat as the Member of Parliament for Morecombe and Lonsdale from 1958-64. From July to October 1962, he was Parliamentary Secretary, Ministry of Aviation, but he resigned to avoid conflict of interest. He was President of the British Computer Society for 1968-9. He is a Fellow of the Institution of Electrical Engineers and became an honorary doctor of science of City University in 1970.

Geoffrey Holland (Service bureaux and time sharing) graduated in electrical engineering in 1959 and then spent three years in the electrical industry before changing to computer services in 1962. He has held appointments in sales and marketing with ITT Data Services, Management Dynamics and English Electric Computers.

Peter Hunt (Survey of computing systems) is Managing Director of Leasco Systems and Research Company Limited which he has developed into one of the largest software houses in the UK. He is also Managing Director of the Leasco software subsidiaries in Germany, Holland and Belgium. Before joining Leasco, Mr Hunt was in charge of all software development at ICL for the 1900 series computers.

G P Jacobs (Computers for managing information) has worked with computers for ten years as a programmer, systems analyst, lecturer, manager and consultant. His experience covers a wide range of applications, both batch processing and real-time for commercial organisations and service bureaux. He is currently a Senior Consultant in Logica's Turnkey Division.

Alan Jenkin (Choosing software) graduated from Oxford University with an honours degree in physics in 1956. He worked for eight years with Esso in England, the USA and Australia. During this time he worked on process engineering, planning and economics work, and the use of computing in both the oil and petrochemical industries. He joined Scicon in 1964, and has worked mainly on mathematical modelling and large system implementation. For a period he was manager of the Division responsible for the development and marketing of packages. He is currently Sales Support Manager of Scicon Computer Services. He has lectured to various organisations and government departments, has published several articles and is a part-time lecturer and examiner in computer science at the University of London.

Murray Laver (Facilities management) began his career in 1935 at the Post Office Research Station, first developing standards of frequency and time; later coaxial-cable systems for speech and television. He moved to the Radio Planning Branch in 1951 to work on radio, broadcasting and television systems. In 1956 he began the engineering appraisal of commercial computer systems, and helped to launch the use of computers by the Post Office. He transferred to H M Treasury in 1963 in charge of the O & M Division responsible for advising on the use and purchases of computers by government departments. Mr Laver moved to the Ministry of Technology in 1965 to set up its Computer Advisory Service and was later Director of its Computer Division. He returned to the Post Office in 1968 as Director of the National Data Processing Service, and is now the Board Member for Data Processing.

S J Macoustra (Training for data processing) is a supervising consultant with Brandon Applied Systems Limited. He holds a master's degree in business administration and has been responsible for the design of career structures and training programmes for the European staff of an international computer manufacturer. Mr Macoustra has worked on almost every aspect of computer development during the last ten years. His career has included original research in programming and he has lectured throughout West and Eastern Europe.

John Roger Mills (Choosing software) is currently a director of two software houses and has application package development and marketing responsibilities. Educated at the LSE and the Graduate Centre for Management Studies, Birmingham University, he has had an extensive data processing career, starting in 1960 with the CEGB. He has also held senior appointments in British Rail, the National Computing Centre Limited and the Post Office National Data Processing Service. As a Fellow of the BCS he serves on the Systems Examination Board and also acts as an examiner to the Society.

D A Milner (Computers in production management) is a graduate of the University of London. He started his career as a trainee engineer with a medium-sized firm manufacturing a wide range of products. Subsequently he spent further time in the engineering industry engaged on mechanical and production systems. Mr Milner then entered the teaching profession and has lectured extensively to mechanical and production engineering students. At present he is engaged on computing and control theory lecturing to the undergraduate and post-graduate students in the Department of Production Engineering at the University of Aston.

D W Moore (Computer consultants) is a partner of the management consultancy firm of Peat, Marwick, Mitchell & Co. Before joining the firm, he was the manager of the Data Processing Development Department of Shell Mex and BP and before that he was responsible for the Royal Army Pay Corps project at Worthy Down. In addition to being the partner primarily responsible for data processing, Mr Moore is also involved with studies in several overseas countries and courses of the Institute of Chartered Accountants, British Computer Society and a wide range of clients.

Michael Naughton (Installation audits) worked in finance in Shell International in various overseas postings after graduating from Oxford. He then joined GEC, and worked in programming and systems analysis before becoming Manager of a major computing centre. There he directed the implementation of a wide range of systems including an engineering data base, stock control, network-based production control, costing and financial suites. Joining Brandon Applied Systems, he worked on the installation of Brandon standards and project control in various major companies, carried out installation review and forward planning assignments, and controlled a number of consultancy and implementation tasks including real-time multi-VDU systems.

Eric Oliver (Security of the computer installation) is Security Adviser to Unilever Limited. He served in the Metropolitan Police from 1930 to 1959 and gained extensive experience of commercial security, whilst in charge of investigating offences against banks at the Central Department, New Scotland Yard and as detective superintendent in the Yard's Company Fraud Department. Mr Oliver is a Governor and Fellow of the Institution of Industrial Security. He and John Wilson wrote *Practical Security in Commerce and Industry* (Gower Press, 1972) and *Security Manual* (Gower Press, 1968). Their chapter in this handbook is taken from the second edition of *Practical Security in Commerce and Industry*.

R J Oliver (Third-party computer leasing). After an Honours Degree in English at Lincoln College, Oxford, Richard Oliver joined IBM in 1955, where he served in a variety of management and marketing functions, until joining Leasco in 1968. He is now Managing Director of Leasco Limited, and Executive Vice President of Leasco Europa Ltd.

Eddie Parish (Computers in inventory management) joined International Computers Limited from the measurement and control industry in 1955 after a number of years in works management. Since then his main interests have been production and inventory control systems. After nearly ten years advising on customer problems, he led the development of the ICL SCAN applications package for inventory control. He has lectured widely both at home and abroad and is currently developing and running new-style courses using company models for business systems training at ICL's training centre near Windsor.

John Smith (Computers for planning and control) was an operational research consultant with Scientific Control Systems Limited (formerly CEIR Limited). He was previously employed as an operational research analyst at BEA, which he joined in 1960. He has spent most of his time working in the field of computer simulation and has had extensive experience of developing and running models to solve many types of problems. He has recently been concerned with the Roskill Commission on the third London Airport and is currently Software Coordinator with the Plessy Electronics Group.

Kenneth Smith (Survey of computing systems) graduated as an electrical engineer at Kings College London in 1946. After an initial career in communications engineering, he entered the computer industry in 1954 with Powers-Samas where he was responsible for electronic computer research. Since 1958 he has been with IBM UK Limited, initially as Manager of Special Engineering at the Hursley Laboratories, and has occupied many positions in the Marketing Division of that Company since 1961. Currently he is Product Line Manager for Communications and Special Systems. A member of the Council of the British Computer Society, he is a serving member of the Membership Board and Chairman of the Publications Committee and has been actively involved in many other groups within BCS.

Richard Soper (Choosing software) graduated from Imperial College London in 1956 with a degree in mathematics. After spending four years with the De Havilland Aircraft Company as an aerodynamist he joined IBM (UK) Limited as a systems engineer. Later he became a systems engineering manager and then

Branch Manager in Welwyn Garden. From 1967 until leaving IBM in December 1969 he was a Staff Marketing Manager in IBM (UK) Head Office. Richard Soper was until recently Managing Director of Hoskyns Systems Research Limited and President of Hoskyns Systems Research Incorporated, the American subsidiary.

Humphrey Sturt (Staffing and job specification) is Personnel Planning and Salary Policy Manager of IBM United Kingdom Ltd. After graduating from Oxford University he worked in South-east Asia as a manager in an insurance group before entering data processing as a systems executive with International Computers Ltd. Subsequently he founded and was chief executive of ASAP Limited, a consulting practice specialising in the selection of computer staff and technical management.

David Tebbs (Selecting a computer & Control and management standards) is a director of Brandon Applied Systems Limited. After graduating from Cambridge, he started his career in data processing in 1958. He has carried out, supervised and directed a wide range of computer projects including feasibility studies, system design, programming and implementation work. He has directed the development of standards for controlling data processing departments and has installed these procedures in various organisations. He has been particularly involved in computer production control and real-time applications. Prior to joining Brandon he created a real time system and programming centre of competence for a major manufacturer. He has lectured extensively on data processing subjects and has presented a series of lectures in Australia, New Zealand, South Africa, Eire and Holland on real time and data base systems.

Michael Thornley (Budgeting, planning and control of computer activities) first became involved with computers in 1959 after a period in professional accountancy. His initial experience concentrated on the application of large-scale computers and real-time systems. He has spent some six years as a management consultant and, for two years, was a director of the Diebold Group operating in the United States of America. He is now Management Services Controller of The Rank Organisation.

John Wilson (Security of the computer installation) is Company Security Officer for Yorkshire Imperial Metals Limited. He is responsible for the overall security of the company's Leeds site and advises the managers of other factories on prosecutions and security aspects of new construction. Mr Wilson was a detective chief inspector in Leeds City Police. He and Eric Oliver wrote *Security Manual* (Gower Press, 1968) and *Practical Security in Commerce and Industry* (Gower Press, 1972) from the second edition of which their chapter in this handbook is taken.

D A Yeates is Training and Standards Coordinator in the Central Computer Services Department of the British Oxygen Company. Following a degree in economics and seven years' business and DP experience with a major user in engineering, he spent nearly four years with National Computing Centre Limited, finishing as the head of the Professional and Schools Education Department. Other activities include membership of the Council of British Computer Society and of the Education Board and Systems Analysis Examination Board. He has contributed a number of articles in journals and is joint editor of a book, *Basic Training in Systems Analysis.*

Foreword

B.Z. de Ferranti

A brief look at the likely responsibility of the data processing manager will reveal that he is probably undertrained, and perhaps even underpaid, for the job that he is expected to do.

He will be expected to advise on the department budget, on the selection of staff and on whether to use applications packages or write programs in-house. He may be expected to evaluate proposals from different manufacturers and possibly organise benchmark tests to assess performance. He will be responsible for ensuring that his staff receive adequate training to keep them fully conversant with the state of the art, and he will also want to ensure that they observe well-defined standards in all their working procedures so that disruption is minimised in the event of staff leaving. He will also be expected to be realistic enough to recognise when his in-house capability is inadequate to meet requirements, and in that case to be able to assess software companies, bureaux and consultants. He will be expected to advise on data input methods, on file organisations and data bases, and on which high-level languages are implemented in the system. Above all, he will be responsible for establishing the place of the data processing department within the organisation.

The data processing manager's problems are not confined to man-machine communications, but extend to human problems not only within but outside his own department. When new systems are being implemented delicate negotiations may have to be conducted with unions, for example, and while the data processing manager may not be directly responsible, his advice will be vital. And in carrying out these activities the data processing manager in a large organisation will rub shoulders with specialists from many different disciplines—engineers, accountants, production men and so on. He will need to be able to translate their often obscure requirements into concrete data processing proposals.

The present trend towards multi-access systems may also exacerbate the problems of the data processing manager. Where a system of this type is implemented the user cannot be kept out of the computer room while his job is being processed as in batch processing installations—he will be there in the spirit if not in the flesh and when things go wrong he will want them put right there and then.

I hope I have said enough to indicate that the role of the computer manager has become a vital element in running a modern business. Unfortunately it is a field where very little expertise has crystallised, largely because data processing has been moving too fast for this to happen.

I am sure that this handbook does not set out to convert the computer tiro into the computer manager par excellence overnight. Instead it has filled a noticeable void by bringing together, in concise form, up-to-date knowledge and views from recognised authorities on virtually every subject that is of direct interest to data processing managers. It will be a valuable addition to their bookshelves.

Editors' Preface

This book offers between two covers the quintessence of some of the most recent developments in computer technology. It was originally compiled for the senior manager—the person whom research has shown is most in need of this information but has the least chance of obtaining it. There are two equally significant sectors of business towards which this volume is also directed. First, the specialist or staff manager who seeks an understanding of the general patterns of computing which impinge on his current work. Secondly, there is the rapidly growing body of HND, undergraduate and postgraduate students of business and management to whom this book will be useful—sometimes as an introduction to, and sometimes for a quick appreciation of, the techniques described.

Computers are used in commerce in a variety of ways and it is the inflexibility of the machines which make them a problem to the businessman. Here is a machine which can be programmed to perform a wealth of different tasks, many of which will not have been thought of when the decision to install a computer is taken.

In this book we look at some of the commonest areas of computer application and see the sort of problems that computers are being asked to solve. The very nature of these routine commercial tasks has forced great changes on the evolution of computers, which began life as laboratory calculators. Probably the greatest development that has taken place is the change of emphasis from the speed of calculation, so vital to the scientist, to the size and accessibility of data storage facilities, so important to the businessman.

The files stored by computers may contain data for accounting, marketing or manufacturing applications; they may be full of names and addresses, or stock records, or overseas orders. Whatever their content, as well as being files of data they hold information that is useful to management. But can the computer organise and present this information when it is required—which is often at very short notice? It is not a static problem, because as files of stored information become larger and more complex, so the science of information processing must become more sophisticated.

The commonest area for the application of computers is in accounting. This is because there are strong historical reasons for starting with accounting work when a computer is first installed. It may be replacing existing accounting machinery, it may be that the most obvious savings can be made in the accounts department, it may be that the computer comes under the direct control of the chief accountant. Whatever reasons, and they are not necessarily the right ones, computers spend a great deal of time on accounting work.

It is now widely appreciated that computers are far more than just accounting machines, keeping track of and reporting on events of the past. They are much more likely to show real profits when they are used to control events of the present. Their response to external factors which affect a system which they control is so much faster and more accurate than that of a human controller that for the day-to-day decisions involved in the operation of a warehouse or factory they can be far superior.

The book covers the role computers are playing in controlling the men and machines involved in manufacturing processes. Again it is the speed of response together with the ability to hold and consider incredible quantities of detail that enables the computer to be such a valuable management tool.

Other projects which have to be controlled are not of a day-to-day nature and require special treatment. They may be the launching of a new product, the building of a new factory or even the installation of a computer. Techniques to help management to control such 'one-off' projects have been evolved under the general heading of critical path techniques. Again the quick response of a computer, enabling the whole plan to be reappraised and rescheduled when outside influences rock the boat is of vital importance.

Management must, however, do more than control the present. There is a constant need to predict the future as well. Very often the facts are available in order to make a reasonable shot at this, but the mathematical techniques are so involved and laborious that there is neither the time nor the calculating power available to make use of them. Management then has to plan using experience and intuition as guides, usually arriving at a satisfactory solution but seldom at an optimum solution. Mathematicians have inevitably moved into commerce along with computers, and under the general title of operations research have evolved exact analytical methods by which optimum solutions can be obtained to many of managements' problems of prediction.

However, in some cases exact methods of solution are not available, or the problem is so involved that to obtain an exact solution would take many days of calculation even on a computer. Computers can still assist management to plan for the future by means of simulation techniques. This means making the computer simulate the problem; literally building a model in mathematical terms which behaves as closely as possible to the real-life situation. Management can then experiment with the model, trying the effect of various courses of action and using the computer's speed to condense the timescale into a few seconds or minutes.

Computer technology itself is no panacea for the problems of management today. What is needed is the realism that can only be generated from a position of *understanding* the technology which exists for professional management.

The Editors
London, March 1972

Acknowledgements

We wish at the outset of this book to acknowledge the help and encouragement we have received from our colleagues in Brandon Applied Systems Ltd. Many have been in no way directly involved in this book, but it was through their continual support and encouragement of our efforts that we undertook to extend this understanding of management technology. We wish also to thank our wives for their assistance in the preparation of typescripts, bibliographies, and the glossary of terms.

In the editing of this volume our work has been greatly facilitated by the ready cooperation of all our contributors—busy men, many of them authors already in their own right. Their enthusiasm has once again emphasised the deep sense of frustration so many specialists feel when confronted with a lack of understanding of their subject on the part of general management. We should also like to acknowledge, on behalf of the authors, the debt we all owe to the originators of many of the techniques and concepts discussed here. It is in the nature of this volume that we have not included extensive references.

PART 1

Survey of computing systems

1

Modern Computing Systems

K.L.Smith and P.M.Hunt

The electronic digital computer has developed dramatically over the last twenty-five years from the simple programmed calculator of the late 1940s to the sophisticated real-time system of today. The industry surrounding the computer has developed equally dramatically until today we see it challenging the size and growth of the automobile and petroleum industries. However, the computer has a far more profound effect on the society and industries it serves and many managers feel they can only retain (or perhaps regain) control of their operations through the use of data processing systems. A gourmet can enjoy his food without understanding the physics of digestion, but a wise gourmet at least understands enough of the physics to avoid indigestion. Likewise a manager must understand the basic principles of data processing system if he too is to avoid the very uncomfortable indigestion which can result from their ill-informed and incompetent application.

The objectives of this chapter are to present the essential features of modern computing systems in a simple concise form to help in a better understanding of the type of services such systems can offer a business in today's very complex environment.

Basic principle of register-to-register arithmetic

The simplest form of mechanised calculation is to be found in the traditional desk calculator. In this a number is set up manually on a keyboard (or input register), added to the contents of another register via a simple adding device

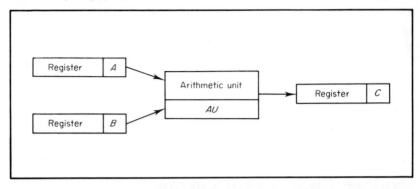

Figure 1:1 Simple register-to-register arithmetic. In a practical machine, registers *B* and *C* are the same physical device. The contents of *C* represent the new state of *B* after *A* has been added to it.

(arithmetic unit) and the results passed to a further register (the accumulator) whose contents are displayed on a simple indicator.

The principle is demonstrated diagrammatically in Figure 1:1.

Several important principles can be identified in this simple device:

1   Transferring data from register to register via an arithmetic unit, enables that data to be manipulated. A range of arithmetic operations (addition, subtraction, multiplication and so on) can be provided which are limited only by the cost of constructing a device to carry them out and the ingenuity of the designer.

2   The operator can implement a large number of complex calculations by a sequence of the primitive operations described above. Such a sequence of operations is known as a *program.*

3   The speed of operation is determined by the technology used in the physical implementation of the principle. In a desk calculator the technology is based on mechanical gears and gives a speed which is quite adequate for the type of direct manual control employed. The overall performance of the calculator is equally determined directly by the technology employed.

Simple electronic computer

The electronic computer uses exactly the same principle of register-to-register arithmetic as employed in the desk calculator. The use of electronic techniques to implement the registers and arithmetic units permits much faster operation, but no longer permits the sequencing of the calculation to be under direct operator control. A means has to be found to instruct the machine at electronic speeds. The obvious extension is to store the instructions or program within the machine in exactly the same way as the data is stored. It is this simple principle which made the electronic computer technically feasible in the first instance and is the basis of its tremendous power and flexibility.

The method of use of the computer differs completely from the desk calculator because of the need to determine, beforehand, the sequence of calculations to be carried out and the associated need to have the data itself already available in the machine before the start of the calculation sequence. Clearly more storage units than the basic three registers of the mechanical calculator are needed. The technique is to make available a bank of a large number of storage units. In modern machines, as many as a million storage units (or locations) are provided in the store. Each of these locations is given a number, called its address.

The electronic computer can be represented diagrammatically as in Figure 1:2.

The circuitry of the arithmetic unit carries out the basic operations (addition, multiplication, and so on) that the computer can perform.

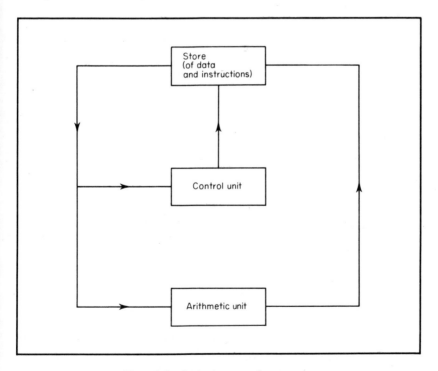

Figure 1:2   Basic elements of a computer

The control unit takes instructions from the program in the store, interprets them and initiates the appropriate operations.

Both the control unit and the arithmetic unit operate at very high speeds (up to ten million operations per second) but the speed of operation of the computer is limited by the time it takes to obtain data from the store to operate on (the *access* time). Rapid-access stores are expensive and so it is usual to divide the computer's storage capacity between a small, rapid-access store (the *memory*) and cheaper stores with slower access, called backing stores. The backing stores are based on magnetic recording, and are either tape recorders or 'disk packs', which look like large auto-change record players.

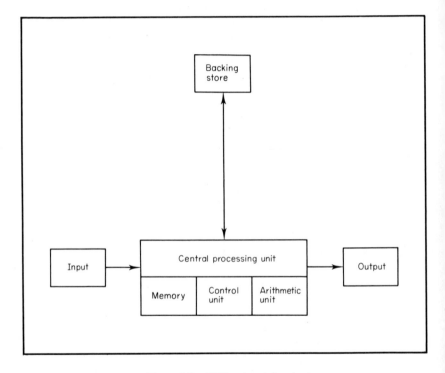

Figure 1:3   CPU and peripherals

The central memory, control unit and arithmetic unit are known collectively as the central processing unit (CPU) and form the 'brain' of the computer. The three units are usually housed together in one cabinet. The slow-access stores and devices for reading data into the computer (input) and for the computer to produce the results of its operations in a form that humans can read (output) are known as *peripherals* (see Figure 1:3).

Programs

The machine executes a calculation under the control of a program. The program itself comprises a number of individual instructions. If we consider the form of instructions we note that we need to specify:

1   The address of the locations containing the two operands *A* and *B*.
2   The addition or other operation to be executed.
3   Address of the location in which to place the result *C.*
4   The address of the next instruction in the program.

Thus a typical instruction would appear as in Figure 1:4. Different computers employ instructions of different format to that shown in Figure 1:4. Thus, in some machines the result *C* is sent back to one of the operand locations *A* or *B*. This enables the designer to reduce the size of his instruction and hence reduces the storage required for the program. The penalty is the loss of one of the original operands in the process.

Another form of simplification is to execute instructions sequentially. In this case, one does not need to specify separately the address of the next instruction. Instead a register records the number that is the address of the first instruction in the program. When that instruction has been read and performed, the control unit automatically instructs the register to add 1 to the number it is storing. The control unit then reads the register, which now gives the location of the second step in the program, and so on. If one needs to change the order of instructions from the strictly sequential mode then a simple instruction can be introduced which will tell the control unit where the address of the next instruction can be found. For this purpose, one of the operand addresses can be used.

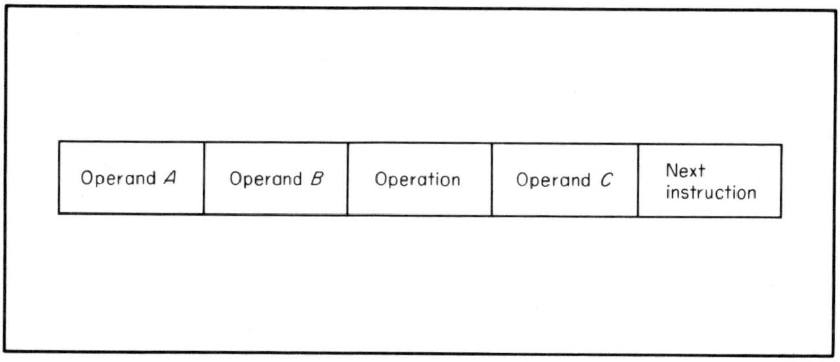

Operand *A*	Operand *B*	Operation	Operand *C*	Next instruction

Figure 1:4   Format of a typical four-address instruction

This permits the development of a powerful facility in all modern computers known as *branching*. Branching permits a programmer to switch the sequence of instructions to one of several alternatives according to the value of a particular parameter. This could be the amount of total income to decide which method of calculating tax should be employed. Another example could be different forms of calculating bonus according to the number of hours worked. The essential principle is that the value of a selected parameter in the data produced by the program can itself be used to switch the sequence of instructions in that program.

Furthermore since the instructions are recorded in exactly the same way as data, they can also be modified by the arithmetic unit. Thus addresses of instructions in the program can be changed by simple arithmetic manipulation. This enables given programs to apply to different data by modifying the addresses arithmetically. Many powerful computing techniques can be built up on these very simple principles.

Instruction set

The essential character of a computer is determined by the range of instructions made available within its repertoire. Thus a scientifically oriented machine will have a number of instructions to simplify the manipulation of mathematical formulae. On the other hand, a commercially oriented computer will have an instruction set to simplify the manipulation of files of data. Early computers were specialised to one type of application or the other. However, the development of micro-programming at Cambridge, gave systems designers a powerful tool to enable general-purpose computers to be oriented to a scientific or commercial performance under the control of the computer itself.

Micro-programming

The principle of micro-programming is simple to understand. Complex instructions, such as multiplying, can either be simulated within the machine by a sequence of more primitive instructions, such as addition, or can be implemented directly by a special-purpose electrical circuit in the machine. Micro-programming extends this principle one stage further. Most complex instructions can be built up from a primitive instruction set, the combination being known as a micro-program. The power of the technique, however, comes in its implementation. Instead of storing these series of primitive instructions which comprise the micro-program in the memory like other data, they are held in a special read-only store which can be accessed at a speed far higher than the basic rhythm of the machine. Thus it is possible to execute a micro-program at a much higher speed than a normal group of instructions (a sub-routine). Systems design in modern systems is invariably based on micro-programming, using a basic instruction set which probably has little resemblance to the more usual instructions in everyday arithmetic and selected to simplify the implementation of the micro-programs. The nature of the machine can be changed conveniently and cheaply by replacing the micro-program or allowing the user to select those he requires from a store.

Programming languages

Machine code

We have seen that a computer's program is stored in the memory and consists of a sequence of instructions to the control unit.

Memories are usually constructed of a number of pieces of magnetisable material called cores (hence the alternative name, core store, for the memory). The information that each core can give to the control unit is whether or not it is magnetised. Similarly, the elements of the arithmetic unit are designed to react, essentially, only to the presence or absence of electric current; the result they produce is either an electric pulse or nothing.

This binary—yes-or-no, presence-or-absence—characteristic of the elements of a computer forms the language in which it stores information. Each piece of data and every instruction must be coded as a string of 0s and 1s, each of which is recorded as one or other of the possible states of one core. Each item in the string is called a *bit* (from *bi*nary digi*t*, that is either 0 or 1).

To simplify the handling of information, storage locations in many computers are grouped together to store *words*, each of a standard number of bits. The control unit then deals with whole words. A particular size of word, the eight-bit 'byte', is used by a number of computer manufacturers.

A program that is written as a string of 0s and 1s for immediate execution by a computer is said to be in *machine code*. Each line of the program represents an instruction in a format like that shown in Figure 1:4. Different models of computer require different codes to initiate the same operation, depending on the design of the central processing unit. Also, different computers have different instruction formats. This means that a program written in the machine code of one computer is likely to be unintelligible to a different computer.

Autocodes

The opportunities for error when writing a program in binary notation are very great. The mere copying of an instruction such as:

$$101101 \qquad 100011001011$$

will induce errors of transposition and misplacement which are not evident until

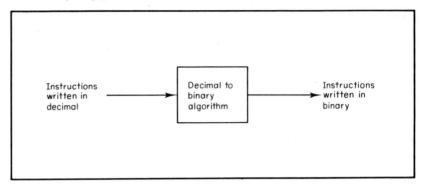

Figure 1:5   Principle of a translation program

the program fails to behave as intended, and even then it is extremely difficult to track them down.

Binary, however, is merely a number system based on 2, just as decimal is a number system based on 10. If the program could only be expressed in decimal rather than binary, the programmer would be dealing in terms with which, having ten fingers, he had been familar since childhood. Instead of the instruction:

$$101101 \qquad 1000110011011$$

he could now write the exact decimal equivalent:

$$45 \qquad 4507$$

It does not require an advanced knowledge of mathematics to realise that there must be a simple rule for transforming decimal notation into binary. Of more importance, any decimal number can be transformed into the equivalent binary number by application of this rule. Such transformation rules are called *algorithms*. In this case an algorithm, is needed to transform decimal into binary.

Figure 1:5 shows this concept in diagrammatic form. It is important to realise that the algorithm is accepting *data* and transforming it, although we know that this data will, when transformed, be used as a program. The program which is input to the algorithm is called the *source program*, and the result of the transformation is called the *object program*.

To enable a computer to undertake this transformation process, the algorithm has to be expressed as a series of instructions (an *assembly* program) which are loaded into the memory and executed. On execution, each source program instruction (written in decimal) is read by the assembly program, converted into binary, and loaded sequentially somewhere else in the memory. When all the decimal instructions have been converted, the resultant binary object program can then be obeyed by the computer. This is shown in Figure 1:6.

The principle of using the decimal equivalent of a binary instruction can be extended by using alphabetical representations (such as ADD and SUB) which can also be translated by the assembly program and which are easily memorable.

Another tedious problem concerned with programming is to allocate addresses for the various instructions and operands. Even a medium-sized program can be extremely difficult to organise in terms of address assignment. Again the computer itself can come to the aid of the programmer. He can assign symbolic addresses to various operands and leave the assignment of a particular address in the machine itself to a program called a *loader*. The loader will keep a record of addresses it has assigned and avoid duplication. This also facilitates modification of the program and insertion of additional instructions should these be needed after program tests. The loader and assembly program are often combined.

Programs written with simple decimal and alphabetical equivalents of the machine code are said to be in *autocode*. Each autocode needs an assembler to

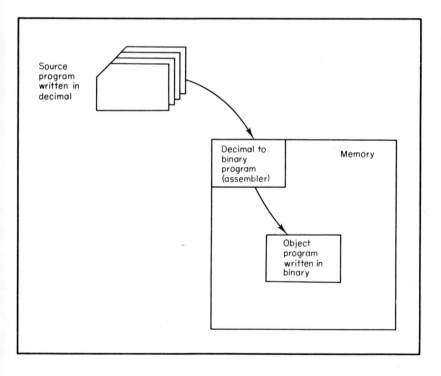

Figure 1:6 Assembly program

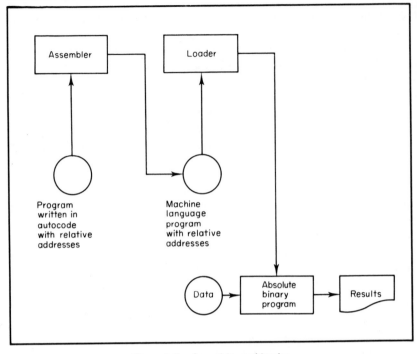

Figure 1:7   Assembler and loader

translate it into the machine code of the computer being used. The sequence of operations is shown in Figure 1:7.

It is a matter of pride for some programmers to be able to program a system using the autocode available for that machine. Its use demands a considerable level of skill from the programmer and also demands detailed knowledge of the central processing unit's structure and organisation. Programming at the autocode level is only possible if both skills and knowledge are available to the programmer. However, such use is justified only in those instances where the response time of a program or the economy of use of storage and other machine facilities is absolutely essential. Generally speaking, most programming in modern machines is best done by the use of high-level languages which will now be discussed.

High-level languages

A program written in autocode is still very unwieldy. It is in a form dictated by the computer itself; each instruction that the computer requires has to be written as a separate statement in the program.

The principle of a translation program can be considerably extended so that programs can be written looking like English statements or mathematical statements. Such programs are said to be in a *high-level* language (autocodes are low-level languages). High-level languages are designed with the computer user in mind. Typically, each instruction represents a number of machine-code instructions. The object program produced from a high-level language is often rather longer and less elegant than that produced from autocode because the programmer has less direct control over the machine-code instructions.

The four principal high-level languages are:

COBOL (COmmon Business Oriented Language) which is suitable for programming commercial problems and looks like a stylised form of English.

FORTRAN (FORmula TRANslator), used in scientific and mathematical work. It consists of a combination of algebraic and English statements.

ALGOL (ALGOrithmic Language) used (less extensively than FORTRAN) for scientific and mathematical work. Consists of a mixture of algebraic and English statements.

PL/1 (Programming Language 1) has been developed to combine features of COBOL, FORTRAN and ALGOL.

The translation program used with a high-level language is called a *compiler.* As with assemblers, a different compiler has to be written for each type of machine. With some machines, it is too difficult to write a compiler that will translate every available statement in a particular high-level language. This can mean that a program written for one machine will not work without modification on a different machine.

Input and output units

Having implemented a means of very fast calculation, our next problem is to provide a means of feeding data into the system before the calculation starts and also another means of taking the data from the computer after calculation and presenting it in a form readable by human beings.

Early computers were developed for scientific applications where the volume of input and output was quite low. Accordingly very simple paper tape devices were used for both.

However, when the computers were used for commercial applications the high volumes of data involved necessitated the use of more sophisticated input and output devices. A further factor was the existence of large numbers of unit record machines based on punched cards as the recording medium. Consequently, many commercial computers have been characterised by the use of punched card input devices.

Typical speeds for card input/output equipment are up to 2000 cards per minute for input and up to 300 cards per minute for output.

For normal commercial application, high-speed line-printers capable of up to 2000 lines per minute provide enormous printing capacity.

To reduce the high cost of data entry into the systems, specialised document handlers and character reading systems permit the direct entry of data on forms using a common recording method acceptable to both human beings and machines. Typical of these devices are the bank cheque sorting machines used to read the magnetic ink characters which are now standard on British cheques.

Multi-programming

During the 1950s, the development of digital storage and circuit techniques brought about enormous increases in the power of central processors. The power derived from the speed of basic operations and from the amount of immediate-access storage that became available at reasonable cost. It was also increasingly clear that the productivity of large computers was better than that of small ones; in other words, the larger machine could do the same work more cheaply.

By comparison, computer peripherals that descended from electro-mechanical accounting machines were already well developed and offered nothing like the same scope. The introduction of magnetic storage overcame the worst bottleneck—the punching of computer output for re-input—but still left an imbalance between processor and peripheral speeds for many types 'of data-processing operation.

It was in this context that multi-programming was seen as a means of matching of varying workload to the larger—and more productive—computer and the array of peripherals which such a computer could support. For the work done on one computer calls in most cases for a variety of facilities. One job demands a large memory; the next generates a large volume of printed output; a third may be devoted to reading and checking input data. If these jobs are run in sequence then, at any one time, some of the facilities of the installation are idle and the full speed of the processor may seldom be exercised. In multi-programmed operation, the installation is shared by two or more 'streams' of work proceeding in parallel. Storage and peripherals are allotted to each job and the time of the central processor is divided between them, being directed always to a job which is not awaiting a peripheral action. On completion of a job, its core allocation and peripherals are freed for use by a subsequent job, while the other concurrent streams continue in operation.

The control cycle in the classical form of multi-programming makes use of a 'priority', specified when the job is presented. A list is also maintained of jobs which are currently awaiting completion of a peripheral action. When a job initiates an action, it is marked in the list as suspended; when an action is

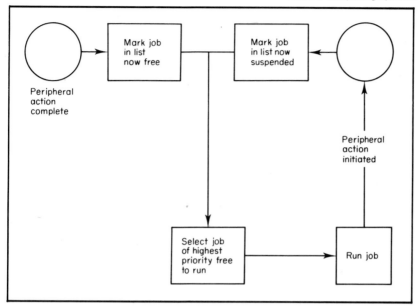

Figure 1:8   Control cycle in multi-programming

completed, the job which originated it is freed. After each change in the list, the central processor is directed to the job of highest priority which is free to run (see Figure 1:8).

An ideal balance of jobs will keep all the peripheral channels active. The redirection of the central processor must be done often enough to maintain this activity; on a minimum multi-processing configuration this would be in the order of 100 times per second. Thus the impression given to an observer is of the jobs proceeding simultaneously.

Safeguards

When two or more job streams are sharing facilities of the machine in this way, it is important that program errors or shortcomings should not be able to result in one job interfering with another. There are three methods commonly used to trap errors before they can cause trouble.

1   The job is allocated a partition of the working store, and hardware is provided which checks that every reference by the current job is to an address within its own partition.

Where the job refers to individual input/output devices, a combination of hardware and software is used to check the validity of each data transfer in terms of device and store area involved before it takes place.

3　For units such as disks, the space may be subdivided and treated as a 'number of separate entities. The check used for individual devices is then extended to include the validity of the disk address referenced.

An attempt by a job to transgress the limits of its stated requirements is intercepted before damage can result, and reported by the supervisor (see below) to the machine operator.

Control of multi-programmed operation

Control is exercised by a program called a *supervisor,* monitor or executive. The functions of the supervisor may be briefly summarised thus:

1　Upon presentation of a new job for execution to check that its demands for storage and peripherals can be met from the pool of currently available resources.

2　To share the time of the central processor among the current jobs.

3　With hardware assistance, to intercept any attempt by a job to use facilities (for example, peripherals) other than those allocated to it.

4　To communicate with the operator, giving him information to help his management of the job streams, and accepting commands (for example, to initiate a new job).

Some special problems of operation are introduced by having more than one job running at once, and these can be eased but not eliminated by the design of the supervisor. It is necessary to establish, for instance, which printed output is to be associated with which input; output files present a similar problem, complicated by the fact that visual inspection of the output is not possible. Preliminary organisation of the job is needed if proper advantage is to be taken of multi-programming, so that a workload is presented which is balanced in terms of memory and peripheral requirements. In a commercial data-processing environment, with a regular pattern of work week by week, this balance once achieved can be maintained without much subsequent attention.

Besides these general difficulties, there were others which arose from the original methods of implementing multi-programming. Most jobs, for example, produce some printed output even if the volume involved is quite small, so the number of streams tended to be limited by the number of printing devices. This disadvantage is overcome by the facility for 'off-lining' input and output, whereby magnetic filing facilities (tape or disk) are used for intermediate storage of the information. Standard routines transcribe the data between files and input or output devices; the job itself may address the files, or a command to any input/output device may be intercepted and a file transfer substituted.

By this point, the function of controlling the multi-programmed operation becomes one aspect of a comprehensive operating system. The facilities of the supervisor are extended to ease the routine processes of operation (automatic off-lining, program complications, remote communication), and a 'job-control' or 'command' language is introduced to direct the operating system in the detailed processing of each job.

Extending the system

We have so far evolved a typical modern computing system capable of processing several jobs concurrently. We now have to consider how to supply it with data.

From the systems point of view, we have to consider how to simplify the access of the various operating functions in the business to the vital data-processing services on which their effective operation depends.

Data entry

Our first problem is to capture data at source and to enter it into the system. Traditionally the simplest method of data entry was to punch data onto cards (or paper tape), verify the data for security reasons and enter it into the system via card readers.

Recent developments make it possible to enter data directly onto magnetic tape. This has the advantage of using a cheaper medium, which can be re-used, is easy to handle and provides far higher entry speeds into the system. Claims are made for greater productivity through the use of such systems, but these are not always supported by practical measurements.

More recently, subsystems in which a cluster of several keyboards can enter data onto a common tape via a small controller, lead to cheaper data entry systems.

The systems described tend to be located next to the computer room and operate under direct control of the data processing manager who maintains responsibility for the processing of data from its original capture through to the processor output.

More recent developments in data transmission, coupled with a wider appreciation of the role of data processing in modern business control, make it possible and desirable to move data entry devices closer to the data source. Not only does this place responsibility for the control of accuracy where it matters,

17

i.e. in the user department, but also improves the response of the system to each new event.

Sometimes the data entry devices used in the dispersed user areas are similar to those used in the data processing department itself. However, a whole range of sophisticated, specialised data transmission terminals have evolved.

Data transmission

The need to extend access to a central system from a remote point necessitates the use of a communication medium with wide geographical coverage. The obvious selection is to use the existing telephone (and telegraph) services.

Unfortunately the telephone system has been designed primarily for the transmission of speech and its adaption to the transmission of data requires several important modifications.

1   Data signals from computing systems will not pass directly through the telephone circuits. Accordingly an artifice has to be adopted in which the data signals are used to modify one characteristic of a carrier signal which itself will pass through the network. Devices for modulating and de-modulating the carrier are known as modems.

2   Significant circuit deficiencies exist in telephone systems which, while having little effect on speech signals, have a devastating effect on the transmission of data. They manifest themselves as errors and hence any system for the transmission of data over telephone circuits must include facilities for detecting errors and arranging for their correction, either by re-transmission or by sophisticated error correction coding techniques.

3   The remote terminal has to be provided with a range of supervisory and control signals by which it can control its own operation in working with the computing system.

All of these facilities are incorporated in what is usually known as a *data link control* system with each family of devices employing the most primitive data link control adequate for their class of service. Thus while devices of the same family can readily communicate with each other, devices employing different data link controls just cannot communicate.

Many different types of data transmission terminals have been developed each corresponding to a unique class of service.

Data collection

Data collection systems are characterised by a flow of data in one direction only—usually into the data processing system. The terminals themselves are usually very simple, comprising key boards, card readers and identity badge readers etc. Data transmission speeds are typically 10-20 characters per second, although speeds of up to 60 are sometimes employed.

Enquiry system

Terminals again are simple and usually comprise a keyboard and means of displaying a response from the central system. Visual displays using television-type tubes are becoming commonplace but, for permanent copy, typewriter-like printers are employed. The visual display unit provides a most powerful form of sketch pad in which the situation relating to a particular problem can be developed by interaction between the terminal user and the central data-based system.

Order entry system

These are similar to enquiry systems, but provide a means of entering transaction data after determining the system's ability to react positively to it. They often employ punched-card and plastic-badge readers in addition to the simple type of enquiry terminals.

Satellite operations

The main objective in using such systems is to provide data processing facilities at remote points at a level equivalent to those available at the central system. The main features of terminals in such systems therefore, correspond to the typical input output facilities used at the central processor. These normally include high speed card readers and punches and line printers.

Analysis of such systems shows that much of the data which is sent down the line from the terminal, is returned by the processor for print-out without any processing. This means that such data occupies the line unnecessarily. Efficiency can be improved by editing the data before transmission and extracting non-processable information, and retaining it in a local store. This can be collated with the processed data on its return from the central processor and printed out or displayed in the local output unit. Thus the local terminal has input, output and processing capabilities, in short, it has all the attributes of a computer itself. Consequently, most small computing systems have the capability of attachment to communication systems, so that they can behave as remote terminals to a central larger computing system.

A further extension of such concepts enables large computers to be interconnected on a common data transmission network. Modern operating

19

systems permit the sharing of workload between large systems of this kind, enabling jobs to be entered into the nearest convenient system without regard to load balancing.

Multiplexors and concentrators

Frequently, terminals will be attached to communication systems and operated at speeds well below the capacity of the communication circuits employed. Multiplexors enable traffic from several low-speed circuits to be merged onto a common high-speed circuit for greater efficiency. Frequently, too, the traffic from each of the low-speed circuits will contain much redundant information, such as blanks inserted by the terminal for purposes of data transmission. Sophisticated multiplexors with the ability to edit out such redundant information are called *concentrators* and are to be found in modern complex data transmission networks.

Message handling

The attachment of data transmission systems to a computing system, places additional burdens on this system. In addition to processing the jobs entered into the system from the remote terminal, the system has also to assemble the messages into one of its work areas prior to processing. It has to check the accuracy of the received data and call for re-transmission of the message if an error is detected. It has to interpret the information contained in the header to the message which will identify the nature of the data within the message and hence how it is to be processed in the computer. In the event of the failure of either the transmission line or the system, it will ensure continuity of operation, keep remote terminals informed of the systems status, if at all possible, and restore the systems functions to a full service level in an orderly manner after repair.

The usual method of handling this type of system is to dedicate a region under the operating system for the purpose of message handling. Input data is assembled into an input job queue via the message handling routines and from the input job queue it enters the normal job stream under operating system control. After processing, output messages are fed to an output message queue and, in turn, are handled by the message handling routines and sent to the appropriate remote terminals (see Figure 1:9).

In modern systems the volume of message handling is sufficiently large to justify the provision of a separate computing system, known as a *front-end processor*. This handles messages in the same way as the region under the operating system in the single processor system, and enters jobs into the main system along a channel by which it is connected to the main processor. In this way the front-end processor acts as any other input/output device but relieves the main processor of the burden of handling messages.

Time sharing

A *real-time system* is a communications-based data processing system in which the response to an enquiry is developed within the system within a time period acceptable to the originating user and regarded by him as immediate. One of the most sophisticated forms of real-time systems in use today is a *time-sharing system*. Sometimes these are known as interactive or multi-access systems to describe their method of use and the nature of their applications respectively. Interactive systems recognise that the user is probably not skilled in the use of a computer, but at the same time needs to be encouraged to use its facilities. Accordingly they lead the user gently through the intricacies of its use and give him adequate guidance information as to what is needed next in the sequence of operations involved. Although a large number of terminals will be connected concurrently to the same system, nevertheless the system itself must respond to each as though it is dedicated entirely to his sole use.

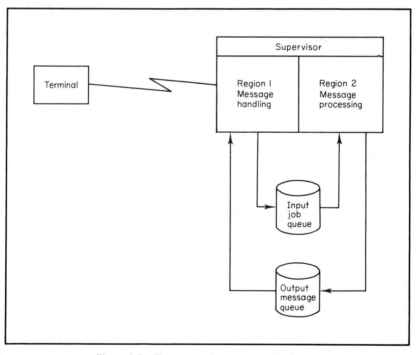

Figure 1:9   Tele-processing systems organisation

The basis of the technique is a regular scan of all the users, to determine those who are currently requesting service from the system (entry, compilation, job run, output). Each active user is given attention up to a predefined 'time slice', after which the scan continues.

Thus no one has to wait more than a predictable time for processing, though inactive users are passed over quickly and, in a period of light usage one's 'turn' comes around again sooner. This shows itself in the time taken to respond to a request, which tends to increase considerably as the system becomes crowded.

This time-sharing principle has been taken up in a number of more recent operating systems, both as a special service and also in combination with the conventional batch mode of operation. In the combined form, the keyboard user may operate in the time-sharing mode, or he may initiate jobs to be run in batch mode. The system provides facilities for filing programs and data, incorporates safeguards against misuse (the user will probably be required to type in his individual 'password' when he logs in), and will provide accounts for the time used by each terminal.

Several time-sharing services are available on a commercial basis, using telephone lines for data communication. A programming facility may be offered, a specialist service, or a choice of ready-programmed applications.

The major problem in the design of such systems is associated with space management. Clearly, the system cannot afford to dedicate a partition of main storage adequate for each problem of each user 'logged-on'. Such an allocation of space would demand storage capacities considerably in excess of those achievable with current technology. The solution is to divide each program into much smaller segments, usually known as *pages,* and typically of capacity of 1000 words. The programs are then held in a backing store known as a *systems residence* file. Only that page of the user program which is actually active is entered into the main storage in a space allocated to it. When a terminal ceases to send data into its associated page, then that page is rolled out of the main storage back into the systems residence file, and the space it occupied in main storage is allocated to another terminal which has become active. When the first terminal is again active, its page is again entered into main storage, but this time into a different space. A special device known as a *Dynamic Address Translator* (DAT) manages space in such systems, keeps track of all storage allocations, notes the availability of space and translates the addresses used by the actual programs to fit the page to that space in the main storage allocated to it. The user, however, need not know about this operation at all and, instead, uses addresses in his program itself in a quite arbitary manner. These are known as *virtual addresses* and can assume a capacity considerably in excess of the physical capacity of the actual main store. The DAT then modifies the addresses to fit the virtual address assigned by the user to the physical address in the main store.

Multi-processing

Under this general heading, two main trends can be distinguished. The first is towards using specialised stored-program processors for functions, often associated with input-output, which have conventionally been performed by hardware. The second involves bring together two or more similar processors to provide extra power or improved reliability. In practice, a large computer system may involve both types of combination. Further, the component processors may be on one site, or they may be dispersed.

Specialised processors

The minimum case of multi-processing is the specialised processor (referred to above as a 'front end') which controls a peripheral or communications subsystem, with the object of relieving the main processor of repetitive interruptions for simple organisational tasks. It will be provided with features to enable it to perform its specialised function efficiently, but will not have the speed or general computing capability of the main processor in the system. The stored program which controls its operation may be standard, or may well be tailor-made for the situation; in either event, it is likely to be permanently resident in the machine.

A small remote processor may operate as a sophisticated terminal, controlling, for example, a reader, keyboard, and slow line printer. Again, one resident program communicates with the main computer, performing checks on the data transfers, buffering messages, and directing the operations of the devices attached to it. Such an arrangement may well suit an organisation with a central computer and a number of geographically dispersed factories, for example. There are also bureau computers which offer terminal facilities for small-scale commercial users.

Dual processors

Two similar processors accessing a common main store have been seen as one means of increasingly the capacity of a configuration. Genuinely simultaneous performance of two jobs is possible (in contrast to sharing the time of one processor, as in simple multi-programming), under the control of a supervisor program held in the common store. However, there are problems in store accessing and in use of the supervisor which tend to make the 'dual' arrangement less efficient than a single processor of equivalent cost. If the peripherals are connected through the main processors, rather than through separate channels to the main store, a fault in one processor may effectively render the whole installation of little use. There must also be safeguards against mutual interference in the event of a fault.

Thus, for a variety of reasons, the dual processor has not been popular as a means simply of increasing capacity on batch work. Where it has proved its value is in the more specialised field of real-time applications, with the necessary attention paid to hardware and software to allow advantage to be taken of the inherent safety duplication.

Fail soft and fail safe

The standard of reliability which is acceptable from a configuration of equipment is determined by an economic balance. On the one side is the cost to the user of the delay due to a breakdown (and it is necessary to evaluate separately the frequency and the duration of interruptions); on the other is the expense of reducing these delays by duplication of equipment, choice of a more expensive maintenance service, extra care in programming, and so on. For batch work, an average 'uptime' in the region of 90 per cent will probably be as good as can be justified, so long as the interruptions are not more often than about one per shift, nor exceeding a few hours' duration. In the field of real-time applications, however, the implications of such a level could not be contemplated, and breaks in service must be held to less than a few minutes to be acceptable. The cost of handling each transaction will be higher than by batch methods, and must be justified by the circumstances.

In the early examples of real-time applications, exemplified by the airline seat reservations systems which were established between 1960 and 1965, a 'twin' main processor was commonly provided as a standby. Each processor is self-supporting, with its own main store, and there are means for switching the backing stores which hold the current files, and the line equipment connecting the terminals, from one processor to another (often manually) at short notice. A variety of hardware and software checks are provided throughout the system, and a malfunction in part of the communications network, for example, is contained, and that part disconnected until the fault is remedied. If a processor error is suspected, a changeover to the standby can be made within a minute, with a further minute for the standby processor to retrieve the situation that obtained before the failure occurred. It will be seen that great care is needed in design of the system to ensure that the necessary backtracking can be performed from information recorded on the common storage. (Some terminals may in practice be asked to repeat their last transmissions, but corruption of the files can normally be avoided.) There may also be some duplication of file storage devices and channels, since these are as vital to the system as the processor.

It is necessary in some real-time applications (though not all) to provide a 24-hour 7-day service, and the second processor, as well as being an emergency standby, permits the first to be taken out of service for routine maintenance. At other times, it will probably be used on batch work, thus helping to cover its cost.

A more flexible approach to providing reliability in real-time applications has come from a development of the dual processor discussed above. Two units are again employed (occasionally more), but instead of having separate main stores they are each connected to a common store which is modular, ie being possible to isolate either processor or any store module if a fault is suspected or for routine maintenance. Both processors are normally engaged on handling transactions from the terminals, the effect of removing one being to reduce the capacity without any perceptible interruption. The peripherals are connected to the main store, rather than to either of the processors, probably again through duplicate channels. A specialised supervisor routine allows batch jobs to be run at a lower priority than the real-time work, to make use of any spare capacity. It will also help to limit the amount of error handling that needs to be built into individual applications programs. The Univac 1108 is one example of this type of multi-processing.

A standby processor, or a multi-processor configuration which gives reduced performance in the event of a fault, is described as providing 'fail soft' capacity. (Automatic reconfiguration and resumption of service is sometimes referred to as 'graceful degradation'.) Where the utmost reliability is essential a greater degree of redundancy must be provided—three processors, for example, may independently perform each calculation so that in the event of one error the correct result can be determined without delay. If a failure results in neither interruption nor reduction in service, then the system is 'fail safe'.

Networks

A further development of the 'intelligent terminal' described above under specialised processors is a terminal capable of itself running small jobs. A number of such terminals may be connected to a large central computer, and jobs outside the scope of the local machines are passed to the centre, processed there, and the results returned. The essential distinction between this situation and the intelligent terminal is that special programs are used for the job processing, rather than having one control program in permanent residence.

For data-processing applications there is a fundamental problem in deciding whether files should be held centrally or at the terminal site. The economics of line transmission discourage excessive passing of data, although techniques exist to ease this problem in certain specialised fields. The use of computer networks is therefore normally confined to the scientific field, where a high ratio of computation to data is typical.

The central and remote processors may be of the same type, but this is not essential when the problems are expressed in a high-level language such as FORTRAN.

2

A Manager's Guide
to Systems Analysis

D.A.Yeates

It is difficult to define the word 'system' in the sense in which it is used in phrases like 'systems analysis'. Perhaps 'system' should be left undefined, so that its meaning can be acquired and consequently understood by observing it in use. In business, however, we commonly use 'system' to mean a procedure or a set of rules which govern the behaviour of people and things. If we expand this we can say that a system is a collection of people or things which receives inputs and by observing a set of rules acts in an organised fashion on the inputs to produce certain outputs with a view to maximising some combinations of these inputs and outputs. We can now begin to see what systems analysis is; it is concerned with optimising the relationship between inputs and outputs. Systems analysis attempts to devise the best set of rules so that maximum output can be obtained from the minimum input. Relating this to a business system, such as invoicing, we can say that systems analysis attempts to get the most invoices produced and dispatched at the least cost within a given time period.

This chapter is not concerned, however, with the broad principles of systems and their analysis. It takes 'systems analysis' as defined in common, everyday use to apply to that range of tasks and skills concerned with the investigation of business systems and their specification in terms that make it possible for them to use a computer. To put it at its very worst, systems analysis is concerned with getting systems put onto a computer.

The difficulty with accepting common, everyday usage is that 'systems analysis' does not completely describe what the systems analyst does. The title itself is a misnomer, as all the analysis in the world is of little use unless we learn from it and design something better for the future; hence systems analysis and design. If we also include the implementation of the newly designed system we have a broad description in three words of what systems analysis is all about—analysis, design and implementation. It is these three major task areas within which a systems analyst will employ his skills. It is, however, an amalgamation of skills.

Most early uses of computers were in technical and scientific areas, and early computer people usually had qualifications relevant to their fields of work. In their own areas, physicists and mathematicians handled problems by using computers themselves. They analysed their own problems, specified how the computer should be used, and programmed the computer to do the job. Gradually, the spread of computer use moved into the wider field of business data processing where problems were not so easy to define and where no specific discipline provided all the skills. In this way systems analysis was born. This new function was an amalgamation of skills many of which were themselves part of other disciplines. Many people became systems analysts from other disciplines, picking up the skills which were outside their experience as they went along. Over the last five to ten years, however, this picture has changed radiacally and we are now able to point to many university, college and industry based training programmes in this new discipline.

What is a systems analyst?

Before examining the attributes and skills of a systems analyst in detail, there are a number of important general matters to consider. A systems analyst is usually working or should be working on the frontiers of knowledge—not the frontiers of knowledge in the true scientific sense, but as far as his organisation's business systems are concerned. With the support and the encouragement of his management his job is essentially creative and innovatory. A systems analyst's job is to create change and to assist his organisation in the achievement of its goals and targets. If he is not making profitable change he is not fulfilling his primary purpose. To achieve this purpose he will need special skills in disciplining his creative instincts to profitable goals and in communicating his ideas to people different from himself.

In spite of, or perhaps because of, this wide-ranging change-making role, a modern systems analyst works within an environment of limitations. The systems with which he is concerned will have to meet defined output demands and work from specified inputs. From management the analyst receives requirements, targets and objectives which he must meet. To do this he will need to get his facts straight, record them unambiguously and analyse them critically. This will require him to have knowledge of a number of techniques ranging from interviewing to activity sampling. The creative tasks of designing and specifying new systems will require him to have abilities as diverse as an understanding of human motivations and of sophisticated computer equipment. Finally he will need to be part salesman to present and convince people of the effectiveness of new systems. Needless to say such paragons are hard to find.

The job specification for a commercial systems analyst is shown in Figure 2:1 and is reproduced from *The Training of Systems Analysts (Commercial)* published by the Department of Employment. It is not based on any one job description of any one organisation, but shows the kind of detailed specification which is needed before the job of systems analysis can be defined. The way in which this skill and knowledge is used can best be seen by looking at the stages of systems work.

Stages of systems work

In this section it is assumed that a systems project will be carried out by a systems team headed by a project leader, and that the user departments are represented by a user project leader. For small projects, or in smaller organisations, the systems team may easily be one person, but there must always be a senior person from the users' side to represent the 'client' for whom the systems team is working. This client is often referred to as the sponsor, as, in some organisations, he will be charged on an interdepartmental basis for the services of the systems team.

The first step will be to establish the project's 'terms of reference'. These are essential as they set the boundaries within which the systems team may work and will focus the team's attention upon the precise task and prevent time being wasted on areas outside the study. Many of the projects which start badly are begun with the analyst being told to 'go down to accounts and have a look at costs'. Terms of reference should be prepared by the user and accepted by the systems team and it is to the advantage of both groups to confirm these agreements formally.

Following the establishment of the terms of reference, the systems team will begin their investigations with a view to issuing a feasibility study report. This initial investigation, or feasibility study as it is often called, usually attempts to do one of two things, either to determine whether or not a computer could be of value to the organisation or to determine if it is worthwhile to computerise (a word for which I apologise) the system under review. This example will consider the latter case, although the methodology is basically the same for both. The systems team will be aiming to find out precisely what the system does at the moment and exactly how it does it. Some of the questions which have to be answered are:

JOB DESCRIP- TION	TASK ELEMENTS	KNOWLEDGE	SKILL
1. Fact finding Recording and Analysis	1.1. Find out the objectives of the activity to be analysed and confirm findings with management 1.2. Interview key staff and prepare a plan of action. 1.3. Find and check: *(a)* The organisation of the area concerned. *(b)* The policy on the system to be designed. *(c)* Information flow. *(d)* The procedures in current use. *(e)* Volumes and frequencies of information. *(f)* All documentation in use, obtaining copies. *(g)* The audit and legal requirements. 1.4. Obtain management confirmation that the facts in 1.3 above, accurately reflect the situation and that there are no omissions. 1.5. Document the facts recorded in accordance with established standards.	The organisation of the area concerned. The span of responsibilities of the departmental managers concerned. The consequences of decisions. Business/Commercial Industrial background. Communication methods. Basic office systems and procedures including: *(a)* Manual systems. *(b)* Accounting machine systems. *(c)* Unit record systems. Basic office organisation. Systems standards.	Human relations including interviewing techniques. Data gathering and recording techniques. Data organisation and analysis. Organisation and methods techniques including: *(a)* Work sampling. *(b)* Flowcharting. *(c)* Documenting. *(d)* Procedure records. Evaluation and design of forms. Self-management.
2. Design alternative systems and select optimum system	2.1. Establish the feasibility of computer based systems in the area under consideration. 2.2 Outline alternative computer based systems, collecting additional	Balancing the costs of developing and operating data processing systems against management objectives and operational	Techniques for costing the development and operation of modern computer-based systems. Making the best use

JOB DESCRIP-TION		KNOWLEDGE	SKILL
	information where necessary and consulting appropriate specialists. 2.3. Select the optimum system. 2.4. Obtain management approval for the development of the new system. 2.5. Design the selected system. 2.6. Obtain management approval for the implementation and operation of the new system.	requirements. The capabilities and limitations of varying configuration of computer systems and an awareness of future developments Principles of good systems design. The capabilities and limitations of personnel involved in data processing systems. Appreciation of modern management techniques. Audit and legal requirements. Communication methods.	of available hardware and software. Forecasting resources required and establishing time scales. Report writing and case presentation. Block diagramming.
3. Develop, implement, operate and maintain the system.	3.1. Present to, and discuss with the user department the new system. 3.2. Prepare detail plan for implementation. 3.3. Prepare program specification. 3.4. Write job procedures for user department. 3.5. Write job procedures for data preparation and computer departments. 3.6. Arrange for program and system testing. 3.6. Arrange for program and system testing. 3.7. Specify training of staff in user departments. 3.8. Arrange for customer and volume testing. 3.9. Maintain and monitor the system.	Programming strategy. Systems and programming standards. Communication methods. Systems procedures. Data preparation and computer organisation. Possible error conditions. Basic principles of computer education and training. Planning and monitoring of computer-based systems.	Writing program specifications. Report writing and case presentation. Procedure writing. Planning flow of work through data process-ing department. Control techniques.

Figure 2:1 Job specification for a commercial systems analyst

1   Why does the company or organisation have this system; what purpose does it serve?
2   What is the relationship between this system and other systems in the business?
3   What data does this system collect, use and distribute? Does it need all the data it collects and is all the data it distributes useful?
4   What volume of work does this system handle: How many orders does it receive, how many customers' records does it maintain, how many dispatch notes does it produce?
5   Are there any delays in the system between the arrival of the input and the production of the output? Do invoices wait a week before they are dispatched?
6   What does the system cost and how are these costs made up; is the labour high calibre; is there a great deal of overtime?

This list is by no means an exhaustive one, but will show at least the lines along which the system team's investigation will proceed.

The feasibility study report is made to the project sponsor and will tell him what happens now, what could happen if the system were redesigned and some estimate of the benefits which this could bring. It will usually cover:

1   The true objectives of the system which has been studied. These objectives should be quantified wherever possible.
2   A description of the present situation, which should take account of the external environment within which the company operates: for example the system may be affected by legislation or by special competitive factors.
3   How well the present objectives are being met. This should also be quantified.
4   An action proposal. This could be a recommendation to abolish the system completely, to amalgamate it with other systems, to seek immediate conventional improvements or to explore new system possibilities.
5   Financial information. This information will show the expected costs and benefits of suggested improvements and should also give an estimate of the time and the costs which will be incurred in the development of a new system.

The next stage is to prepare a number of outline designs for alternative new systems which should be compared and ranked according to how well they meet the objectives of the area of the business they are to serve. It is uncommon to find systems staff truly designing alternative outline systems which may be compared and evaluated. It is more unusual but less desirable to find a systems analyst working towards what he regards as the best solution by making many small decisions along the way, which then lead him to only one solution of the problem, and only one outline system design.

At some stage the systems team will need to report back to their sponsor. A logical place for this is when outline systems design is complete. In my own organisation, the report and presentation which is made to management aims at agreeing a 'statement of requirements'. This will effectively agree the basis with the sponsor for the design and implementation of a new system and becomes a contract between the client department and the systems department. The final statement of requirements will almost certainly contain the following basic information:

1   A restatement of the systems objectives and the present situation.
2   A summarised description in layman's language of the agreed new system outline.
3   How the new system meets the objectives better than alternative new systems. This records for everyone's benefit that a sound and thoroughly thought out choice has been made.
4   An action plan showing the time and cost budgets for all subsequent work. This should also cover proposals for project control.
5   A financial appraisal of the project which usually requires the use of an appropriate cash flow discounting technique.

All the preceding stages have occupied both the systems team and the user. The next stage which involves detailed systems design and programming is the concern mainly of the computer department.

The activities of this stage are aimed at the production of a detailed systems specification, user and operations procedure manuals, program specifications and computer programs. The systems specification will be produced by the systems analyst; probably in conjunction with an experienced programmer who will be able to advise on how to get the best out of the computer and so produce the outputs which the user requires in an economical way. He will almost certainly then produce program specifications for each of the individual programs which the system requires. It is not unusual in small organisations to find all of the above tasks being carried out by the systems analyst. He will also almost certainly prepare the user and operations procedure manuals.

One additional factor worth mentioning is that of new problems and ideas which arise during detailed design. Although many of the problems will need to be solved during design there will be some which can put to one side later for solution. Although new ideas may constantly present themselves, the temptation to constantly redesign already specified parts of the system should be resisted. These ideas should not be forgotton, however. They should be held over in a project diary for future use unless by implementing them now a significant saving can be made in overall project time or cost.

A great deal of the work at this stage will be concerned with computer programming with which the analyst will not concern himself. During implementation and handover he will once again be considerably involved. The programmers will have presented him with fully tested programs which produce the required output based on test data which they have prepared. The systems analyst will need to subject these suites of programs to further tests based on real data which he has collected from the user departments. Considerable testing will take place until the sponsor is satisfied with the test results. Then will follow the setting up of computer files eventually to replace existing clerical files, and the running in parallel of both the new and old systems until the user is happy to discard the old in favour of the new.

The time and effort of this testing and implementation procedure is considerable. It involves both the systems team and the management and staff of the user areas whose system it will be. A major effort will also have to be put into the training of user staff. This is an important area and often neglected, but poor implementation and lack of user education often leads to well-designed systems not achieving their potential.

When the system has been operational for around six months, a system audit should take place to determine whether the system meets the statement of requirements and whether the statement of requirements is still valid.

The development of new areas of computer application and certainly the introduction of computer systems for the first time are major projects requiring time, money, effective control and management involvement, if expensive systems staff are to produce the profitable change which it is their job to deliver.

Where do systems analysts come from?

Because systems analysis is a new discipline which already qualified or experienced people take up, there are many ways of becoming a systems analyst. It is possible, however, to point to two main routes: through some other branch of computer work or through general business experience, although this latter route is heavily populated by ex-O&M and work study people.

A good systems department will contain a variety of people from a mixture of backgrounds. Although it is useful to recruit new blood with good experience from outside the company (this is essential if no experience is available within the organisation), it is desirable to mix this with staff experienced in the organisation who have an aptitude for and who have been trained in systems analysis. There are no proven aptitude tests which will pick out good systems analysts although a number of organisations offer reliable general aptitude testing services.

Many organisations offer good-quality systems analysis training and this includes computer manufacturers and consultants, polytechnics and colleges of technology and government sponsored bodies like the National Computing Centre. Not every course will be applicable to every organisation, however, and a careful study of the syllabus and timetable, and some investigation of the teachers' experience will prove worthwhile. A number of universities are also offering first and postgraduate degrees in systems analysis.

As a supplement to using one's own staff, organisations may also employ outside computer consultants. Opinions about consultants quite often fall into two distinct—and unfair—groups: the first group dismisses them as incompetent and inexperienced charlatans, while the second group, although agreeing that consultants may do useful jobs for other people, 'aren't really needed here'. Needless to say neither of these opinions is the whole truth. Undoubtedly there are bad, inexperienced consultants, who will do a poor job. Equally there are good consultants who will deliver the goods, on time, at the agreed price. The problem lies in choosing the right consultant and controlling him effectively. There are now a number of organisations who can help in this area and notable perhaps are the National Computing Centre, the Management Consultants Association, the Software Houses Association and the Computer Service Bureaux Association (COSBA). This whole subject is covered in greater depth in Chapter 6.

Development of good systems

There is no easy way to develop good computer-based systems, but there are three essential ingredients which must be included in every successful recipe. They are:

1   Make a realistic plan
2   Ensure continued management involvement
3   Use competent computer staff

and the ommission of any one of these will have serious consequences.

Realistic planning

This is not the place to explore in detail the methods of computer project planning and control. There is little difference between a project to install a computer and a project to install any other comparably expensive piece of equipment. The project can be divided into phases each of which can be controlled independently. In addition there are a number of specific well-tried and proven control techniques which may be used. Most organisations plan in a disciplined way for the physical installation of their first computer and make considerable use of the assistance which the computer vendor can provide. There is usually similar control exercised over the transfer of initial applications to the computer. All this is, however, trivial when compared with the work which should precede it. This work is the development of the organisation's overall systems plan. This overall planning operation will consider at least some of the following points:

1   What are the requirements of the organisation in terms of its business and control systems. It is expanding so quickly that it needs a computer to help it keep up? Are present systems too slow and unresponsive?

2   What priorities does the organisation have for systems development?

3   Is the aim long-term integration or short-term problem solving?

In other words, the organisation must develop an overall systems plan, before it can decide if there is a place for a computer.

Management involvement

Getting and keeping management involvement is often thought of as the panacea for solving all computer systems project problems, but this does not invalidate its importance. A growing number of surveys are highlighting the importance of management commitment to systems projects. McKinsey in 1968 reported, 'the profitable exploitation of computers hinges on people, not upon the nuts and bolts which make up the computer equipment' and this was further emphasised in a joint Brandon BIM survey, *Achieving Computer Profitability,* published in 1971. Of more significance is the fact that many companies surveyed by the BIM had taken formal steps to increase management involvement both in selecting areas of potential computer application and in controlling computer projects.

Competent computer staff

There is no substitute for competent technical staff. Mention has already been made of the skills and attributes required by good systems staff. The BIM survey already quoted states that the best advice existing users could give to potential users concerned the critical position of computer staff, and most important in this area is the position of the computer or data processing manager, who, the survey points out, should be a manager first and a computer man second. The competence of computer staff is not easily assessed, although aptitude tests will identify likely potential, providing personality factors and the like are satisfactory. Emphasis in selection should be on securing evidence of actual skills possessed, of tasks completed successfully, and progressive experience.

PART 2

Buying computer services

3

Selecting a Computer

David Tebbs

The selection of a computer and, more importantly, a manufacturer is one of the major decisions in to be made in formulating an organisation's computer policy. The decision is important for two main reasons: the equipment itself is probably the largest individual expense in the computer department, and the selection of manufacturer and a specific computer in his range sets a constraint on system development that will probably last at least five years.

Project justification

It is important to differentiate between 'computer selection' and 'project justification'. The investment in a computer is normally made against some business objectives and, therefore, the evaluation of these objectives and the cost of achieving them are frequently carried out in combination with manufacturer selection. Nevertheless it is important to differentiate between deciding 'is it worth doing' and 'which then is the best way'. For example, in deciding on the cost of a new system a company may set the policy that manufacturers' software still in production must be costed as if still to be developed by the company itself. This certainly is a reasonable, cautious attitude in the light of frequent late deliveries of manufacturers' software. If a particular item, say a real-time monitor is costed at £50 000 then should two manufacturers with monitors in development be treated equally? Especially if the first is providing a full monitor in three months' time and the other is providing a monitor that will need £25,000 of user programming and is not available for six months.

Recognising this possible overlap of interests this chapter concentrates on equipment and manufacturer selection assuming that the project has been justified. The evaluation of a new computer raises three key questions: what will it cost? how will it carry out the work planned? how will the computer (or reasonable enhancement thereof) cope with a future (perhaps unspecified) workload? Evaluation procedures are necessary because these questions have inexact answers. 'How much does it cost?' is a fairly straightforward question to answer for a specified configuration although there are various options of purchasing, renting, leasing and mixtures of these to be considered. However, while the computer may be the largest individual item of cost it has represented historically only about 50 per cent of data processing department budgets, a figure rapidly dropping to 25 per cent. Nevertheless the selected computer, its software and the manufacturer's supporting services make a considerable impact on the other costs of operation and systems development.

The efficiency of the computer in carrying out immediate or future work is, as far as evaluation is concerned, a problem of first defining the work and secondly measuring (or more typically calculating) the expected performance. The problem is that the simple equipment specification is a poor guide to actual system performance especially when comparing two similar machines from different manufacturers. This chapter therefore sets down guidelines to equipment selection in two main stages. The first stage considers the procedures required in an equipment selection project while the remainder of the chapter discusses a number of important subjects that arise during those procedures.

Before beginning the computer selection project it is important to stand back and answer the question, 'Why a new computer?' in as broad terms as possible. Too often in the past the 'real why' has been the skill of a good salesman or the internal desire for a new hardware rather than a requirement of the business. Having determined the 'broad why' the more detailed justification can be examined. Unfortunately, the answer is not always to do job X more economically.

Planning the evaluation study

Having determined that a computer selection project is justified—on its own or as part of the basic computer feasibility project—the next step is to plan the evaluation study. The first difficulty is in staffing the evaluation project. Most companies, as yet unfamiliar with computers, or about to take a major step up in their computing activity, are unlikely to have prople with the relevant experience on their own payroll. Six years' computer experience with a company may be an excellent base for systems analysts or data processing management but unfortunately it seldom covers experience in the process of computer selection or in the scale and technology about to be investigated. Because it is an infrequent task in individual installations, it is well worth considering external assistance over selection. Assistance here is the key word as abdicating such a project to a consultancy means that although their knowledge of the relevant techniques and computer technology may be excellent, true company knowledge will not be imparted to the project team and the user company looses a valuable opportunity for internal training.

Job specification

Having made a plan and allocated responsibilities the first task will be to produce a job specification for the work to be carried out. The level of detail will depend on the situation but in any case sufficient information should be determined if only in a summarised form, for the performance of a particular system, under evaluation, to be measured. The purpose of the job specification is to be the base workload which can be used to

1 Check that the proposed computer is adequate.
2 Evaluate the performance of competitive machines.

The level of detail depends on the situation. An organisation starting with computers that has identified a number of genuine economical applications and is choosing its long-term manufacturer so that the short-term work can start on a bureau basis is justified in saying, 'The precise work content will be worked out in individual applications projects. At present I need only determine the order of magnitude.' However, the installation planning a new dedicated application, say real-time order processing, will need to produce a very accurate job specification.

In addition to a job specification, some thought needs to be given to forward plans. Such plans are characterised by the statements 'know but not yet specified' and 'may be if'. Here it is necessary to differentiate between important and useful. An organisation based in the UK with continental aspirations may specify, 'Equipment should preferably be supported in Europe, Commonwealth and USA.' However, this should only be treated as an aspiration with little weighting in a final analysis.

Ideally the foregoing plans should be completed without too much discussion with manufacturers who would clearly emphasise the applications and requirements that best suit their product. Before progressing any further it is worth recording various constraints that might exist. Examples are:

1   The company will only purchase an *x* computer.
2   The existing installation is a *y* computer. Choosing any other manufacturer will invole staff and system conversion costs
3   The space available for a computer room is limited to 999 square feet.

Political pressure outside the control of the evaluation team should be recognised. It is no good spending ten weeks proving *x* and *y* can do the job and *z* is 10 per cent cheaper if it is already known that the organisation will choose *x* (for some nontechnical reason), in which case the evaluation could be made in five weeks to check that there is not an overwhelming advantage to *y* or *z*.

Tender specification

The next stage is to request selected manufacturers to submit proposals against a tender specification. This simple statement begs two questions, which manufacturers? and what is a tender specification?

Generally the evaluation process is broken into two steps, the first being shortlisting. It is, therefore, worth inviting a wide range of manufacturers who are known to be potentially capable of meeting the requirements, to tender. Usually the manufacturer will be proposing a common (philosophical) approach to a commercial system. Occasionally there are significantly different potential approaches such as the use of mini-computers. The danger in this situation is seen where three medium-sized commercial computers are compared against each other and one mini-computer. In this situation if the mini-computer becomes the favourite then it is not a sign to choose that manufacturer but rather to investigate mini-computers more closely.

One final point about selecting manufacturers to tender is that it is becoming increasingly straightforward and certainly more economical to buy peripherals provided by a third party. Tapes, disks and terminals are particularly worth considering from a third party and can change the balance between two main computer manufacturers.

The tender specification should be a definition of the planned business and computer system. In circumstances where the buyer has a thorough understanding of his requirements and potential suppliers he may wish the manufacturer to quote against a defined equipment specification, thus saving some evaluation time. However, getting the manufacturer to quote against a system specification has the following advantages.

1   Manufacturers often suggest useful new ideas that are still relevant if a second manufacturer is selected.

2   The manufacturers' reaction to the specification provides some guide to his support capability.
3   Timing the performance of the system by the manufacturer indicates his view of software overheads, simultaneous activity and so on.

In addition to a job specification the invitation to tender should insist that the manufacturer estimate all costs associated with his equipment, including space and air conditioning, and answer a number of specific questions on such factors as:

1   Availability and cost of support services
2   Precise performance figures including reliability
3   Maintenance terms—all shift variations
4   Variety of purchase and leasing terms
5   Projected performance of the system against the tender specification.

During the shortlisting process it is best to allow the manufacturers to quote with the minimum of guidance. This approach at this stage gives the best indication of manufacturers' general capability, although it should be remembered that only a local sales office and one account representative will be seen. While the manufacturers are preparing their proposals, two to three months will probably be needed before significant further steps can be taken in the evaluation. The time between meeting manufacturers is best spent in furthering general systems development and upgrading the tender specification from points raised by the various manufacturers and possible greater internal investigation.

Eventually all the manufacturers will submit their proposals, probably preceded by a number of items of sales literature, technical literature, visits etc. This is now the time to carry out the evaluation in detail. This subject is covered later in the chapter. The aim at this stage is to reduce the number of manufacturers to two or at the most three.

Once a shortlist is produced, the final manufacturer should be asked to make a final tender. This is the stage to ensure that the manufacturer puts forward the best proposals as opposed to the earlier stage when it was worthwhile risking a manufacturer missing out because you had a bad representative.

Although the final tender is against a specification it is not the time for surprises. This means that the user will need to discuss the probable configuration, services, special prices etc. with the shortlisted manufacturers so that the final tender is much more of a confirmation of the earlier proposal as amended in discussion. Certainly during this period terms need to be clearly discussed. In one particular case the two shortlisted manufacturers changed the following items in their proposals during the discussion: computer enhancement announced, new computer announced and proposed, new terminals announced and proposed, new real-time software, change of rental terms, extra free services.

Once the final tenders have been provided then the selection can be made.

Evaluation

To turn now to the evaluation process certain factors need to be borne in mind.

1   The purpose of evaluation is to select the 'best' manufacturer/-computer
2   Measurement of cost/performance will not be precise
3   Minor differences are best resolved by a reasonable pragmatic decision
4   Although the sales offices are representative of the manufacturer it is dangerous to buy on the best sales campaign.
5   There is no obligation to give every manufacturer a chance to show his best. But it is in the buyer's interest to choose the 'best for them' and thus all need a full opportunity to present their case.

The purpose of the two stages of the evaluation process is not only to reduce the number of manufacturers on whom a close study has to be carried out, but also to give the manufacturer the opportunity to show his ability without being influenced by the buyer's views in the early shorttesting process.

One task during the evaluation process is to determine whether the computer proposed is powerful enough for the job and, where pertinent, how much spare capacity will remain after handling the precisely determined workload. From a buyer's point of view, the smallest (and cheapest) *viable* configuration is required while the manufacturer will wish to keep his bid as low as possible with the common danger of under-bidding. It is therefore important to check and compare the projected performance of the computers under evaluation. This can be achieved in a number of ways:

1   The job specification is translated into computer terms and the performance calculated by system designers. Although the manufacturer may be requested to carry out this work it is important for the user to double-check the calculations of the chosen manufacturers.
2   In more advanced systems, manual calculation of system performance can be particularly complex. In such systems the

performance can be simulated to greater accuracy than by manual calculation. In both cases the accuracy is very dependent on the quality of the initial data used.

3   A number of standard work units have been defined for the purpose of comparing raw computer power. Units such as the Post Office Work Unit and Gibson Mix are defined in terms of the time taken to carry out a set of predefined logical operations such as adding and moving data. Common measures such as these have the advantage that calculations have generally already been carried out by the manufacturer.

4   Benchmarks are a set of tasks which are run on a computer under evaluation to provide comparative measures. A benchmark may consist of a mix of standard manufacturer's programs and other programs specified by the buyer and written either by him or the manufacturer. Chapter 4 covers this subject in more detail.

Having determined which machines satisfy the loading requirements, the final stage is to evaluate costs. Here a form of balance sheet needs to be drawn up for each machine under consideration. The first part of the balance sheet is straightforward and consists of the definite costs which depend on the choice of manufacturer/machine. Items that are machine independent (such as systems analysis, data processing manager's salary etc.) need not be included in the balance sheet as it is for comparison purposes only.

The balance sheet must be drawn up over a period of years to get a true comparison as different machines will have peaks in their costs at different times, especially if there is an ongoing data processing activity. Definite costs will include such items as:

1   Central computing equipment and later enhancements.
2   Communication equipment if required.
3   Maintenance.
4   Computer room and services.
5   Costs of conversion from current systems.
6   Training of data processing and user staff (less free services).
7   Pre-delivery computer costs (less free services).
8   User software (against manufacturers' packages).
9   Unbundled software costs.
10   Programming costs (if language dependent).

The more difficult part of the balance sheet consists of the items whose occurence is not certain. These items are well worth listing but their analysis needs to be on a risk basis. (Note that this is uncertainty of occurence rather than inaccuracy of estimates.) The types of factors that need to be considered at this stage can be illustrated by such examples as:

1   Cost of user software if a manufacturer package under development is delivered late.
2   Effect of enhancement one year earlier than forecast (if performance does not meet that forecast).
3   Consequential loss of later delivery of product.
4   Overheads of using an existing compiler rather than a scheduled improved version.

One problem with evaluation is the uncertainty of several vital factors. Nevertheless it is vitally important that the procedure is carried out in a specific carefully recorded manner. Manufacturers will continually change their bids in later stages and a formalised approach at the earlier stages will make the evaluation of last-minute changes much easier. However the final aim is to choose the best computer which is the one that will do the job and provide reasonable forward potential at the overall least cost. Therefore the scientific approach needs to be tempered with pragmatic decision when margins are close. But even pragmatic decisions need recording.

Finally, while the cost of computers make manufacturer and computer evaluation important subjects, the environment in which the computer is used—the data processing staff and company environment—remains the critical factor affecting success or failure. In many ways the choice of the right seniors in the data processing department is a far more important decision that the choice of the manufacturer.

4

Choosing Software

A. Jenkin, J. R. Mills, and R. T. Soper

Operating systems, compilers and the high-level languages discussed in Chapter 1 are examples of the basic software generally provided by computer manufacturers with their machines. The purpose of such software is to assist in the use of the computer; the level of software provided will vary with the manufacturer and with the degree of sophistication of the machine. Software provided with the medium- to large-sized machines will normally include an operating system, several compilers for high-level languages, an assembler for the mnemonic machine code and general file processors. On the small, typically dedicated, machines little if any of this software will be present, since the same needs do not exist.

Basic software

The purpose of basic software of the type described so far is either to assist the programmer by the provision of language facilities, or to help the operator by providing an operating system. Programmers' aids may include an assembler for the mnemonic version of the machine language and its associated macro facilities and high-level language compilers, such as those for COBOL, FORTRAN, ALGOL and PL/1; other languages which may be supplied include BASIC, which can be used as a medium for training programmers, and special-purpose languages designed for particular applications. The file-processing facilities usually supplied with a medium to large machine are of two types: those which are associated with programming languages, and those which are designed as stand-alone utilities for operator use. The latter properly belong to the operating system and its associated facilities.

Basic software, then, can be regarded as providing an interface between the computer technician (programmer or operator) and the machine. It is, of course, quite possible to program and run a computer without the aid of these facilities, but few people would dispute that the advent of operating systems and high-level languages has improved the efficient use of computers and the rapidity with which programs can be produced.

Packages

The next higher level of software is provided by packages. These may be supplied by the manufacturer or purchased from a software house. The major computer manufacturers employ teams of programmers who are mainly concerned with writing packages for users of their installations, but many software houses were set up for this purpose alone; their original aim was largely to provide user-oriented packages to supplement those designed by the manufacturers. Such packages may be programmed with a particular user in mind, or for a particular manufacturer. Some packages have been developed by software houses speculatively to meet a supposed general need.

Some packages are designed to be used by programmers, but the purpose of most packages is to enable people who are not familiar with the detailed workings of a computer, or with programming, to process their data effectively. Packages are normally designed for specific applications or for mathematical purposes. The conventional distinction between these two groups, however, is artifical, and in this chapter we shall attempt to extend these concepts.

Applications packages

Applications packages are designed to handle specified standard jobs: examples are accounting, invoicing and payroll. Generally, the intention of such applications packages is to avoid the necessity for writing a program specifically for each separate installation to handle routine calculations. Most user-installations have a number of standard applications which are treated as initial work when the computer is installed. The use of standard applications packages at this stage is frequently seen as a valuable aid to accelerating effective use of the equipment. Consequently, such packages are often useful as a first step to getting an installation on the air.

Unfortunately, early experience in the use of these packages has often been disappointing. The difficulty is that the details of procedures usually differ between companies and even within the departments of a given company. There is no reliable estimate of the number of payroll programs which have been written for companies; it is clear, however, that very few installations have been successful in applying a standard payroll package. There are so very many different methods of calculating pay according to industry and locale; even within a single organisation this can present a problem: for example, Dr Herb Grosch, in evidence to Sub-Committee A of the British Government in the Spring of 1971, has stated that the US Government have 105 different payroll systems.

Different local and national practices have limited the practical use of applications packages, particularly different practices in the calculation of taxation, overtime payments, book-keeping and depreciation. This is not to say, however, that applications packages are valueless; several organisations have been successful in using standard applications packages, and certainly many companies have found that quite small changes have been sufficient to make them effective. It is most important to examine very carefully how the package under consideration will be used. It is often possible to modify a package, but one of the fundamental problems is that of assessing the feasibility of making the necessary changes.

The implementation of such changes will involve a number of factors, not all of which may be obvious. These include how well written the original package is, and in particular whether the design is sufficiently modular to allow for quite simple amendments. The standard of documentation is also important, both at the user and at the programmer level and the degree of interaction with the operating system and other software is critical. An apparently well-designed applications package is often so sensitive to the peculiarities of the operating system and the assumptions made in other basic software that even superficially trivial changes may necessitate major redesign and programming work.

Mathematical packages

We have seen that the term 'applications packages' is normally reserved for packages which are designed for conventional commercial purposes. The term 'mathematical packages' covers a wide range from packages for calculating standard mathematical functions to larger and quite complex systems. The former are normally designed to be used by programmers as an adjunct to their normal programming function, while the latter are designed for mathematical analysts. In general, mathematical packages have now gained fairly wide acceptance and are usually well tested and reliable.

Examples of mathematical packages of the first type include the common functions available in FORTRAN or ALGOL for calculating square roots and trigonometric functions. No programmer would dream of writing such a routine nowadays if it were available in the language library unless he had good reason to believe that the stndard package was inadequate for his purpose. A slightly higher level of mathematical package is illustrated by the statistical routines provided by many manufacturers and software houses. In general these are designed so that they do not require a knowledge of computer programming, although some are designed simply as facilities for programmers.

The statistical packages provided by most manufacturers include those for such activities as tabulation and analysis of surveys, simple regression and significance tests. Most of the standard statistical facilities described in the elementary statistics textbooks are now available on the full range of equipment from the major computer manufacturers. They may be designed as 'stand-alone' packages, with their own input and output requirements, or in some cases as callable functions for inclusion within larger program modules. More powerful and varied packages are generally provided by bureaux and software houses. These may include facilities for factor analysis, cluster analysis, time series analysis and other, less frequently needed, statistical purposes. Such packages represent an intermediate stage between simple callable mathematical subroutines or functions and the large-scale mathematical packages such as mathematical programming systems.

Mathematical programming systems

Mathematical programming systems are normally provided by the manufacturers on their large machines only. They are usually designed for handling optimisation problems and, in particular, problems which can be solved by the technique of linear programming. Such systems were formerly prepared only by software houses, and many are still software house products. Mathematical programming systems are probably the most technically sophisticated packages today. They are designed for use by mathematical analysts and, in theory at least, require only a very limited knowledge of the computer. However, the complexities of modern operating systems, and the degree with which such powerful packages interact with these systems, generally makes it necessary for the user to have considerable familiarity with the operating system. Most mathematical programming systems are fairly well proven, but there is still some variation in quality.

The development of mathematical programming systems has been one of the more interesting facets of computing. During the 1950s it was primarily a question of using simplex and revised simplex-based programs which were capable of solving linear programming problems of some tens or hundreds of constraints in a reasonable time. By 1959, for example, it was possible to solve a

200-row linear programming problem on an IBM 704 in about twelve hours of computing time with a considerable chance of success. The possibility of solving problems larger than about 500 rows did not exist. The 1960s saw a rapid growth in the size of problems which could be solved. This was due partly to the enormous increase in machine power and partly to the growth of fairly small teams of programmers dedicated to the art of developing specialised systems of this type. By the end of the decade, 2000-row problems were commonly solved on the larger machines and it was possible to solve 200-row problems on these machines in minutes or even seconds.

The end of the decade saw the extension of the simpler systems into the areas of non-linear and integer programming, and the beginning of the process of simplifying the use of these large systems. It seems unlikely that the same rate of increase in sheer problem-solving capacity will be maintained in the 1970s, but it is probable that work will progress more along the lines of improved communication with the user. In this sense, mathematical programming packages are representative of the trend in packages generally and, indeed, of the overall trend in computing.

Other packages

In addition to applications and mathematical packages there are a large number of packages which do not fall obviously into either catagory. Particular examples of packages of this type are those used in engineering work and critical path analysis. It would probably be logical to consider engineering packages as applications packages, although their applications are limited to very specific tasks. These tasks are essentially quite different in nature from those of conventional commercial applications packages. Successful and widely used packages have been designed for structural engineering and stress calculations as well as many other engineering and scientific tasks. The growth of advanced engineering projects in the past decade would certainly not have been possible without the use of the electronic computer and the powerful engineering packages which have been developed for design work. Innovative engineering, from design of new automobiles and aircraft to that of bridges and other civil engineering structures, leans very heavily upon the use of engineering packages.

Large construction projects are usually controlled nowadays by some form of network technique. This is frequently carried out on a computer using a critical path or PERT package. Packages of this type have been in use for several years. PERT originated with the US Navy's needs when they first commissioned the Polaris Project. As with mathematical programming packages, most manufacturers now provide some variety of critical path or PERT package; these packages are not always limited to use on the medium- to large-sized machines only, but are often available on quite small computers. Critical path or PERT packages are well tried and in frequent use but some of the criticisms made of mathematical programming packages apply also to these packages. In particular, it is often difficult to use PERT packages without detailed knowledge of the operating system of the computer.

The more developed PERT packages include facilities for resource allocation and scheduling, and for job costing and cost control. The reporting and updating facilities included in these packages, together with the means of producing histograms and bar charts, enable PERT packages to be used as quite powerful data processing and information systems.

Recent developments in the PERT and CPM packages have been mainly in their associated reporting systems. Improvements of this type have enabled the better packages to provide very effective means of summarising information for higher management levels and of segregating information for dissemination to appropriate lower levels. Consequently, the modern PERT and CPM packages are extremely effective and powerful tools for the planning and control of large projects, and can form a key part of a total management information system.

Advantages and disadvantages of packages

Looking at packages as a means of bridging the gap between the computer and the user, one of the most notable difficulties is that the use of the more complex packages, such as mathematical programming and PERT, almost always calls for a good knowledge of the computer's operating system. This constraint has almost certainly limited the use of such packages in the past. It is to be hoped that future developments will tend to relieve the user of this need for systems knowledge. The other major difficulty, especially with applications packages, is the variable quality of the packages themselves.

Despite the reservations which have been made concerning their value, packages are now gaining a very wide acceptance, and are undoubtedly beginning to prove their worth. There is no doubt that the future will show a rapid growth in the availability and use of computer packages. Consider, for example, a situation in which an organisation is considering a new product, and examine how the use of computer packages might assist in this and subsequent events. First, a market survey might be carried out and various statistical packages could be used on the results to determine the new type of product which would be most suitable for the current and predicted markets. Having carried out the survey and determined the type of product required, one might then design a process for manufacturing the product. The use of engineering design packages can assist this technical design work. One might then use a mathematical programming package to determine the optimum siting and timing of the investment in a new factory. The construction of the factory could be planned and implemented with the aid of PERT package. Once staff were taken on, one would then require a payroll package and a number of other conventional accounting applications packages. A management information system using various packages would be required in running the factory. Finally it would no doubt be necessary to acquire a package for calculating the pension requirements of the staff as they retire from the factory!

It is clear that the intelligent use of packages can lead to considerable savings in programming costs and in software development. Often, too little attention is given to the packages offered by a manufacturer when the installation of a new machine is considered. To some extent machine selection should be geared not only to the hardware and basic software available, but should also take account of applications, mathematical and other packages which the manufacturer will provide. The judicious use of these facilities can lead to significant savings in in-house or outside programming effort.

In addition to these benefits, the buyer is generally safeguarded against the risks associated with maintaining the system. If he loses or fails to develop the ability to maintain the package in-house, he can usually rely on the supplier to maintain or modify the system for him.

Packages are not without their disadvantages, but they are viable for the same reasons that make any manufactured product cheaper than specially designed commodities. Unfortunately, they cannot satisfy all requirements, and the user has to decide whether to use a package performing, say, 95 per cent of a specified function at 50 per cent of the cost of a tailor-made system which will provide 100 per cent of his requirements.

Evaluation of packages

The decision to make or buy a given package is a matter that has to be resolved by each user independently. Usually, the criteria will be cost, time, resources, characteristics and expediency; most likely the result will reflect a combination of these factors. Once the need for a package has been determined the evaluation process can commence.

Systems evaluation requires knowledge of the intended applications, general systems design and programming. Experience has shown that the project-team approach is very successful: the team usually consists of data processing personnel and persons who have had experience in the required application areas. The larger the organisation the greater the opportunity to draw upon the facilities of various specialist sections. Ideally the project team should consist of three or four persons representing the following functions: systems/programming, software, operating and marketing. Not all organisations will have such resources to draw upon and in the case of a user installation, representatives of the user department should be invited to participate in the team. In organisations with no data processing personnel, the system user may have to perform all functions of the project team. If none of these capabilities are available, an independent consultant should be employed to provide the missing abilities.

Before any decision is made to buy a package, a proposal should be submitted to management for approval. This can be very comprehensive exercise and a detailed report is usually required covering finance, personnel and operations. Where packages are being acquired for bureaux the report must also cover marketing and supporting functions. The report will indicate the following:

1   Scope of the system—what functions will it perform and, for a bureau, what areas of the market will it fulfil?

2   System characteristics—what features, options abilities and flexibility will be required?

3   Resources for system operation—what manpower and finance will be needed for implementation and operation of the system?

4   Anticipated benefits and, again for a bureau, the marketing/profitability plans.

In order to communicate the system requirements to the prospective package suppliers, it is advantageous for the potential buyer to prepare a statement of requirements for each application area. This statement is usefully divided into two parts or specifications namely:

General operating system—setting out the operating and implementation conditions and limitations under which the package is expected to perform.

Application system specification—specifying the features and contents of the application area.

General operating specification

Broadly, the aim of this specification should be to define the environment in which an application package would be expected to operate and what would be expected of the package itself. These overall requirements for a package can be summarised as those which:

1   Are sufficiently flexible to meet 85-90 per cent of the requirements of each application area—for bureaux this would mean 80-90 per cent of the potential market.

2 Can be operated efficiently and economically with particular reference to:
   (a) Minimisation of job set-up time.
   (b) Ease of statonery changes and handling.
   (c) Simplification of implementation.
   (d) Restarts in the event of hardware failure.
3 Can accommodate multi-client files and processing and ensure:
   (a) The security and confidentiality of data.
   (b) Reasonable running times.
4 Are designed to meet in-house standard operating practices in multi-programming mode by adopting:
   (a) Specified kit sizes
   (b) User-developed utilities.
5 Are compatible with user's hardware configuration by using specified:
   (a) Programming language(s).
   (b) Operating system(s).
   (c) Manufacturers' standard utilities.
6 Have a proven record of successful operation.

Application system specification
The level of detail to which a specification is taken can vary from a brief description of the desirable characteristics normally encountered in an application to a detailed systems specification. It is preferable to prepare a fairly detailed list of features—distinguished between essential and desirable—since this method will not inhibit suppliers offering packages for consideration or, alternatively, not inhibit a software house in system design. This latter point is particularly important as all too often software houses have to design systems within so many constraints that their originality is restricted with possible subsequent effects on the efficiency of the system.

The contents sheet of a payroll application system specification is shown in Figure 4:1 and this indicates the kind of detail level to be provided. A specimen section of the specification is given in Figure 4:2.

Finding a suitable package

How does a buyer find out who is willing to supply packages of the type he needs? An initial step is to write to all suppliers who are known to possess or likely to have the package required. Computer trade journals provided a good deal of information or potential suppliers but, as communication is far from perfect and it takes time for information to circulate, it may be some time before a number of lesser known suppliers are identified. The initial reaction of most suppliers will be to arrange an early meeting by sending a sales representative to demonstrate their products; this should normally be rejected and instead they should be issued with a copy of the general operating and application system specifications. If they are able to fulfil the specification requirements, each potential supplier can be invited to make a presentation to the project team. Each supplier could be allowed approximately two hours for a presentation during which time he should be expected to answer any questions. The objective of the exercise is to elicit technical and economic facts and, therefore, time should not be wasted on irrelevant matters.

INTRODUCTION

SEARCH PHILOSOPHY AND PROCESS
    Required feature of the application service
    General operating specification
    Application system specification
    General criteria for search

PACKAGES INSPECTED
    Salient features
    Defects analysis
    Comparative assessment

THE SYSTEM RECOMMENDED
    System design
    Inputs
    Outputs
    Delivery
    Implementation

FINANCE
    Development costs
    Processing costs
    Data preparation costs
    Training costs
    Charges
    Breakeven point and return on investment

RECOMMENDATION

Figure 4:1   Contents list of a payroll application system specification

The first part will deal with the overall systems philosophy and design in broad terms so that each component part can be put into perspective within the whole system.

The second part looks at the functions of each program including the inputs and outputs.

APPENDIX II

5.9 Pension/Superannuation Schemes

A client may have up to nine pension schemes but an employee may only belong to one scheme. The superannuation scheme contribution is based on one or more of the following elements:

1   Flat-rate standard contribution held in the employee's master file.
2   A flat-rate standard payment applicable to all employees in the scheme and held on the group control file.
3   A percentage (held on the group control file) of pensionable pay.
4   A flat-rate supplementary contribution held on the employee's master file.

The calculation is subject to:

1   An earnings level below which percentage calculations do not apply. This value is held on the group control file and could be zero.
2   A maximum earnings level above which the percentage calculation ceases to apply.

The employer's contributions will be calculated in the same way as the employee's except that the supplementary contributions would not apply.

Net pay arrangements for tax are provided for in the system and are specified on an employee basis. The following cumulative totals are maintained:

Employee—contributions during tax year
            contributions during pension year.
Employer—contributions during pension year.

Figure 4:2   Section from payroll application system specification

Finally, general discussion can proceed on any aspect, including cost, documentation, contract conditions and operational history.

Within a reasonably short time, a position can be reached in which a shortlist of suppliers likely to fulfil the specifications can be compiled. Experience with several packages has shown that the list will usually contain three to six suppliers. All suppliers on this second list should be invited to make a further presentation. The second presentation, repeats the contents of the previous occasion but systems, programming and operation are discussed in greater detail. As each package is examined, the application system specification can be reviewed. Very often it can be usefully amended to include new features or modify existing features.

The results of this process in relation to the first three packages acquired by one organisation are shown in Figure 4:3.

SEARCH PROCESS	APPLICATION		
	PAYROLL	SALES ACCOUNTING	PURCHASE ACCOUNTING
Letter of invitation	25	15	16
First presentation	16	11	12
Second presentation	3	4	4

Figure 4:3 Numbers of suppliers selected at each stage of package evaluation

The first presentation could be avoided by sending the operating and application system specifications with the letter of invitation. It could be made clear that they need only reply if they could fulfil all the essential features and, say, 50 per cent of the desirable features. However, the first presentation can still be useful, particularly in seeing what is generally available.

Although the above process may seem onerous it can be achieved in a very short time and yield excellent results in terms of product and market knowledge. Other evaluators of package material prefer to carry out a preliminary screening process based on the descriptive material submitted by each supplier. Whichever method is adopted, each package must be evaluated independently and then comparatively. During the second presentation, a simple analysis of the merits and demerits of each package in relation to the specification should be made. The comparative assessment is made by preparing a chart which lists criteria on one axis and competitive packages on the other. Criteria can be weighted according to importance and it is simple to compare the resultant totals. Weights will, of course, very according to the requirements of the person carrying out the evaluation. It must be stressed that this method will not tell the buyer whether he made the correct decision or not; at best, it will enable him to make his subjective assessment more objective. This is even more important where several people are participating in the evaluation.

From a technical standpoint, it should then be possible to decide which package will be most suitable for acquisition. Clearly, other factors influence the decision to buy and it is necessary to assess such things as the financial position of the supplier and his support capabilities. Cost enters into every consideration and there is no point in considering packages if they cost more than the organisation is prepared to spend, no matter how technically suitable they might be. Remember, the total cost of buying a package and getting it into an operable condition is far more than the buying price, as will be shown later.

Negotiating for packages

In the course of the presentation carried out by each supplier, it is necessary to examine packages not only for their technical merits but also from other standpoints. The following attempts to illustrate what technical and other factors must be considered and the range of variation which a buyer may encounter:

Systems philosophy and design

This should be studied very closely in order to ensure that there are no major defects in the overall design. A copy of the overall system design flowchart should be acquired at the first presentation by the suppliers. Particular aspects to search for are:

1   The length of the error detection/correction cycle and the number of processes involved—extremely important in a bureau environment as the time available for data correction is usually less than that allowable in the normal user installation.
2   The number of times data is input into the system—ideally this should occur once.
3   The total number of programs in the system and their estimated running times on given volumes of data.
4   The effective use of acceptable program architecture, such as modularity and overlays.
5   That file organisation techniques are appropriate to the application area requirements.
6   Adequacy of security, control and reconcilation checks throughout the system.

The foregoing are not exhaustive or conclusive, but they represent the basis of typical buyer questions.

Cost

This is always important and there is a need to know the exact amount and, perhaps more important, to establish what the buyer gets for that price. Usually, the price has very little relationship to the development cost of the package or its profitability requirements. Very often it represents the 'going market' price, or it is negotiated according to the seller's assessment of the buyer's ability to pay.

Prices for packages can be expressed in several ways, some of which are:

Fixed sum   Buyer can make a single payment upon delivery and acceptance. Alternatively, progress payments can be made with a retention payment—

usually 10 per cent of the total price—payable (say) three months after delivery and acceptance. Where fixed prices are involved, a warranty or guarantee against defects is provided in the contract for a specified period after acceptance.

Lease (or rental).   A monthly or other periodic payment is made over a specified term of years. Very often a maintenance or updating service is included in the terms of the lease.

Lease plus royalty.   A fixed amount payable monthly or annually together with a royalty payment on processing usage. Usually the royalty is calculated on an agreed parameter rather than elapsed time; for example, men per week/month for a payroll package.

Royalty.   User pays on usage of package only and usually installation of the package and maintenance is included in royalty payment. Also, invariably includes system enchancement.

Of course, several variations of the foregoing main types exist, but whatever pricing mechanism is encountered, it is extremely important for the buyer to determine exactly what is included in that price. He should ask whether the contract price includes:

1   Pre- and post-installation support.
2   Provision of computer time for system trials testing.
3   Documentation for systems, programming, operating and implementation purposes.
4   Maintenance of the system.

There are wide variances in the prices of available packages and there are as many reasons why this is so—remember you only get what you pay for. Experience suggests avoiding contracts which allow the supplier to have most of his money before the system is accepted. It is quite clear that non-payment is a great influence in ensuring that the supplier does his job well.

Performance

It has to be resolved how good the package is in operation and much depends on how 'performance' is defined. The problem is that package systems seek a compromise solution between wide applicability and excludive design. Therefore, there is a tendency for performance to be relative to the degree of applicability; thus the higher the performance the lower the applicability and vice versa.

Performance is very often measured by throughput, particularly for tasks that have to be carried out regularly. In the case of a payroll system, a buyer should want to know the number of employees which can be processed per hour. Naturally, overall system performance can be affected by other factors and the following are a representative selection:

Program sizes—most installations, particularly those with multi-programming operations, possess program kit standards—and, of course, there is the maximum size limitation of an installation.

CPU dominance—basically, CPU usage should not dominate peripheral facilities and vice versa. Ideally, the two should be balanced, but this is unlikely to be attained in practice although all systems should get as near the ideal as is possible.

Re-starts—very essential for operational programs particularly those with running times in excess of 30 minutes. Re-starts should have been incorporated in the basic system design and should be constructed to operate at periodic intervals, for example every 30 minutes running time.

Program options—many packages contain optional subsystems and it is very hard to assess realistic running times since different options can have very different effects on performance. At best, the buyer should attempt to obtain approximate minimum, average and maximum running times in order to assess the effect on existing production schedules.

Program languages—most languages possess different efficiency ratings and there are wide differences between low and high-level languages. So much depends on the languages involved and the machines employed that each case must be looked at separately.

Some package suppliers will allow potential buyers to run specimen test data through the system before a decision to buy is made. But again, the system tested has to be exactly the same as the one to be purchased if the comparison is to have value.

Maintenance

What is maintenance and why is it necessary? Initially, a distinction has to be made between system defects and system enhancements. The fomrer should cover any defects and bugs found in the system after delivery and acceptance. Usually, a minimum free guarantee period of one year should be demanded (to cover for example, preparation of end-of-year tax returns). On expiry of the free guarantee period, most package suppliers can provide a maintenance contract at reasonable rates. Recent evaluation exercises have shown that the type of maintenance facility closely follows the origin of the package (see Figure 4:4).

System enhancements are improvements to the system usually made at the user's request, although enhancements necessiated by statutory legislation (which are really systems updates) should be covered by the maintenance agreement. Payroll and social security requirements illustrate this point.

ORIGIN OF PACKAGE	CORRECTION OF DEFECTS	UPDATING	GUARANTEE PERIOD	ON-GOING MAINTENANCE AVAILABLE
Software house	Yes	Yes	6-12 months	Yes
Service bureau or Program broker	Yes	Maybe	6-12 months	Maybe
User installation or Cooperative scheme	No	No	None	None

Figure 4:4   Maintenance facilities offered by various suppliers of packages

New releases of operating systems may cause modifications to an application package and it is advisable that this type of modification is included in the maintenance agreement.

Installation and user support

First and foremost, it is essential to define whose responsibility it is for installing the package. It could be the package supplier or the user or the originator (where the package is being acquired through a broker). Much depends on the price paid and the terms under which the package was sold. Normally, outright purchase includes installation and user support, but where modifications are involved extra charge will usually result. Raw computer time for system trials is usually provided by the buyer free of charge.

User support should also include provision for training the buyer's data processing and user personnel. Again, this may be an extra, chargeable at consultancy day-rate.

Documentation

Any computer program is only as good as the documentation provided with it. If the buyer wishes to modify the package in the future without the assistance of the seller, then the buyer must have full documentation including the overall systems design flowchart, program flowcharts, file specifications and operating instructions. Some package suppliers will not release source listings and thus the buyer is unable to amend and adapt the package. Therefore, any modification must be carried out by the supplier and this might prove to be expensive.

As a minimum, every buyer has a right to expect that the following will be available after the software supplier has finished implementation:

Systems manual–showing the functions of the package and every program.

User manual–indicating and illustrating how to use the system, particularly optional features.

Operating instructions–instructing the operators what to do and when. Very important since the package merely becomes another set of programs to operate.

Operational history and origin

It is important to determine who was responsible for originating the package since this has been found to have immediate effects on maintenance and installation support. Other than packages emanating from the computer manufacturers, there are five possible points of origin:

> Service bureau.
> User installation.
> Cooperative scheme.
> Software house.
> Program broker.

A sixth case could be added, one which has happened and is still occuring all too frequently: divine revelation—the bright idea still on the drawing board. Whatever the origin of the package, it is still a good idea to obtain references from other users and if possible carry out some kind of benchmark test. It is recommended that at least two references be obtained and systematically checked.

When ascertaining the operational history of a package it is also very useful to determine the credibility of the supplier. This is particularly important where maintenance agreements are involved and full documentation is not available to the buyer for him to carry out future modifications. Therefore, the following questions should be asked to evaluate the package supplier:

1   When was the company established?
2   Does the company have proprietory rights to the system or is it only marketing the system?
3   How many employees does it have?
4   What is the business, technical and applications background of the members of the company?
5   What is the profit record like?
6   How many other buyers have bought the package?

Before buying any package, it is advisable to carry out a thorough financial search and technical assessment of the selected supplier before a final decision is made.

Contract conditions

Almost without exception, package suppliers will have a standard contract to conclude the sale. As expected, it will contain several conditions on the way the package can be used. Usually, the seller seeks to protect his proprietary rights. The user is normally forbidden to reproduce the package except for his own internal purposes. The use of the package may be restricted to a single installation. A user with several installations will normally be expected to pay a special price for operating the package throughout his network.

Written documentation is often copyrighted to prevent reproduction and distribution to third parties.

Operational problems

The main problem areas in getting packages operational are: acceptance trials, provision of computer time, delivery and documentation.

Acceptance trials

Whatever package is being bought and no matter from whom it is purchased, the buyer should be prepared to conduct comprehensive acceptance trials before making final payment to the supplier. This will involve the buyer in a great deal of hard work in assimilating the documentation, preparing test data and arranging for the necessary computer runs. Nevertheless, the investment is well worthwhile for the following reasons:

1   Most package suppliers are more optimistic about package performance than the results justify.

2   If properly conducted, the standard of documentation will be checked just as much as the system provided. This is important as, in an emergency, the documentation will prove the user's sole source of reference.

3   It will familiarise staff with the intricacies and operational characteristice of the system in advance of handling work.

4   The standard of service of the package supplier will be tested in advance of a 'live' situation.

The attitude of the package supplier to the acceptance trials is important. Some will dispute that such trials are necessary and may offer to take a prospective purchaser to an installation which is using the package already. Such visits can be of great value *but* they will not necessarily prove that the programs as supplied to the buyer will work as specified.

The service obtained from the supplier in clearing up errors found during acceptance trials is of key importance if the buyer is likely to require additional packages. A reputable software house will be anxious to clear errors as soon as possible to preserve its reputation. In some cases, it will prove most difficult to get the supplier to agree that an error condition exists and it will be necessary on these occasions to supply irrefutable evidence. This may not prove quite as simple as it sounds, particularly if tests are being conducted at a computer installation a considerable distance from the supplier's premises.

Despite the difficulties, the buyer should not, under any circumstances, allow himself to be persuaded that acceptance trials will be unnecessary and he must be prepared to make available sufficient high-calibre staff to conduct such trials in a professional manner.

Computer time

Sooner or later the buyer will have to make computer time available to the supplier. This can cause severe problems, particularly if the supplier is based some distance from the computer centre. He will almost certainly expect to be given a block (or blocks) or guaranteed time on a specified day. This may appear straightforward, but not all computer centres running time-critical jobs are willing or able to do this. Even if the work schedule is favourable, hardware failures can create havoc with such arrangements. Failure to provide time in this way can create a growing backlog of problems as the supplier's staff will rarely be in a position to wait more than a few hours for time to become available. If they depart having achieved nothing, it may not be possible to get them to attend for another few days as they will have other commitments to meet. Two failures like this can add two weeks or more to delivery schedules. It is also relevant that not all suppliers react favourably to guaranteed time being available only on the 'graveyard shift' which may be taken as anywhere between 22 30 and 07 00 hours. On many large installations guaranteed time bookings may only be available during this period, where the day shifts are used for production jobs and most testing is done remotely on the night shifts.

Delivery

The package. If arguments are to be avoided it would be wise to stipulate in the contract a definition of 'delivery' and of the method by which the package is to be delivered. For instance, if you do not wish the system to be delivered on cards, say so, before it is too late. It may also be wise to consider what is meant by 'delivery' as the buyer's definition may differ from that of the suppliers. If, for example, delivery is intended to mean receipt of source, object and loadable programs for the whole package, it would be wise to specify this in the contract. If this is not done, it may be found that only half the package is 'delivered' with other portions, such as end-of-year programs, following at random intervals. Alternatively, only loadable programs may be initially installed with source/object coding following at a later time. It is recommended that buyers should define 'delivery' as sending or taking of all source, object, and loadable programs on magnetic tape or disk to a centre specified by the buyer.

Amendments. The delivery of amendments after acceptance is normally best handled by the user agreeing to accept amendment card packs from the suppliers and then updating the programs on his own installation.

Good software houses will normally wish to hold, at the very least, source listings of their customers' programs and may also require a magnetic tape copy of the programs. Therefore, it will be necessary for the user to supply these each time a program update is executed. The small amount of extra effort to do this is worthwhile in that the supplier is thereby placed in a much better position to deal with any telephone queries that may arise out of the production running and can carry out enhancements without necessarily having to attend the buyer's computer installation. This can be highly advantageous to both supplier and buyer.

Documentation

Experience has shown that it is useful to insist (preferably in the contract) on the provision of user documentation *before* the system is delivered. This allows test data to be prepared in time for delivery, for support staff to familiarise themselves with the system and settle many queries before reaching the 'live'-run stage. If the supplier complains, he may not have adequate documentation. This should be regarded with suspicion. Either the buyer is pioneering a new system or dealing with an unprofessional firm. The latter is likely to give rise to continual problems. The former may be perfectly acceptable—provided it is known and the price allows for it.

The standard of documentation supplied varies enormously. Some is excellent but in other cases documentation can be almost nonexistent. Obtaining documentation well in advance of the system also enables the project team to make a better evaluation of the package before the decision to buy is made. Attention should also be made to the way in which amendments are circulated to users.

Overall cost

Probably because of extensive publicity, a general impression has been created that packages can be purchased and used as easily as most consumer products. Therefore, there is a tendency to regard the cost of a package as the purchase price only. Of course, there are many other costs to consider. At least one person within the buyer's organisation should be fully conversant with the package. This is important not only for making modifications (if the buyer decides to take this action), but also to carry out the necessary acceptance trials. Computer testing facilities impose a very real cost and the buyer will have to provide several hours of time. If modifications have been made to the package, program trials in addition to system trials will be necessary. The preparation of test packs is an exhaustive and time-consuming job if carried out thoroughly— again, detailed knowledge of the package has to be gained by those persons preparing the test data. Documentation may have to be rewritten by the buyer to his own in-house standards and format.

The total cost of a package will vary according to how much work the buyer elects to do himself. If carried out realistically, a user-installation buyer could normally expect the total cost to be approximately twice the purchase price of the package itself. One very large user installation in the UK, which recently required a package, compared the cost of the most attractive package *(X)* with the costs of contracting out the development work *(Y)* and the cost of the internal development *(Z)*. The ratio was approximately $X: Y: Z = 1:3:2$ which confirms the view above. A bureau package would show somewhat higher costs, but this would result from additional costs not encountered by user installations.

Customer-supplier relations

Much has been said about the points to look for when package acquisition is contemplated. However, one last criterion and one difficult to determine—find a supplier you can work with. Acquiring packages has continuing responsibilities and obligations and, therefore, a satisfactory working relationship has to be built up and maintained. There are and always will be differences in the use of terminology and the computer industry has probably sponsored more jargon than any other insustry. As a result, problems will continually occur and even the best-drawn contract cannot cover every eventuality in a highly technical product area. Thus personal relationships between supplier and buyer are of the highest importance. At present, many user installations are reluctant to commit themselves to external software purchasers. This situation is very often bases on a lack of confidence in the software houses and the general view that any job is best done in-house. However, software houses are becoming more professional and businesslike in their practice and market forecasts suggest upward trends in their growth.

The practice of developing all systems in-house can create insular attitudes to new ideas and techniques. This situation is all too common in many career jobs within one organisation with the result that flexibility and vitality are inhibited. The placing of contracts with software houses does have many subsidiary effects other than costs. The package supplier will use knowledge and experience gained on many contracts which should reflect in the package being purchased. Also, the constant communication between personnel from the supplier and the buyer will have its benefits in terms of systems and programming know-how.

The general quality of packages varies enormously, and there still are too many 'original user' programs being offered as packages. However, there is increasing evidence that these are disappearing and are being replaced by very flexible and powerful generalised programs. The anticipated future growth for packages will create a major product area for the software industry of the 1970s.

5

Benchmark Testing

Alan H. Duncan

The benchmark test is, as its name implies, a standard against which one can test a computer to assess its performance. As with most tests, the benchmark test tends to be indicative rather than an absolute measure. The finesse of the game of benchmark testing is in devising tests that are truly representative.

Before giving examples of tests a few words are relevant on the circumstances under which tests are used. Benchmark tests are generally used either to gain an idea of the likely potential of a machine or as part of acceptance testing. It is fairly common practice for big computer users to have their set of benchmark tests and to hawk these around the manufacturers so that some measure and guide may be obtained of the power of new machines on the market. Manufacturers in general welcome this practice for it gives them the opportunity to show off their products. The second use of benchmark tests is the formal acceptance testing of a machine installation before paying for it. This is a more serious business. If manufacturers were prepared to guarantee the performance of their machine when doing a job and to agree to pay damages in the event of the machine falling short of a stated level of throughput, then there would be no point in running an acceptance test. As almost without exception they will not, then the customer is forced to accept the responsibility of testing the machine to the best of his ability before parting with his money.

Simple forms of test: mixes

In performing a job, such as a payroll, on the computer, one uses many hundreds of separate instructions, adds, multiplies, compares, subtracts, etc. Early machines had a limited number of types of instruction, perhaps sixteen. It was, therefore, possible to take a typical job, add up the numbers of each type of instruction and define the proportion. A typical mix might be in the proportion of five adds, two compares, one subtract, one multiply. This, then, might be described as a mix of instructions. By multiplying the frequency for which the instruction is typically used by the time a particular machine takes to perform the instruction and adding these together for the mix, then one can arrive at a sum total which represents the time for the mix on the particular machine. This sum can be done for various machines and thereby the machines compared for a mix appropriate to a particular type of job. This type of test was used widely in America and the UK to compare machines.

These figures can be arrived at from the theoretical timings for instructions of the machine or they can be actually measured by running a mix containing the appropriate number of instructions on the machine.

As instruction times are in milliseconds or microseconds, it is convenient to run the mix, say, ten thousand times in loop consecutively so that the start and finish can be measured in minutes on a stop watch.

Some of these mixes have been commonly adopted as means of comparison. Perhaps the best known for university use is the Gibson mix.

Figure 5:1 shows the calculation of the mix time and Figure 5:2 shows some approximate Gibson mix times in milliseconds for a number of machines.

INSTRUCTION	MILLISECONDS	SECONDS
5 adds	10	50
2 compares	5	10
1 multiply	10	10
1 subtract	50	50
		0.120

Mix time 0.120 seconds

Figure 5:1   Calculation of mix time

PROCESSOR	GIBSON MIX MILLISECONDS
ATLAS	0.23
7094	0.28
1106	0.24
360/65	0.17
1108	0.11
360/75	0.11
1906A	0.10
6600	0.09
1110	0.025
370/195	0.02
7600	0.01
370/165	Approx. 0.07
370/155	Approx. 0.15
370/145	Approx. 0.30

Figure 5:2 Approximate performance figures

Influence of hardware: work units

Mixes are a means of comparing the speed of doing arithmetic in machines. Even so, this simple form of comparison may be prejudiced by dissimilarities between hardware which, perhaps, are advantageous to one machine and not the other. For instance, word length (the size of number which is normally handled electronically by the hardware) varies between machines. To the user this is of some importance from the point of view of accuracy. For example, in a process control application it may be perfectly adequate for the hardware normally to handle four decimal digits. For numerical analysis ten decimal digits may be required. Quite obviously a simple comparison of addition times is valuable only with other information.

The variation in addition times between machines also depends on the way the number is presented to the machine. Numbers presented in binary may be added many times faster than numbers presented in decimal. The number presented in floating point may take several times longer. It is, therefore, important to ensure that the mix used is appropriate to the particular type of scientific or commercial job for which the computer will be used.

The performance of a machine in the scientific environment is affected primarily by the central processor speed. In the commercial environment, there are many other factors which affect machine performance. In addition to arithmetic speed there is memory access speed, channel speeds, disk-access times, printing speeds and tape speeds, card and paper-tape reading speeds. Performance is also affected by the efficiency of the operating system and by multi-programming and multi-processing. Furthermore, the majority of jobs are now run in high-level languages, such as FORTRAN, COBOL, ALGOL or PL/1, and the machine performance is dependent on the efficiency with which the compiled instructions are generated. In some environments the important thing is the time which is takes to compile rather than the efficiency of the program when it is compiled. This is particularly true of installations that are used for training students.

In the United Kingdom the Post Office were, perhaps, among the first to appreciate that comparison of simple mix speeds was possibly not the best criteria to judge the performance of one machine against another. They, therefore, developed the work unit which was comprised of a mixture of small job units, these units being comprised of a number of instructions. It was a successful means of making the measurement more appropriate to the type of work that the Post Office undertook. This, then, was the second stage of development in benchmark tests

Benchmark tests

The third stage is what is known as the benchmark test proper, and comprises a mixture of jobs which are appropriate to the general run of work in a particular company. The benchmark test, one might say to a computer company, is a typical sample of the type of jobs that we would run on our system. It is, perhaps, best illustrated by two examples. The first, from the academic world, is known as the Oxford benchmark test and is still widely used, and the second is a typical example from a bank.

In order to have a means of assessing the potential of new machines, Oxford University produced their benchmark test. This benchmark test was considerably more comprehensive than previous university benchmark tests. It comprised one day's work for a KDF 9, now an obsolescent machine. The work on university machines generally consists of a mixture of very short jobs and very long jobs. The very short jobs are compilations and students' examples, whereas the long jobs tend to be numerical analyses or simulations designed by physicists. The rules for the Oxford benchmark tests give considerable detail on exactly how the day's work should be run. Although on modern machines it would be preferable and more efficient to run the work in another way, the

Oxford benchmark test is nevertheless still widely used as a means of comparing machines.

The point is made that the most representative benchmark test is a typical day's work. In a bank much of the day's work is of the same type. Perhaps one-quarter of the workload is testing and a fair proportion of the testing load is the compilation of COBOL programs after they have been amended or corrected.

Another operation carried out many times a day on computers in banks is sorting. Every account has an account number, every branch a branch number, each credit card has an individual number. There are many other unique numbers used to identify the customer's use of a particular service. The work is generated and comes into the bank in a ramdom order and there are, therefore, many sorting operations carried out each day in order that the transactions may be allocated methodically to the right customer and account. Sorts of some considerable magnitude are commonplace; it is not unusual to have to sort a million customers into alphabetical order.

The payment of standing orders is a typical bank computer application. Held on the computer is a file of standing order instructions. This file contains the customer's instructions to pay standing orders, to whom they should be paid, the frequency of payments, the amounts and the date of the last payments. Each day the computer runs through this file and extracts the standing orders which are due for payment on that day. It creates a debit for the customer's account and a credit to be paid to the recipient of the standing order. Every day the workload for the standing order computer run contains a large number of amendments to existing standing orders. The day's work, therefore, commences with an input of amendments and instructions. These are then sorted into account number order and whilst applying them to the file those standing orders due for payment today are extracted. This process is in essence the same as the branch book-keeping application, a credit card application and a number of others.

To test the multi-programming capacity of a machine one might run a compilation, sort and an update at the same time or one could run a number of copies of the sort at the same time. With multi-processor machines one can run the same job with one, two or three processors switched on.

Figure 5:3 illustrates the results of some comparative benchmark tests employing a compile, a sort and an update run. It shows the comparative performance of the machines quoted at a particular stage in their development.

Detailed analysis of the results and of the comparison requires considerable investigation in the weeks following the tests. It is, therefore, necessary to record carefully not only the timings but the circumstances of the tests including comments on the individual tests and the units in the installation on which the tests were run. A typical form is shown in Figure 5:4.

MACHINE	360/50	360/65	B. 5500	4/70
Operation				
Sort	2.40	1.70	4.55	2.20
Compilation	5.27	2.50	2.24	5.63
Run job	12.44	6.84	12.70	34.83
Multi-programming				
2 x compilations	6.90	5.52	3.47	8.72
3 x compilations	-	8.42	-	12.68
Run job and compilation	13.75	7.70	13.52	32.97
Run job and sort and compilation	-	8.62	28.28	33.80

Figure 5:3   Comparative results in minutes

The results in Figure 5:3 were obtained some while ago, but they indicate how at that time the Burroughs B. 5500 compared with the IBM 360/50 for the banking type of job. The Burroughs B. 5500 was almost twice as fast for compilations and might, therefore, be expected to halve the time spent on this type of work. The reason for this was the efficient re-entrant coding of the Burroughs compiler. At this time the ICL 470 showed up poorly although the sort was reasonably efficient, but it is stressed that any conclusions that may be drawn from such a table are only applicable in a particular banking environment.

It is worth stressing the point that the results of benchmark tests are appropriate only to a particular set of tests and circumstances. Under slightly different circumstances they can show a completely different picture. Part of the value of benchmark tests is also in the interpretation of the results. There is no reason why they should not be freely exchanged between manufacturers and very quickly the reasons are revealed for one installation being at a disadvantage when used in a particular manner, or for another installation being advantageously, but not representatively, used.

Benchmark tests, therefore, are of value in themselves as an exercise and as a means of eliciting information on particular machines and gaining a deeper knowledge of their operation.

In performing these comparisons many interesting facts come to light and it is easy to get lost in the esoteric and almost philosophical pursuits of chasing the reasons for the differences and to lose sight of the general objective which is to produce a comparison or an assessment under a very special set of circumstances representative of a particular job.

Machine _____		Date _____	
Operation		Time taken	Comments
1.1	Sort		
2.1	1 x compilation		
2.2	2 x compilation		
2.3	3 x compilation		
3.1	Run program		
3.2	Run + compile		
3.3	Run + sort		
3.4	Run + sort + compile		

Equipment	Made available	Operation							
		1.1	2.1	2.2	2.3	3.1	3.2	3.3	3.4
CORE									
DISK UNITS									
DRUM UNITS									
TAPE UNITS									
PRINT UNITS									
CARD UNITS									

Figure 5:4   Form for recording results of benchmark testing

77

It is worth stressing the point that the results of benchmark tests are appropriate only to a particular set of tests and circumstances. Under slightly different circumstances they can show a completely different picture. Part of the value of benchmark tests is also in the interpretation of the results. There is no reason why they should not be freely exchanged between manufacturers and very quickly the reasons are revealed for one installation being at a disadvantage when used in a particular manner, or for another installation being advantageously, but not representatively, used.

Benchmark tests, therefore, are of value in themselves as an exercise and as a means of eliciting information on particular machines and gaining a deeper knowledge of their operation.

In performing these comparisons many interesting facts come to light and it is easy to get lost in the esoteric and almost philosophical pursuits of chasing the reasons for the differences and to lose sight of the general objective which is to produce a comparison or an assessment under a very special set of circumstances representative of a particular job.

Benchmark tests must be viewed in perspective. They are a comparative measure of performance and this measure of performance must be taken into consideration with the cost of the installation and reliability. The measurement of component and system reliability is another subject which, nevertheless, is ot vital importance in selecting or accepting a system but, to an increasing extent, the benchmark test, including perhaps a simulation rather than a typical job, is becoming increasingly more important as a means of giving an indication of the capability of a system.

With multi-processors and multi-programming, it is no longer possible to estimate from theoretical considerations alone how much work a manufacturer's product will handle. One must, therefore, expect the science of benchmark testing to become more formalised and to increase in importance during the next few years.

Further reading

J Meredith Smith, 'A review and comparison of certain methods of computer performance evaluation', *The Computer Bulletin,* volume 12, number 1 (May 1968).

6

Computer Consultants

D. W. Moore

The range of services available from consultants to an established or potential computer user is very wide. Consultants' services include advice to management on, or assistance with, an overall survey to establish a medium- and long-term computer usage plan, design and implementation of particular applications, facilities management, efficiency auditing, advice on particular hardware, software, personnel and training problems.

The reasons why management seek advice and assistance from computer consultancy firms can be classified under the following broad headings:

1   Objective and impartial advice. On many occasions management is called upon to make decisions on reports and recommendations prepared against a politically and emotionally charged background and needs advice from disinterested parties. Management may also, on occasions, wish to have a second opinion on some particular problem and proposed solution.
2   Need for expertise not readily available within the organisation.
3   Short-term professional assistance to data processing managers who require expert support beyond the resources of their own organisation or department.
4   Expert and urgent assistance to organisations that find themselves in severe difficulties with the development and implementation of systems. Where consultants are asked to help, they have the dual responsibility of establishing the system on a sound footing, and of ensuring that any loss of prestige or morale suffered by the DP staff is restored.

Computer consultancy services are provided by the leading firms of established management consultants who, in the main, are members of the Management Consultants Association and whose staff have the experience required by the professional body. Apart from these general consultancy firms with specialist staff, there are a number of established specialist firms that concentrate on computer hardware and software problems and solutions. The current market demands and opportunities are also leading to groups of people, with varying amounts of experience in computer usage, establishing small organisations and offering a wide range of specialist services. The computer manufacturers also provide advice and guidance pertinent to the use and exploitation of their own hardware.

A list of the services and the type of firms providing the services is shown in Figure 6:1.

Services provided

Formulation of computer policy

Computers are now recognised as an integral part of the data flow systems of the companies that use them and the actual or potential source of a great deal of the planning and control information required by management.

The design, implementation and development of such systems is complicated, expensive and has a significant effect on the organisation structure, planning and operating procedures of the company. The pattern over the period since 1960 has been to start using computers for well-defined, self-contained tasks such as payroll, stock-recording and accounting procedures. There have been some advantages in following this course as it has given the user some experience in developing systems in well-defined areas with which he is familiar. Manufacturers have been able to build up some expertise which they have made freely available to their clients.

Experienced users are now recognising that these systems perpetuate the situation where the information that is being, and able to be, made available is often only suitable for the department or function for which the system was originally designed. An expensive and fundamental change of approach is now required in order to exploit the potential uses of computers with data bases structured to serve a number of departments, telecommunications and rapid response systems.

The change of approach has led to the need for the establishment of the basic systems architecture on which future systems will be designed and implemented. People with both commercial and industrial systems experience,

CONSULTANCY SERVICES	MANAGEMENT CONSULTANTS	COMPUTER CONSULTANTS	SOFTWARE HOUSES	PERSONNEL RECRUITING SPECIALISTS	COMPUTER MANUFACTURERS
Management					
Company computer objectives	X				
Company plans	X	X			
Organisation	X	X			
Control systems	X	X	X		X
Systems audit	X	X			
Efficiency appraisals	X	X	X		X
Standards	X	X	X		X
Systems design					
Information systems	X	X			
Application systems definition	X	X	X		
Analysis and specification	X	X	X		
Software					
Operating systems	X	X	X		X
Packages	X	X	X		X
Program writing	X	X	X		X
Turnkey and project management	X	X			
Personnel					
Recruiting	X	X		X	
Job specification	X	X		X	
Training	X	X		X	X

Figure 6:1   Services offered by various types of consultant. Not all companies with the classification shown provide all the services. Some companies advertise a wider range.

together with a knowledge of computer capabilities and problems, will be required to formulate the fundamental pattern of the structure and agree with management that the design meets their current and anticipated commercial and industrial requirements. This structure will become the basis of a long-term computer usage development plan and provide the criteria for the formation of a hardware acquisition policy.

Such plans and policies are likely to have a long-term effect on the company and the support of suitably experienced consultants, not associated with any manufacturer and able to give objective impartial advice, is a service for which senior management recognise a need.

Project selection

The corporate policy of a company will establish the objectives for all subsequent plans. Examples of such objectives are:

1   A defined rate of return on capital invested in projects.
2   Provision for anticipated staff losses arising from an unbalnced age structure.
3   Improvement in customer service which will lead to a better environment for the marketing and sales staff.

These studies will disclose unexpected management requirements, redundant work, and a series of data cells used to provide management information. These small data banks are to be found in every area of the company and are thought to contain identical factual information until the information that they generate is compared. An example is the sales figures independently provided by the sales manager, the accountant and from the finished stock records.

The existence of these various data cells, and their manipulation to provide information in which a wide range of decisions is made, leads to difficulties in identification and subsequent selection of projects. The introduction to a project of artificial boundaries, which pay insufficient attention to the environment and with the need to integrate with the other activities of the business, leads to discrete, self-contained and inflexible computer systems. These, in turn, lead to unsound hardware acquisition policies and the probability of very expensive redesign and reprogramming projects when the constraints are no longer tenable.

Management often becomes aware of this difficulty only after they have been committed to computers for some years and a great deal of money has been spent. They realise that they have created the wrong type of systems and may well have to replace it completely.

It would not enter the heads of the same management to have built a new factory, depot or office block without engaging an architect. This professional would have spent considerable time in comprehending the manufacturing and assembly processes, the stock plans and personnel traffic before he started to design new premises. He would have no preconceived ideas about the size of fabric before he fully established the needs of the business.

This task could be undertaken by management but they generally accept that they lack the time and quite often the objectivity and experience to perform it effectively.

The same requirements obtain for data processing systems and the provision of these services is the function of the management consultant who is qualified in information processing. He needs to understand all the processes of a business and be able, figuratively, to put himself in the place of the managing director when formulating his recommendations. He needs to be able to outline all the systems that will or could be introduced in the next five to ten years and to rate them in an order of priority based on the best interests of the business and the practicability of implementation. He will recognise the need for immediate improvements and rationalisation of procedures in certain areas and his solutions should not be biased towards any particular method of processing, department or personality.

The product of this type of consultancy assignment is a blueprint for systems development, an outline of the products of each phase of the development and a flexible timetable based on the resources that the organisation is prepared to afford and can reasonably be expected to be available.

The assignment can be undertaken by the organisation's own staff, provided they have experience, objectivity and the necessary time. In common with the structural problem mentioned above, this is most unlikely in an organisation that fully occupies and absorbs its senior management.

Consultants who are most competent to undertake this type of assignment are likely to be or have the qualifications to be, members of the Institute of Management Consultants, which requires a broadly based knowledge and experience of management and its problems. This qualification should be combined with a wide experience and involvement in the design and implementation of data processing systems.

This competence is a requirement of the specialist data processing consultants in most of the firms that are members of the Management Consultants Association. It also exists in some individual independent consultants and in some smaller firms, but an organisation seeking consultancy services should make the necessary investigations to satisfy themselves on the background and experience of the firm and the methods it uses to control its assignments before entering into any commitment.

83

Hardware selection

The blueprint, the project list and the agreed implementation timetable establish the basis for a definition of hardware needs. It should be the aim of the consultant to limit the amount and capacity of the computer to the day-to-day requirements. Obviously precise matching is not practicable but everyone involved should recognise that any excess is redundant and is an unjustifiable expense. This approach has to be balanced by a recognition of the need for increased capacity as further applications are developed. It is very expensive in cost and elapsed time if a change in hardware, as opposed to enhancement has to be made during the development unless the change is carefully phased. Formulating a hardware policy and phasing its implementation to ensure adequate available power, without incurring unnecessary cost, is a complicated operation. Effective processing of the workloads during the early phases of development and at times of peak loading thereafter might well be undertaken at a bureau or use made of the spare capacity of another user. Provided adequate precautions and controls are established and the application can be transferred to the in-house machine when an economic workload sufficient to justify further equipment has been built up, considerable cash savings can be made.

In the more complicated situation requiring larger computers with a wide range of terminals and other input and output equipment the potential user is faced with another type of problem. All computer manufacturers will welcome the opportunity to specify equipment to meet their definition of the requirements. None of them is likely to have a full understanding of this requirement when their proposals are submitted unless they are given a detailed specification and in order to make a saleable proposal, they may make assumptions which are not apparent to the customer or of a significance that they do not readily recognise.

The customer is, therefore, faced with the problem of establishing his requirements and finding the best supplier to meet his needs in the short and long term. This problem is becoming more complicated because there is a wide range of specialist computer equipment produced by manufacturers who do not market complete systems. Furthermore, some items in the range of one manufacturer might be superior for the needs of the customer than those of the manufacturer from whom he proposes to make the major acquisition.

To ensure that the implementation of the hardware acquisition plan will integrate with the development of systems, precise specifications need to be submitted to the manufacturer of the company's choice or to a selection of manufacturers if a tendering operation is to be undertaken. The preparation of specifications, ensuring a standard interpretation of the detail and liaison with manufacturers during the tendering phase takes time, patience and dogged determination if the proposals are to conform with the specified requirements.

The involvement of a consultant to assist in these negotiations and with the subsequent machine selection should ensure that the whole operation is undertaken in a planned and professional manner. The personalities of the parties involved and other subjective criteria will not be allowed to affect a decision which could have a significant bearing on the success of the company. The knowledge that a reputable consultant is involved often leads to greater care and objectivity being maintained by the manufacturers, as they recognise that recommendations will be based on impartial assessments of the facts appertaining to the situation and the client is aware that the principle of caveat emtor applies equally to computer acquisitions as it does to other products.

The range of consultants operating in this field extends beyond the member firms of the Management Consultants Association and it includes organisations specialising in this particular operation. Information about firms providing this form of consultancy is available from the Management Consultants Association, the British Institute of Management, the National Computing Centre and a number of publications issued from time to time by the computer press.

Software services

The increasing complexity and expense of computer software, its importance for the effective operation of a business or service and the effect on costs of hardware operation through indifferent software, has created the need for a service to management to provide advice and guidance on the subject.

During the early days of computer development, this service was available only from the manufacturers. The rapid increase in the number of computers in operation and the manufacturers' problem of training an adequate number of experts readily available to the users has led to the formation of small teams of independent specialists who are to be found in software houses.

These organisations have formed themselves into an Association with the following objectives: to make people understand what a software house could do and to improve standards of performance.

The Association has formulated a code of conduct covering such matters as contracts, confidentially, quality and recruiting. The code is intended to maintain established standards of professional integrity and technical competence.

To assist with his software problems, the user now has the manufacturer, software houses and package suppliers. The manufacturer's software has to be generalised to provide for a wide range of users and potential users and this inevitably leads to some redundancy for the individual user. This redundancy can lead to the user having to acquire more hardware than would be necessary for software 'tuned' to his own requirements. The people who designed and wrote the manufacturer's programs are usually remote and not available to the user and he is subjected to every conceivable discouragement from interfering with the manufacturer's software. He is also unlikely to have staff in his own organisation with the degree of knowledge, experience and confidence to make the changes that are known to be necessary.

The advice, guidance and assistance with implementation that the user needs is in limited supply and will be contained in the specialist consultancy firms that employ professional staff with experience in designing and implementing specialist software for particular machines and environments. This is not a task for the gifted generalist and the user will be advised to exercise caution in the selection of individuals or companies whom he will permit to make the adaptations that are necessary.

Users should recognise that the most commercial packages are made to operate in a people-dominated environment and the staff required to use the products of the package will generally need to modify their current methods, procedures and attitudes if the implementation and operation of the package are to be successful.

The planning and implementation of these environmental changes often creates problems for management. Assistance may be necessary or helpful to overcome 'emotional' problems and firms of management consultants are usually prepared to help.

There are a large number of small, specialist firms, classifying themselves as computer consultants, that provide a wide range of packages and others that provide, in addition, direct personnel support to write programs to their own or to their customer's specifications.

Personnel services

Advice, guidance and assistance beyond the resources of the personnel of the user organisation are often required in the recruiting and training of staff and the provision of individuals for a limited period to assist with the implementation of systems.

In addition to firms engaged in the full range of management consultancy services, specialist companies will assist in recruiting staff. They will discuss the requirements, draft and insert press advertisements and, if required, deal with replies and create a shortlist of suitable applicants for the client to interview. The shortlist is created using the criteria agreed during the initial discussions and the consultant's assessment of the characteristics of the person most likely to succeed in the client's environment and with the current management and staff.

Other computer personnel recruiting agencies maintain a register of individuals who are looking for a change of employer. These lists are scanned at the request of a potential employer and after consultation and agreement of each individual, a list of suitable candidates is submitted to the client.

Some agencies will circulate details of staff on their registers to potential employers whether or not they are advertising or seeking staff at the time.

A refinement of the executive selection function is 'head hunting'. This is an operation undertaken by some agencies which, rather than advertise, make deliberate approaches to individuals who may not even be considering a change of employer. The agency needs to have contacts which will lead it to the type of individual required, be able to provide sufficient knowledge to assess their suitability and be able to provide jobs with sufficiently good salary and development prospects to titillate the interest of the individual when he is approached.

Another form of personnel service provided by some agencies, which often classify themselves as consultants, is the provision of analysts and programmers to make good temporary shortages in a client's organisation. The individuals enjoy more freedom than they would have with a regular employer and receive a higher income for the period during which they are working. The agency makes its profit from the difference between their charges and the payments they make to the individual. Ensuring that the individual has suitable experience and background and will meet the requirements is left largely in the hands of the client.

Training

Computer staff generally receive less formal training in their particular subjects than people in other professions. Training is often confined to manufacturer's programming courses and limited attendance at short appreciation courses thereafter. Very few staff currently attempt the British Computer Society or National Computing Centre examinations.

Courses are provided by some consultancy firms as a service to their clients in the recognition that unless some basic standards and training are established the likelihood of successful and economic computer development is remote. Without this service, it will not be practicable to implement their recommendations and consequently their reputation is at risk.

Turnkey operations and project management

A turnkey operation involves the design and implementation of a defined system by a specialist staff. The object of the operation is the introduction of a new system with the minimum involvement of the client's staff and with the team leaving as soon as they have handed over to the client. The service is offered by some firms of management and computer consultants.

The idea is attractive in concept but is difficult to implement as it assumes a knowledge of the company's requirements which external personnel are unlikely to have without continuing contact with and appraisal of design features in the context of the company's methods of operating. It tends to alienate and divorce the staff from the design and implementation of a system which they will be required to operate and there is a danger of creating a vacuum due to lack of the knowledge required to maintain the system when the specialist staff have left.

A more acceptable and effective form of assistance is provided by a consultant acting as a project leader. He is responsible for the integration of the systems into the company environment and will have company staff in his project team. This staff may be supplemented by other external staff over which he will also exercise control. As the project develops he should transfer an increasing amount of the responsibility to the client staff until he becomes only an adviser. The project consultant will be able to leave in the full knowledge that an assignment has been undertaken in a professional manner, the staff have been trained during the assignment and they are fully competent to maintain the system.

Efficiency appraisals

There is a need to review regularly the objectives which management has set and the appropriateness of the organisation, procedures, management and staff to meet these objectives. This is an area that senior management recognises as one of its major tasks but the demands made on its time to deal with day-to-day problems frequently lead it to ask for impartial assistance to undertake the task on its behalf.

This assistance can cover the whole organisation or any part of it. A particular area which disturbs a number of boards and senior management is the efficiency and effectiveness of their computer operations. The concern arises from their realisation that the implementation of the promises made during the impressionable phase of negotiating the original contract for the computer have not materialised, have been considerably more expensive or required significantly more time that was anticipated.

The problem for management is compounded by its apprehension about future developments and difficulties in communicating with and controlling a type of department and staff of which it has often had little previous experience. The existence of the problem indicates a need for management action. Its own lack of adequate experience leads it to look for assistance and a number of sources exist. These may include its own management services, those of companies within its own group, where the group is sufficiently large, or consultancy firms with experience in the day-to-day problems of computers and data processing.

Irrespective of the source of the audit team, it is important that it should have experience in the field and be impartial and sympathetic to the problems of management and the data processing staff. The objectives of the team are to identify the reasons for any existing problems, recognise where difficulties are likely to arise in the future and propose remedial action. To achieve these objectives it needs to have the confidence of management and a recognition from the staff, whose work is being studied, that the intention is to help them to establish a firm base for future development.

To be effective, the audit needs to cover the whole range of activity associated with using computers efficiently for the benefit of the business. The main items to be covered are management involvement; the place of the computer in the organisation; projects, their method of initial identification through to final implementation and transfer of responsibility to the operational staff throughout the business; operational efficiency; personnel and communication structures and any associated problems; and the form of controls and budgets required to ensure the achievement of objectives and the optimum use of resources.

The intention of the report of this appraisal is to provide management with a detailed snapshot of its computer operations, indicate its strengths and weaknesses and make recommendations about any action that should be taken to ensure an organisation that contributes efficiently and economically to the success of the business.

This type of service is provided by management consultants with knowledge of and experience in dealing with the problems that are likely to exist and of management and communications. Management commissioning these assignments are aware of their own difficulty in exercising the degree of control they know to be necessary and are seeking methods to establish or restore it.

Systems audit

Management often face a problem of confidence in their future computer systems. They outline their requirements to the professional staff and often little more is heard for months until the systems trials are undertaken. The management has no means of knowing, when the system is under development, whether it will meet the detailed requirements of the business. All too often when systems trials start it is recognised that it does not and months are spent in corrections and adjustments before the system can be brought into production. Taking into account machine rentals or their equivalent, the cost of staff and the value of deferred benefits, the delays are expensive. In the absence of trained staff within the company, the use of trained systems auditors to monitor the content and standard of the work being done by analysts and designers is a sound investment. The service is available from MCA firms and some computer consultants. Software houses will often provide a similar service for the programs that are written by clients' staff.

Standards

Methods, terminology and operating standards are a fundamental requirement of the data processing organisation. When these are established, performance standards for personnel and equipment can be established. The design and introduction of standards tends to be something the data processing manager has to continually defer because of lack of experienced staff. He is fully conscious of the fact that his organisational control and efficiency will suffer until acceptable standards are fully operational. Consultants are available to help overcome the difficulty.

Case for the use of consultants

Figure 6:1 outlines a general list of the services provided by consultanct firms specialising in the computer and data processing functions.

When considering the use of consultants or any other external service, a client is looking for a level of competence that he lacks or does not have in sufficient quantity to meet his particular needs. He also wishes to dispense with the services when the objective for which they have been engaged has been achieved.

Consultants are usually individuals who welcome the challenge of defining problems from ill-defined criteria, designing practical and acceptable solutions and assisting with their implementation. A consultant that cannot implement his recommendations does not merit the title and can cause untold damage to the client and his organisation.

Once a solution has been implemented, a consultant wants to move on to the next problem area. It is this continual challenge in a wide range of situations that provides a consultant with the experience and flexibility of mind and approach that makes his service of particular value. Long-term service in an organisation creates stability; it tends also to lead to inbreeding and the perpetuation of the style of operating management of the type of person that has traditionally held the post.

The introduction of a sound consulting firm provides the opportunity to take an unbiased view of the organisation, its objectives, methods and staffing policy which is always welcome to an enlightened and ambitious management. Although it is made up of individuals, the reputation and method of operation of the whole consulting firm is important to a client. It is the available support of directors or partners, managers and consultants of other disciplines to focus on each client's assignment that ensures mature and enlightened advice and the continuing reputation of the firm that should provide the client with the confidence he seeks.

Mature consultancy will provide management at all levels with another view of a problem and bring to that problem the accumulation of experience of circumstances that may not be completely similar but in which elements have certainly been met before. It should also provide a structured, detailed and disciplined approach to the symptoms of the problem, the definition of that problem and well-argued alternative solutions leading to the choice of the optimum solution for the particular environment and circumstances.

In addition to providing consultancy in this form, consultants will make good, through their own involvement, shortages of project managers and leaders and ensure a professional approach to the achievement of the objectives established by management.

Computer consultancy firms will also often provide, from their own staff, individuals to undertake systems analysis, programming and training assignments. The level of competence of these individuals and their cost should encourage the client to use these individuals on the more complex problems and to support them with less experienced staff to undertake the more routine work.

The case for the use of consultants rests on their competence and ability to indentify problems, structure agreed solutions, and implement them in the minimum of time with the maximum of efficiency. The value of the elapsed time saved by a consultant should more than cover the difference between his fees and the cost of a staff member that might be allocated the task.

Management are also saved the embarrassment of finding alternative employment for a competent and expensive individual when he has completed the task for which he was recruited. Senior staff are often more disposed to cooperate with a consultant whose stay is limited than a specially recruited and expensive technologist because they are aware that the new recruit has to be absorbed into the company structure when the assignment is finished and the lack of certainty of the role he will fill tends to create a sense of insecurity.

Cost of consultants

Consultancy fees structures vary between firms. Some firms quote an all-in cost, others a weekly or hourly rate for all the individuals working on the assignment. Another method is to charge only for the consultant, and for the fees of his supervisors to be included in the consultant fee. Expenses are usually charged in addition to fees.

Consultants that charge on the basis of the time of the consultant will usually provide a client with an estimate of the period that the assignment is likely to last. Regular progress reporting sessions ensure that the client is fully aware of how the time is being spent and provide him with the opportunity of ensuring that any deviation from the prescribed work scheduled is fully justified.

Member firms of the Management Consultants Association are required as a condition of membership to agree fees or the basis for charging before commencing an assignment.

Fee notes are usually submitted each month or other fixed period during an assignment.

Case against the use of consultants

Consultancy fees are usually higher than a client would pay in salary for a staff member of equivalent competence and experience. A staff member would, however, attract significant overheads in the form of management, pension fund, holidays, accommodation and would expect to stay with the firm even if it could not exploit his knowledge and capabilities.

A consultant is always conscious of the fact that when the assignment ends he will move out. He is unlikely to build up personal relationships and become involved in the company's politics. There is therefore a tendency to treat him as an outsider and for him not to be integrated into the organisation during his stay. The consultant would argue that one of his strengths is his detachment and the awareness of management that the views he expresses are not tempered by his promotion prospects.

The consultant is not a member of the company staff and it can be argued that he will never know as much about the business as the staff who have spent a lifetime in it. This may be so, but experience proves that a capable consultant can make a considerable contribution to the efficiency of a business in a comparatively short period provided his terms of reference are well defined, control is exercised by the consultancy firm and the client, and sound working relationships are established and maintained.

Choice of consultants

The selection of a particular firm of consultants for advice, guidance or assistance with computer problems will depend on the type of problem. Figure 6:1 provides a general breakdown of these problems and the type of organisation to which to turn.

Management consultants do not advertise and are precluded from doing so by their established code of conduct. Details of members of the professional body are available from the Management Consultants Association at 23 Cromwell Place, London, SW7.

The British Institute of Management maintains a record of some 1400 consultancy firms including sole practitioners and, if provided with details of the problem, offer to provide from their records a shortlist of firms it considers suitable.

The recently formed Software House Association will provide, through the secretary at 109 Kingsway, London, WC2 a list of its members and details of its code of conduct. Software houses are not restrained from advertising and some details of their services can be obtained from advertisements in the computer press.

Details of computer consultants will also be provided on request by the National Computing Centre at Quay Street, Manchester, M3 3HU.

In addition to these sources, lists of consultants are often published in survey reports by the computer press, for example *Computer Weekly, Computer Survey,* the *Computer Year Book.*

If the reader were to follow up all these contacts and subsequently obtain further details from all the firms whose names are supplied to him, he will still be faced with a difficult selection task. He will, however, be in a better position to make a realistic assessment than if he reacts to the cold canvassing that is undertaken by some companies or accepts the single firm nominated by a professional association or institute.

Having established the field from which the selection is to be made, it is sometimes helpful to refer to other organisations who may have been faced with the same problem or have used consultants recently. A large proportion of consultancy work arises from introduction by satisfied clients and this method certainly helps to establish mutual confidence from the outset.

If these procedures are impracticable, the potential client must make his own selection based on the general experience of the consulting firm, their experience in the particular activity in which he is currently interested, his assessment of their technical competence, staff availability and the firm's methods of operation. This information can be obtained through direct contact with the firm who will almost certainly be prepared to discuss the subject, survey the problem area and quote for the work that is required to be done.

Evaluating the results

An evaluation of the benefits that have been achieved and how these relate to the defined objectives should be made at the end of every assignment. Some of the questions that need to be answered are:

1   Is there improvement in the coordination of the management team?
2   Are goals more clearly defined?
3   Are communications clearer?
4   Are operations more effective?
5   Is there actual or potential improvement?

The final measure of the consultants' assistance is what the company's own management and staff have learnt from their involvement with the consultancy firm. The consultant should leave behind him not only a solution of the immediate problem but also a recognition of the management skills that were used in arriving at the solution.

Management should evaluate how constructively the consultant worked with the organisation's own personnel. Was the assignment carried out with a minimum of disruption in the organisation? What lessons have been learnt that can be applied in the future if consulting services are used again?

A post mortem of each assignment should be undertaken and should include a review of its high and low points, problems that have arisen on both sides and how they have been overcome, and the benefits that have been achieved. Management can then decide whether the use of consultants has been worthwhile. The growth of the professional firms and their continuing contact and involvement with their clients, both large and small, indicate that the service they have to offer is recognised and appreciated.

7

Facilities Management

F. J. M. Laver

In the broadest terms, facilities management covers all of those activities that are necessary to establish and operate a computer-based service for a customer. It assumes that the customer needs or wishes to contract out of data processing either altogether, or for certain functions, for certain activities, in certain territorial regions, in certain company divisions, or whatever. Some restrict their use of the term 'facilities management' to the provision and operation of a computer centre of behalf of a client.

Scope of facilities management

The activities that are associated with the various phases in the development and installation of computer systems cover a wide range which includes:

1   Management consultancy.
2   Computing techniques consultancy.
3   Feasibility and cost studies.
4   Selection and acquisition of equipment.
5   Provision and preparation of computer accommodation, installation
      and acceptance of equipment.
6   Systems analysis, specification and design.
7   Specification, writing and maintenance of programs.
8   Preparation of procedure manuals and staff training.
9   Field implementation of systems.
10   Computer centre operation.
11   Efficiency audit.

The customer may decide to retain each or all of these items wholly within his control, depending largely on whether he chooses to set up, or to continue to operate, a computer development department of his own. In Britain, the majority of computer users still do undertake most of these activities themselves, using specialist concerns occasionally to handle peak loads, to speed the pace of implementation, or to supply particular technical skills that they do not have in-house. For some specialist functions, say items 1, 2, 4, and 5, it is indeed unlikely that any but larger users will be able to afford to maintain their own permanent groups of experts. Where a user does decide to go outside his own organisation he will find a range of specialist suppliers ready to meet his needs. Figure 7:1 displays the different sources of supply, but no supplier would accept that he fitted neatly into any one slot of this schema.

It may be useful at this point to attempt to distinguish between facilities management and the more familiar services offered by computer bureaux. The difference is one of emphasis, for each is concerned with the provision of computer capacity, and most computer bureaux offer capacity either for casual use, or to support a specialist service. Facilities management is not essentially different in this matter, but it tends to imply a longer-term demand and, while its contracts cover the provision of capacity on a pay-as-you-use basis, they generally extend over periods of years. Again, the capacity is commonly used to serve a single user, or a small group of users, and is provided in largish blocks on a computer provided and operated by the contractor either on his own or on the customer's premises.

Alternatively, the customer's machine may be taken over and operated by the contractor—any spare capacity being used to provide service to others, to the mutual advantage of the customer and the contractor. Unlike bureau service, the computer capacity provided under a facilities management contract is tailored to the needs of the customer in respect of the type of machine, its configuration and its location. The facilities are thus personalised, even though they are not owned or leased by the customer; and, more importantly, they are manned and managed by the contractor specifically to meet the customer's requirements. The difference between bureau service and facilities management thus resembles that between a taxi and a contract-hire car service.

Facilities management has been little discussed and little used in Britain so far; but experience in America indicates that contractors in this field often extend their services to cover those of computer consultants and software houses. Equally, some British software and consultancy firms have begun to offer to manage computer operational facilities; and some bureaux, hitherto mainly concerned with providing computer capacity, have begun to cover the development as well as the operational areas of activity.

96

SOURCES OF SUPPLY

THE COMPONENTS OF FACILITIES MANAGEMENT	MANAGEMENT CONSULTANTS	COMPUTER CONSULTANTS	CONSULTING ENGINEERING	SOFTWARE HOUSES	COMPUTER BUREAUX
Management consultancy	x				
Computer techniques advice	x	x			x
Feasibility studies	x	x			x
Selection and acquisition of equipment		x	x		x
Installation and accommodation			x		x
Systems analysis				x	x
Programming services				x	x
Field implementation				x	x
Computer operation					x
Efficiency audit	x	x			

Figure 7:1 Suppliers of the constituents of facilities management

Benefits of facilities management

What benefits can facilities management offer to a customer? The principal ones are discussed under five heads.

Convenience

In their earlier days computers were too often regarded as status symbols, but with more experience many users have come to realise that what they want is not to own and operate a computer, but to have computing done. Facilities management offers the prospect of achieving that result with the least possible trouble. Thus, where a new installation is required, or an existing installation has to be replaced, the customer is spared the tasks of inviting and evaluating manufacturers' proposals, obtaining and preparing accommodation, and recruiting computer staff. He is relieved of staff control, hiring and firing, promotions, career development and training; the responsibility for morale, and for the use of sound operating practices also rests with the contractor.

Capacity

It is extremely difficult to determine in advance precisely what size and configuration of computer equipment will be needed to operate a given system efficiently and economically, and this is especially so when, as is commonly the case, the prospective user is able to specify his requirements only broadly, and in terms of managerial procedures and functions, rather than in the massive and meticulous detail necessary for the preparation of programs. Not uncommonly, therefore, increased capacity and additional facilities prove to be required. The facilities management customer is relieved of the many problems that this causes, for the responsibility for equipment rests with the contractor.

Even jobs which have been accurately estimated tend to grow, and eventually to outgrow, their original equipment. Its enhancement has to take place in jumps whose size is set by the computer manufacturer's catalogue, and this usually results in under-utilisation for some time after an enlargement. Under-utilisation can also arise where equipment has to be large enough to cope with seasonal or occasional peak loadings, which a facilities management contractor may be able to handle more economically, for example, when he has several customers whose peak demands do not coincide. Enlargement involves a more or less prolonged interruption for engineering installation work, and a period of difficulty while the operating staff shake down to the new ways of the new system. A facilities management contractor carries the cost and the worry of coping with enlargements. Similarly, the problems of providing standby capacity will be the contractor's, and when he has several similar installations he can often offer better standby facilities than it would ever be economic to provide in-house. Through shared use, the customer can have access to a more powerful and more advanced installation than he could justify alone. This can result in faster turnrounds on batch-processed work, and the ability to embark upon remote terminal operations either on-line or off-line. Finally, higher standards of reliability may be possible, for the contractor's use of a large installation will often justify on-site maintenance engineers.

Obsolescence

The development of computer equipment has been rapid and continual, and there is no sign that this trend is likely to slow down or reverse: on the whole, it seems more likely to accelerate. The result is that the economic life of computer equipment is determined more by technical obsolescence than by increased maintenance costs or any other sign of wearing out. The economic life of a computer currently lies in the range four to seven years, and the emergence of new models with enhanced performance occurs at times determined by the manufacturer's assessment of his marketing advantage rather than by the user's convenience. Here also, there are troublesome problems which a facilities management contractor offers to lift from his customers' shoulders.

Cost

The range of services available from a facilities management contractor covers items that a potential customer may be inclined to overlook when comparing the contractor's prices with the bare cost of providing for himself.

In his own interest a customer should attempt to assess *all* his own costs, including overheads and indirect costs. The design and implementation of a computer scheme necessarily absorbs a great deal of time and effort on the part of the brighter managers of a company, and the prospective facilities management customer should consider carefully the opportunity cost of deflecting these top-quality men from the main stream of the company's affairs. Some of them may indeed be lost permanently, for computing is addictive and, at present, offers a tempting career profile.

A real incentive is that, because the customer pays only for the items of computer equipment he uses and the periods for which he uses them, idle time can be reduced and significantly lower processing costs may be possible.

Service

Facilities management contractors are professionals whose whole success or failure depends on the service they provide. They have, therefore, a powerful and continual incentive to satisfy their customer and they are likely to be able to do so to a degree that he would find too troublesome and too costly to provide for himself, especially with the greater problems of maintaining continuity in a smaller staff unit in a time of extremely rapid staff turnover. One aspect of particular significance concerns program maintenance, an activity whose importance, or even existence, is too often overlooked. Programs for commercial work are not written once for all time. External circumstances change, systems are enlarged, inefficiencies or errors are detected. Amending and retesting programs to cope with such developments provides a continuing load of program revision and updating. This task is a substantial one, even when the original programs have been well documented—and this is far from being common, especially in small units working under heavy pressure to complete by an imposed target date. When the documentation is sketchy, continuity of staffing becomes vital; but program maintenance has little appeal for the creative, problem-solving minds of most programmers, and it has to be diluted with original work. This is much easier to arrange in a large unit handling a variety of work, and such a unit is in any case less vulnerable to the loss of individuals. Finally, by the very act of contracting out, the customer assumes a position from which he can demand the highest grade of service and seek compensation for failures.

Applications

In what situations can computer facilities management most profitably be employed?

The obvious examples are companies or organisations with little or no data processing capability and experience. Where they are of sufficient size and require service over several years, this suggests facilities management rather than bureau service. Total involvement by the contractor in the entire operation, including the management and provision of systems and programming staff and the machine capacity will enable faster progress into data processing to be safely achieved.

Cost benefits can be derived by customers who are already operating heavily under-utilised equipment, which can be taken over, or replaced by another machine, and operated by a facilities management contractor.

Cost benefits, as well as less tangible advantages, can also be obtained by customers facing the replacement of an existing computer. Over and above the direct cost advantages, the problems of choosing equipment, training staff, converting programs and files, and the re-establishment of operating standards, can be assisted by, or transferred to, a contractor.

Facilities management can help the users of smaller or medium installations who wish to develop a more advanced system for some area of their activities, but are daunted by the heavy costs of development and of hardware, and by the risk of undermining their present success. Contracting out for the specialist skills and a limited slice of a large, sophisticated machine could be most attractive.

A facilities management contract can help companies who as a result of history find themselves operating a number of installations of different ages and manufacturers, with all the problems of compatibility which that can bring. The use of a contractor could speed the rationalisation into fewer, more profitable locations, with common equipment and systems.

A total takeover of a customer's existing installation, including staff, might be appropriate for lame-duck situations, where it could be a drastic, but profitable, step towards the re-establishment of efficient operation.

Certain routine computer applications, payroll and invoicing for instance, are difficult and demanding when it comes to fitting them into computer centre loading schedules. Off-loading these to a contractor—whether facilities management or computer bureau—can hive off some headaches.

This brief survey of some areas for the application of facilities management shows that the decision whether or not to call in a contractor must be one for the senior management of a company. The basis of decision will tend to be economic; and the company's own staff, although able to advise on technical points, cannot be expected to take an entirely detached view of proposals that would deprive them of the computer, and appear to diminish their status.

Problems

Inevitably, there are disadvantages in facilities management. Most of these stem from an alleged loss of control by the customer organisation, or from the separation of the computer installation from the customer's premises.

The disadvantages of remote location are largely overstated—the problems of interface and control are much more important, and exist irrespective of location. Remoteness of the computer is largely an emotive matter, for management and staff alike tend to prefer a machine which they can see and kick! Certainly the transfer of data will require careful attention, but adequate control and clearly defined interfaces can provide satisfactory solutions in most cases. Furthermore, technological advances permitting the direct encoding of data and the increasing use of remote terminal devices over telecommunications channels are reducing data input problems and making the physical location of the central processor a somewhat irrelevant question.

The question of control is a less easy one, for the transfer of responsibility to a contractor inevitably carries some transfer of control. What is required, and what indeed the customer will consider he is paying for, is the transfer of both responsibility and control in those areas which he is anxious to be rid of, but its retention in others that he judges to be more critical to him. It is vitally important, therefore, to define precisely the boundary between the customer and the contractor, and the consequent division of responsibility and control of the work flow between them.

Each party must reach a very clear understanding of the obligations of the other, and this mutual understanding must transcend the contractual documents that bind them together. Experience suggests that detailed understanding and agreement is particularly necessary to:

1   Establish clearly the nature and extent of executive authorities in the contractor's operational and project development areas and in the customer's various departments.
2   Specify completely the flow of work from the customer's work areas through data preparation centres, off-line job control areas and into the computer control room, in relation to the chain of executive authority.
3   Agree timetables of machine loading for the main processing activities before live running of any project begins under the contract.
4   Arrange a procedure for the assignment of priorities, the allocation of trials capacity, and so on.
5   Set out a procedure for the review of operating performance and for effecting agreed changes with the customer.

Where the contractor also assumes responsibility for development, the interface with project development staff is simplified, but an additional customer liaison point is needed to control the progress of development work and to make sure that it meets the requirements of the customer and accords with the priorities and decisions of his senior management. It is necessary to define very clearly the extent of executive authorities and the chain of command for the start of new work and for initiating changes to existing systems. A method for the audit of project development work must be established, with clear procedures for checking, approving and implementing new systems or modifications.

Whatever the extent of involvement by the contractor, the customer will probably want to have a liaison group to work with him. Its functions will depend on the contractor's responsibilities, but it must have executive authority in the customer's organisation and direct access to his senior management. A two-tier system of formal contact between user and contractor can work well with regular user/contractor meetings at management and at senior working levels to handle most day-to-day matters.

The advice which a facilities management contractor can give will be similar to that provided by computer manufacturers or computer bureaux, in that it will always contain some bias towards securing business for the promoter of the service. Customers who are seeking facilities management may, therefore, in their own interests, wish to retain an independent consultant to help them to assess facilities management proposals in respect of viability, costs and the extent to which they should cover the various areas of activity.

Contracts

As has been said, a productive working relationship between customer and contractor will depend on much more than bare legal liability. Nevertheless, a contract will usually be drawn up between the parties. Its nature and terms will depend on the commercial practices and legal styles of contractor and customer, and also on the range of facilities provided. A limited amount of consultancy and technical advice, together with help in procurement and preparation of suitable accommodation, is usually provided by the contractor, and these items may be covered in his accounts as sales overheads rather than as explicit items. The arrangements regarding accommodation may well form an addendum to the contract, or be the subject of a second contract—particularly where the accommodation belongs to the customer who is renting or leasing it back to the contractor.

Fixed-price contracts for computer processing are rare—particularly for the longer periods. The most commonly accepted arrangement is to fix the price for an initial period of one or two years, followed by previously agreed or subsequently negotiated increases for specified reasons and as stated intervals. For some work the processing charges may be based on a rate per account or transaction, but in inflationary times price reviews will certainly be required by the contractor. Charges by a facilities management contractor for project development work cannot be expected to differ essentially from those of computer bureaux or software houses. Prices will be fixed either for an assignment or project, or for the provision of line management and senior staff on a man-day basis, and there will be periodic reviews.

The charges quoted by a facilities management contractor should be attractive to those customers who generate insufficient work to load their existing installations fully, or by those able to transfer work from a smaller well-loaded machine to a larger compatible version owned and operated by the contractor. However, for a large customer whose work will fill virtually the entire capacity of a large configuration owned and operated by the

103

contractor, the charges that can be offered will be less attractive; indeed the costs to the customer may turn out to be somewhat above the cost of do-it-yourself operation. The fact that large concerns in the UK and the USA have, nevertheless, entered into facilities management contracts points to the value to them of other, less tangible, advantages. In the USA, contractors take on new business on the basis of the mutually agreed current annual costs of the installation to the customer. The attraction of this for the contractor lies in the greater efficiency and lower cost at which he expects to be able to run the installation; and for the customer in the greater volume of work that he will be able to handle within the limits of his current investment and in relief from the day-to-day trials and tribulations of computer operation.

The costs of computer facilities management obviously vary over a wide range depending upon the size and configuration of the computer involved, the duration of the contract, and the extent of the contractor's involvement and responsibilities for owning the hardware, proving the accommodation, and supporting and participating in system and program development. Charges for capacity are often based on a reduced rate for the use of common equipment that can be shared with other customers, for example the central processor, plus charges for the sole use of those items that cannot be shared, for example, magnetic disk stores used to hold a customer's files.

Contractors for facilities management tend to be large under-takings by the standards of the computer service industry. They have to be large enough to be able to handle the considerable cash flows required, and to be able to attract and retain staff with the wide range of skills that is necessary. If American experience is any guide, the British market may be able to support only a small number. Dependability is essential, and the contractor must be able to provide a service which equals or surpasses those of customers' existing installations. Furthermore, to be commercially viable, a facilities management contractor must by virtue of his greater experience and his ability to retain and develop the best expertise, be able to operate computer centres and control development teams more efficiently and economically than his in-house equivalents.

Future of facilities management

It is extremely difficult to forecast the future for facilities management, or, indeed, even try to assess the degree of penetration into the computer service industry which it can hope to achieve. Some prophets see computer facilities management as a relatively short-lived phenomenon. They draw support for this belief from the continual hardware and software improvements, and the progress towards increasing compatibility between successive models which, together with relatively cheap enhancement within a computer range, tends to make the profitable achievement of in-house computing a more easily attainable goal. However, in the immediate future a very real credibility gap remains, which promoters of facilities management services will continue to exploit. In so doing, they may well set up chains of compatible large installations across the country, and will thus secure a powerful position from which to develop and specialise their services, perhaps by giving users tailored systems to which they have access by terminals and small front-end computers. In this way facilities management might pave the way towards the long-forecast nationwide computer network.

8

Third-party Computer Leasing

R. J. Oliver

Definition

Leasing contains an ingredient of excitement when associated with computers, which it does not possess in relation to other equipment. The essence of this is that the specialist computer leasing company takes a gamble. It looks upon the computer as a long-term investment, with revenue-earning potential far beyond the period covered by the lease with the first user. The leasing company takes the risk that it will be able to find a second or third user before making its ultimate profit.

When the lease involves this element of risk it is known as an 'operating' lease, as distinct from the conventional 'financial' or 'full payout' lease. The financial lease is a relatively familiar method of financing the acquisition of a wide range of industrial plant and equipment. Over the term of lease, the lessor is paid the full cost of the equipment, the cost of money and an additional margin to cover his own administrative expenses and profit requirements. Since the lessee is endeavouring to conserve capital or credit, he will seek to minimise repayments and therefore spread them over as long a period as is reasonable in relation to the life of the asset, typically five years or more.

The computer user, however, is not normally concerned with the functional life of the equipment, but only how long it will be useful to him. With the ogre of technological obsolescence never far in the future and with a workload which is not only expanding but expanding at an apparently unpredictable rate, he can rarely commit for as much as five years. So another feature of the operating lease is the relative shortness of its duration: commonly three to four years, sometimes as little as one or two.

History

The concept of the third-party operating lease on computer equipment originated in the United States. Indeed, even in Europe, the service has been provided almost exclusively by US-based companies. Its origin can be traced as far back as 1961 when D P Boothe Inc wrote an operating lease on an IBM 7094 for Ling-Temco-Vought. The principal attraction to the user was a saving in additional use charges, then 40 per cent of the primary shift rental.

However, second-generation computers were not really amenable to leasing because any significant increase in power or capacity required a change of hardware, so that even a medium-term commitment would not have been tolerable.

This constraint disappeared with third-generation systems which permit considerable growth through addition rather than change. At the same time, the total cost of running a computer was steadily mounting: because of the increased power and sophistication of the equipment, correspondingly more had to be spent on software and other supporting functions. The overall cost meant that the user had to think in terms of a longer life span for each system he installed, in the range of say three to five years.

The hardware itself was now sufficiently reliable, flexible and modular for a functional life span of at least ten years to be foreseen, against four years for rental to become equivalent to the purchase price. Being prepared to wait longer than this to recover their costs, the leasing companies could provide the equipment at less than the manufacturer's rental.

The state of computer technology and IBM's pricing structure thus created a potential opportunity, but a further vital ingredient was required before the business could take off, namely finance. This too became available from a variety of sources. Initially, US banks provided loan finance on the security of income guaranteed under the lease, typically from major companies with a first-class credit rating. With a relatively small charge for depreciation and smaller interest and administrative costs to set against revenues, the leasing companies quickly showed substantial and rising profits. In the traditionally adventurous investment climate of the US, with the market optimism of 1967-8, with the glamour then pertaining to any high-technology business and particularly to the computer industry, the leasing companies suddenly became the hottest favourite of the US investor and hence attracted huge additional funds.

Soon there were well over 100 companies operating in the US led by Boothe,

Greyhound, Leasco, Randolph and Levin-Townsend, each of these with computer inventories in the range of $100 million to $200 million. Total industry investment has reached $2800 million. Of this, $200 million is in Europe and $100 million in the UK.

The availability of money at the right price had ultimately made the computer leasing business possible. The rise in interest rates and shortage of money, combined and associated with the down-turn on Wall Street in 1969, slowed the business almost to a standstill. Towards the end of 1969 the same influences were at work in Europe, and few new contracts were entered into here after the first quarter of 1970.

In June 1970 IBM announced System/370 and this meant two things for the leasing companies: they had now to view their investment in the context of future competition with System/370, and the 370 itself had to be evaluated for its own leasing potential. Either way, further investment in the 360 would be unwise, so no more operating leases were written.

How did IBM view the leasing company phenomenon? And how did it react? For once it was probably surprised, and not pleasantly surprised either; although it too had something to gain. IBM did not welcome the prospect of future competition from its own equipment at substantial discounts from its own prices. Nor did they like the disturbance of their 'normal' ratio between sale and rental. At the same time they received from this the benefit of an unexpectedly large cash flow and they found further short-term benefits in the market place: their equipment was now cheaper in a competitive situation than under their own rental plan or, looked at from another point of view, their customers could obtain more equipment without spending more than they had planned under previous 'IBM rental' budgets.

Considering the leasing companies as a net disadvantage, IBM found itself with little room for manoeuvre. The Consent Decree of 1956 obliged IBM to retain a 'reasonable' ratio between its rental and purchase prices and although this obligation had formally expired, IBM was under constant surveillance from the US Department of Justice because of its huge share (around 70 per cent) of the US computer market. This deterred any measures which might explicitly undermine the position of the leasing companies, and in fact IBM maintained a posture of equal treatment towards all customers, which meant that the user lost nothing in the way of service by going through a leasing company.

Speculation entertained the possibility that IBM might itself offer a leasing facility, but this would have had more impact on its own high rental revenues than it might have gained by reducing leasing company activity.

So IBM made no difficulties for the leasing companies and even developed a special department to deal with what had become a very substantial new type of customer.

Lessee motivation

However mixed the opinions of the manufacturers, however varied the fortunes of the leasing companies, the computer user who employed a leasing facility has generally found it highly rewarding. Without any significant change in his relationship with the supplier, the user has been able to obtain exactly the same equipment for between 10 and 25 per cent less than the normal rental charge.

Substantial cost savings have, therefore, been the principal benefit to the user. Also, leasing offers a further option in the choice of acquisition method. Traditionally the manufacturer offered two alternatives: rental, usually for a minimum of twelve months only, or outright purchase. Leasing provided a further choice: a lower rental charge for a longer period of commitment. The previous rental user and the previous purchase user both found the leasing proposition attractive. This is because the conventional alternatives are best only in extreme situations which are not the normal user requirements: short-term rental is suited to the user who wishes to make frequent major changes to his equipment, and purchase to the very stable environment where a commitment of six years or more is acceptable and where, also, capital or credit are readily available and not better employed for other purposes.

In practice, even for the rental user, major equipment changes cannot be economically made in less than two to three years so that the flexibility provided with a twelve-month agreement is more illusory than real; it is in fact a relic of the punched card era when change was less pervasive in its effect on a company's overall activities.

The purchase user already realised that the manufacturer's rental terms offered flexibility he did not need at a price he did not want to pay. However, the purchase alternative contained two daunting deterrents: first, commitment to hardware over a period long into the future (at least six years) during which unforeseen requirements could arise for computer processing power, and during which technological advance could make the equipment obsolete; and second, tying up large amounts of capital or credit which could normally be employed better elsewhere in the company, in its own line of business.

Leasing, therefore, provided a very acceptable compromise between the extremes of rental and purchase, and the commitment of two to five years, tailored to the user's plans, was less of a hardship than a correlation with real requirements. Furthermore, different components of the system could be rented or purchased, if these methods of acquisition were selectively found most suitable. For example, if a faster printer is planned one year after the main installation, this could be rented direct from the manufacturer, while the rest of the system is leased.

In addition to the saving against the manufacturer's normal rental charge, leasing contains a further tangible advantage. The leasing company's charge normally covers use of the equipment 24 hours a day, whereas the manufacturer's standard rental is for a specified number of hours per month, roughly equivalent to a single shift five days a week. An additional charge is made for use beyond this period. It is true that the leasing customer will probably incur an additional charge for maintenance, but this again is less than the rental alternative.

There are a variety of ways in which the leasing customer can capitalise on the benefits available. Most obviously, he can reduce the cost of his computer installation. Alternatively, he can have more equipment or more people for the same expenditure as previously budgeted under the manufacturer's rental plan.

In addition, there are more far-reaching opportunities for the user, the benefits of which could far outweigh the direct savings. Through leasing, it may well be possible to install a system of greater power than originally envisaged, and then keep it for longer. A leased 360/40, for example, may cost as little as a 360/30. The user who needs the power of a Model 30 now and a Model 40 in, say, two years' time could afford to install the Model 40 at the outset and then hold it for, say, five years.

The real advantage from doing this is not only in acquiring more power for the same money, but rather in conferring stability on the data processing department. By avoiding frequent changes in hardware the user avoids the concomitant expense of software and procedural changes. Where there are frequent major changes in equipment, the energies and costs of the data processing department are expended on technical transition from one language to another or from one operating system to another. This does not make profit for the company. However, by first establishing a stable technical environment for, say, five years, the data processing staff can then concentrate on its main purpose of increasing the computer's functional contribution to the company's business. In this way, the leasing facility provides the opportunity not only for better value from expenditure on the hardware itself, but for better value from the whole computer investment.

And who is currently enjoying all these benefits? In fact it is the upper echelons of British industry; Boots Pure Drug Company, The British Aircraft Corporation, British Steel Corporation and ICI are among users in the UK. Major companies tend to predominate among the customers of the leasing companies for a number of reasons: they have more to gain in absolute terms, they were quick to perceive the advantages, and they were attractive to the leasing companies because of their credit standing and because they tended to have medium to large computer systems which most lessors favoured.

A 360/50 user could be saving in excess of £100,000 over a three year period and it is estimated that compared with the rental alternative, lessees in this country are saving of the order of £2 million per year.

Lessor motivation

Like the lessee, the lessor is in the business for the money he can make out of it. Already a number of entrepreneurial fortunes have been made (and some lost) in the USA from this business and some companies of substance have emerged, already diversified into other fields.

The lessor's starting point is his willingness to take an eight- to ten-year view of the computer as a revenue-earning investment. He supports this position in a number of ways: first, the computer is an electronic device with little to wear out; second, third-generation computers are sufficiently reliable and modular to have a long working life; third, they have proved to be compatible with the next 'generation' of hardware; fourth, the pace of technological change in the computer industry is slowing down.

The lessor's view of the machine is thus quite different from the user's. It is also quite different from that of the manufacturers. In developing and building a computer, or family of computers, the manufacturer has invested huge sums of money. Even before the first computer of a new 'generation' reaches its first customer the manufacturer has spent millions of pounds on research and development, and on plant and equipment. He has to recoup this within as short a period as the market place will allow, in a market place which is rental-oriented. In practice the selling price of a computer is normally recovered in approximately four years of rental.

So the manufacturer's rental-to-purchase ratio is four years, the user thinks in terms of three to five years, and the lessor believes it will earn reasonable revenues for eight to ten years. Here then lay the opportunity for providing an attractive service which could itself become a substantial business.

Leasing gained rapid acceptance and generated large and fast-growing profits for the lessor. These were to some extent dependent upon the rate of depreciation, and true profits would be obtained only when the lessor had fully recovered all expenses at some time in the future.

And this would depend on the lessor's capability in remarketing his equipment when the first user had finished with it. This capability certainly did not exist, nor was it needed, when the initial leases were being written. The lessor would certainly need this capability and/or other business activities to offset the risk inherent in the leasing operations themselves.

The leasing companies did not have to wait long to satisfy these requirements. The size of profit they were generating and their rate of growth rapidly captured the imagination of the investing public in the USA, providing a high multiple for the company's stock. This is turn gave the leasing companies the opportunity for acquisition and diversification.

Here they faced their biggest challenge. In order to survive, the entrepreneurial opportunists had now to exercise wide-ranging business judgement in determining how to grow, and then in managing the new corporate entity. Here mistakes were inevitably made and diversification for the sake of it produced some strange and undesirable results. The most common, and most successful areas of diversification or internal development have been in the computer services area including software, service bureaux, time sharing and brokerage. Of the pure leasing companies (as distinct from computer leasing subsidiaries of major corporations) the most effective to date has undoubtedly been Leasco. They have not only developed or acquired the services mentioned above, but have obtained consulting organisations with a wide range of industrial expertise and a large insurance company in the U.S. which provides a very substantial base of financial stability.

Outlook

IBM equipment has dominated this review of the leasing companies' activities simply because of their strong majority share of every market in the world except that of the United Kingdom. Some operating leases have been written in this country on ICL equipment, and a very few on other manufacturers' equipment as well, but these account for only a very small percentage of the world-wide leasing inventory. The leasing companies could only afford to take their risk on equipment that is widely popular throughout the world.

When looking to the future, therefore, IBM must still have an over-riding influence on their likely policies. System/370 has in fact been announced with a price structure which makes the operating lease very difficult to write. A comparable rent/purchase ratio has been retained, but the cost of maintenance has been radically increased. This is part of the formula for determining total cost under a leasing arrangement and means either that the lessor has to take a bigger risk or that the term would be of such a length as to be unacceptable to the user. The leasing companies have the advantage that they could, with System/370, start earlier in the life cycle of the machine, but they have still to make a judgement on how long this will be, and to what extent the 370 may or may not be an 'interim generation'. Whatever their conclusions, if operating leases become available they will offer far less dramatic savings and will be for a longer average term than on System/360.

These observations would, of course, require modification if IBM revises its pricing methods for the 370, which is not beyond the realms of possibility in view of the current interest which the Department of Justice is taking in the entire IBM phenomenon.

Another 'phenomenon', at least as seen through the eyes of the USA or continental Europe, has been the investment grant. Many countries imposed a tax on investment, which in the UK was being stimulated by the investment grant. This disappeared for contracts after 26 October 1970 and again diminishes the attractiveness of any lease that could be written in the UK, just as it helped to make computer leasing in this country the most attractive in Europe from the lessee's point of view.

For the user, the most interesting activity of the leasing companies in the future will be as providers of used equipment. Despite the huge size of the computer industry today and despite the fact that it has been commercially significant for as long as fifteen years, very few organisations indeed have been able to acquire a computer at second-hand prices. This is partly a function of rapid technological obsolescence during the early part of this period, but most significantly because rental from the manufacturer has been the dominant method of acquisition. When he has a new generation of computers to sell, it is not in his interest to prolong the life of older machines at lower prices.

The leasing companies, however, have a very powerful motive for extending the life of their equipment: it was part of their original strategy and they need the revenues to offset continuing depreciation charges and the marketing expenses they will incur. In addition, they have a substantial inventory: $200 million at new prices in Europe alone, or nearly 4 per cent of the IBM total in System/360.

The equipment will not be available at knock-down prices but it will provide the user with an opportunity further to reduce his data processing expenditure. The equipment will be attractive for some of the same reasons as the original leasing proposition, not least of which was the chance to obtain profitable work from the computer through a policy of hardware stability. The fourth generation is yet another occasion for exciting technological upheaval in the data processing department. This may be good for the prestige of the technical staff, but it will not help the company's profits while it is going on. Used equipment can therefore by employed to obtain extra power by moving from say a 360/40 to a 360/50 without a parallel systems/programming metamorphosis.

Alternatively, extra power may be obtained be getting a second computer of the same type, thereby providing identical on-site standby. Either way, the user will have the benefit not only of staying with the technology his people know, but he will have hardware and systems software that are thoroughly proven and widely used.

Third-generation equipment may be used instead of fourth-generation machines, or even side-by-side with them, simply because the nature of the workload does not require the sophistication of the latest technological wonders. The mundane high-volume routing applications still have to be done and existing equipment may be perfectly adequate. In fact, lurking inside many a third-generation computer is a second-generation application, not markedly different from its first-generation or punched card precursor. And this is perhaps indicative of the fact that computer hardware technology is frequently far in advance of the user's ability or need to use it.

This may apply not only to hardware but to software. And in the future this distinction may be increasingly important when a change of computer is under consideration. As 'unbundling' begins to bite throughout the industry, existing languages and systems software will begin to have a premium value. It will continue to be available free of charge and will enhance the value of the hardware with which it works.

This may well be supplemented by technical support from the leasing companies which have a software capability, so that third generation machines may continue 'bundled' into the era of unbundling.

With managements' increasing concern over the cost of data processing and their steadily improving ability to control it, a further impetus is likely to emerge in favour of staying with the third-generation machine. This may well, especially when fully loaded, provide the most economic solution to a user's needs even though it does not offer the extreme in versatility and price/performance in a given broad range of equipment cost. Perhaps the very management (or their successors at the same level), who ten years ago were keen to install the latest technological wonder as a matter of competitive principle, may use the same principle, in a more realistic context, to demand a third-generation solution to their problems of tomorrow.

9

Service Bureaux and Time Sharing

Geoffrey Holland

A service bureau is a commercial organisation usually owning one or more computers which offers a range of computing services on a pay-as-you-use basis to industry, commerce and government. Generally, customers of bureaux do not have a computer of their own although many computer owners buy specific services from bureaux. The first bureaux were established in the late 1950s by the computer manufacturers, mainly as a shop window aid to selling their range of computing equipment. However, many of the early prospects for computer purchase found they could obtain a satisfactory service from a bureau without the need to acquire their own computer.

Size of bureaux

The number of bureaux has increased from around 6 in 1961 to over 120 in 1971. 97 of these firms contribute to the quarterly statistical return prepared by the Department of Trade and Industry. Their geographical spread is as follows:

REGION	PERCENTAGE OF COMPANIES
London and South	70
Midlands	12
North	9
Scotland	5
Wales and Ulster	4

The above figures disguise the fact that several of the larger firms have centres in the provinces although their head office is included in the London grouping.

Turnover of bureaux has increased rapidly in recent years as the following DTI figures show:

YEAR	£ MILLIONS
1968	25.3
1969	33.9
1970	46.8
1971	52.0

The two major firms, Baric and IBM Data Centre Services account between them for about 20 per cent of the market. The remaining 80 per cent is shared between the other 95 firms with no firm exceeding a 5 per cent share. The top ten firms account for more than 50 per cent of total turnover.

Owners of bureaux

Bureaux have generally originated with the following five kinds of parenthood:

Computer manufacturers. Bureaux are now mostly established as subsidiary companies or separate operating divisions of the parent company.

Independents. Companies established specifically to provide computer services, often on an international basis. Many were started by groups of entrepreneurs with little financial support.

Large user offshoots. Several companies that have installed larger computers than they need to meet their own processing loads and have built up skilled teams of experienced staff now offer computing services to outside customers. Nationalised concerns. The Post Office, National Coal Board and Central Electricity Generating Board all offer their computing resources on a commercial basis to private industry.

Consultancies, software firms and specialist concerns offer a variety of services on a more limited basis.

The larger companies offer a broad range of services covering remote and batch processing, application software development, data preparation, facilities management and training on a national basis. Several bureaux with a bias towards remote processing can offer an international service. For example, users in, say, Stockholm, Paris and London may share the same computer service at the same time though terminals linked by international telephone network. One company provides a service in Europe linked to its computer in the USA by a communications satellite.

Several companies provide specialist applications, such as payroll and financial services of interest to specific industries.

Future trends

The rapid growth of the industry coupled with fast technological innovation has made forecasting a highly uncertain activity. In 1969 the Hoskyns Group in their report, *UK Computer Industry Trends 1970-80,* forecast a market size for bureaux of £483 million by 1980. With the economic recession in 1971 and the dramatic cut-back in computer orders and expenditure on services it is a bold marketeer who is planning his company's strategy to this figure. However, several trends are apparent.

The industry is generally undercapitalised and is unlikely to attract investment until larger groupings are formed and profitability is improved.

Many of the smaller firms and those pushing back technical frontiers are likely to go out of business for want of better marketing skills to provide the services demanded by users at a price they are willing to pay.

There will be a continued growth in remote-processing services which should become increasingly attractive as the Post Office introduces a data communication network of a switched nature in the late 1970s.

The high cost of original software development will be beyond the resources of medium and small firms. A corresponding increase in standard or 'package' services will emerge where the initial costs are spread over many users.

Some of the bureaux which originated as offshoots of large users will withdraw from the market as parent firms come to realise that they are not really in the computer service business.

Why use a bureau?

The purchase and implementation of a computer installation is a complex process fraught with pitfalls for those companies tackling the task for the first time. Using a service bureau provides a practical alternative which reduces the risk for management gaining their first experience of computers.

Some typical reasons for using bureaux are:

No purchase of capital equipment.
Insufficient accommodation for own computer and staff.
Insufficient workload to keep own computer busy.
The kind of work demands the resources of a large computer on a part-time basis.
Work is irregular, seasonal, or has peaks of activity at a month end.
No desire to tie up own management in administering the day-to-day operation of equipment.
Difficulty in retaining experienced staff to continue with existing clerical or mechanical methods.

Charges for bureau use are made on a 'pay-as-you-use' basis.

A specific application is available only from a bureau.

Own computer is overloaded but there is insufficient additional work to justify replacing it with the next larger model.

A particular set of programs may be more efficiently operated on a more powerful computer than the company owns.

Convenience—it may be easier and quicker to solve a problem using a bureau. This is particularly true with remote-processing timesharing services.

Flexibility—once equipment has been bought it must be used fully to get the best return on the investment. Using a bureau enables shopping around to get the best buy and to take advantage of technical improvements as they become available.

Capacity for growth—an existing clerical system may be fully stretched and cannot cope with expansion without getting more accounting machines and people. Changing to a bureau gives the scope to increase business volumes several times without a proportional increase in cost.

Disadvantages and pitfalls of bureau operation

Level of service   Remember that when work is handed to a bureau it joins that from many other organisations and is competing for a share of the bureau's resources both in computers and people. Most bureaux are efficient in scheduling the work through their centres but if things go awry, such as a temporary breakdown in equipment, a delay in return of completed work is usually inevitable. The current economics of bureau operation do not allow for spare staff to be waiting around for an emergency to happen.

If you are unhappy with the service you are getting from your bureau complain energetically—bureaux do not like having unhappy customers. In general an acceptable service level is a subjective assessment on the part of the user. If you do not complain the bureau will think you are a satisfied customer. Contention for service is being reduced with the increasing availability of remote-processing systems as the scheduling of the work then comes under the initiative of the user.

Control   Inevitably if processing work is contracted out, there is not the same degree of control as when the work is processed in-company. This is not usually a significant problem in practice so long as a good relationship with the bureau is maintained.

Communication   Each service bureau may have several hundred organisations as customers from many different industries. Although some bureaux specialise in servicing specific industries, they cannot understand the intimate problem of one industry or procedures of one firm. Poor communication between customer and bureau is often a cause of misunderstanding.

Applications processed by bureaux

The major applications processed by service bureaux are:

COMMERCIAL	SCIENTIFIC AND ENGINEERING
Payroll	Project control (PERT)
Sales accounting	Scientific analysis
Purchase accounting	Engineering design
Hire purchase accounting	Modelling
Production control	Planning and estimating
Stock control	Optimisation, linear programming
Analyses and forecasting	Transportation
Share registration	General calculations

There are not many activities in research, manufacturing and commerce where the characteristics of a computer cannot be put to good use.

Available services

The range of services available from service bureaux is becoming increasingly varied and covers the majority of ways in which computers can serve management. The services that an organisation is most likely to buy from a bureau are:

Computer time hire   This service accounts for some 35 per cent of current usage and covers the hire of all, or part of the computer's resources for a specific job or agreed numbered of hours. Sometimes the customer provides his own program for the bureau to process or he uses a standard application program from the bureau's library of preprogrammed routines.

Tailormade systems   Sometimes known as a 'full' or 'custom built' service this is where the bureau designs and implements a complete business system to its customer's own particular requirements. The service comprises a detailed investigation of the proposed system, preparation of a specification describing

121

the procedures to be transferred to the computer, programming of the system into computer language, testing the system for accuracy and full implementation on the bureau's computer. Charges are made for the initial work involved in analysis, system design, programming and testing and a recurring charge for the repetitive processing based on a time and materials basis.

Remote processing   This type of service has grown rapidly over the last three years. Its big advantage is that it does away with the need to send actual documents by post or van delivery between the customer's office and the bureau. A terminal is installed in the customer's office, factory or research laboratory which is linked to the bureau computer through the Post Office Datel telephone service.

The terminals may be either simple low-cost keyboard equipment similar to an electric typewriter or more expensive devices which are, in effect, small computers capable of accepting and printing information at speeds comparable to a normal 'batch' computer. The smaller terminals are connected to the computer whenever required by making a dialled telephone call to the bureau over the public telephone network. The larger and faster terminals need a private leased telephone line permanently connecting the user with the bureau.

These services provide immediate access to the computer at any time of the day and, in some cases, night so that processing results are obtainable within minutes.

Standard programs   Many business routines are similar. Payroll is a classic example, particularly the calculation of net pay from gross pay. Scientific and engineering problems often lend themselves to a standardised, accepted method of solution. Many bureaux have reduced the high cost of original system development by designing generalised programs with optional features appealing to a wide variety of different users. Examples are payroll, sales accounting, critical path analysis and stock control. The bureau provides these programs at a cost that is less than for a custom built system.

Contract systems and programming   Many bureaux have staff designing computer systems on behalf of customers to be processed on the bureau's computer. Oftem the workload fluctuates and in order to balance the work schedule the bureaux offer these staff to work either on a temporary basis at a customer location or undertake a specific programming project without the completed work being processed on the bureau's computer.

Data preparation   Many bureaux undertake the preparation of data from source documents into computer-readable form such as punched cards, paper tape or magnetic tape. Some companies offer this service to computer users as a significant part of their business while others only undertake work for customers who contract for regular processing.

Education and training   A few bureaux offer courses in the appreciation of computers, programming and the training of customers' staff in the day-to-day control procedures needed to implement a computer system.

Facilities management   A new kind of service, which is gaining popularity with cost conscious management is called 'facilities management'. This service covers the selection, installation and operation on a continuous basis of a complete computer complex sited within the customer's business location. In effect, the customer delegates, for a fee, the task of providing computer services to its user departments. The advantage is that the customer is guaranteed a prescribed level of service while avoiding the problems of managing a data processing department.

Miscellaneous services   Bureaux normally operate a van collection service for data and for the return of completed results to their customers' offices. Most provide ancillary services such as decollating and guillotining printed reports and addressing envelopes with computer printed labels and a growing number offer a microfilm service for long-term storage of bulky information.

Preparing to use a bureau

Assuming that an application has been chosen which is suitable for transfer to a computer and it has been decided to use a service bureau the steps to follow in selecting a firm and implementing a project are as follows.

Defining objectives

First draw up a written statement of the aims and objectives to be achieved by the use of the new system.

> What is the scope of the application?
> Which departments will be affected?
> Whose work will be altered or eliminated?
> Will retraining of staff be necessary?
> What is an acceptable timescale and schedule for processing?
> Will there be new ways to interpret and use information?
> What training of management will be required?

Try to qualify objectives as much as possible; for example, 'improvement in availability of monthly analysis by four days' or 'reduction in outstanding debtors by eight days' sales'.

Statement of requirements

Next a written statement should be prepared outlining the requirements to be achieved by the system. This document will be used as a basis for inviting tenders from several bureaux. The report should cover the application to be computerised, stating the sources of information, quantities of data involved, both on average and at peak periods, and finally a brief description of the printed reports and documents needed. State clearly all vital deadlines: availability of data for the bureau; time by which completed results must be returned; and a planned start date for the project.

Selecting a supplier

Not all computer bureaux accept every type of work. Some specialise in commercial accounting, some is scientific and engineering work and yet others offer only remote problem-solving timesharing services. It is important to save time by only approaching those organisations which have the experience and competence to carry out the required application.

Salesmen who are generally paid partly on a commission basis are only too anxious to start negotiations if they think there is a chance of business—even though it often turns out that the terms and service eventually offered by the bureau will make their bid unattractive when compared with competitive quotes. It is better to make a shortlist of about six firms from which a full quotation should be invited based on the written statement of requirements. Names of suitable bureaux may be obtained from:

Existing personal contacts and references.
Direct contact by salesmen.
Trade journals and advertisements.
Direct mail literature.
Computer Services and Bureaux Association (COSBA), whose address is Leicester House, 8 Leicester Street, London WC2H 7BN (telephone 01-437 0678), will provide a list of its member bureaux.

Making the right choice of bureau is critical to the future success of a computer application. A bureau service is a continuing relationship where good communication and personal contact between the two parties is paramount. Once a decision is made it is not easy to change suppliers in midstream. Time spent at this stage of the negotiations can be crucial to success later. Invite representatives from each firm to visit a few days after sending them, by post, a request for quotation enclosing your written requirements. At the meeting, be frank with each salesman. Tell him that you are inviting tenders from competitors, set a deadline for the receipt of quotation and advise him of the time needed to reach a decision on the project. Ask each salesman the following questions:

1   Background to his bureau, how long in business?
2   How many staff and where are his computer centres?
3   How long has he been with his company and what is his background?
4   What experience has the company had of similar work?
5   Is he able to name any reference companies which are currently using his service for this application?
6   Has the bureau any 'package' programs for this application?
7   What is their basis of charging and what term of contract are they prepared to consider.
8   What arrangements are there for the transport of information between your office and the bureau?
9   How would his company go about implementing an application of this type within your organisation?
10 What training will be offered to your staff and is this included in his price?
11 Will he be prepared to let you visit his bureau and discuss your application with other members of his company.

These questions will not only obtain information about the bureau but will enable you to assess the general level of competence and familiarity with your particular application.

While you are waiting for tenders to be submitted think about how you will choose between bureaux. One way is to make a list of attributes about the required service so that you can rank the offers and obtain a logical comparison between tenders. Typical headings for such a list are:

1   Proximity of bureau to your office.
2   Previous experience of bureau.
3   Length of time in business.
4   Assessment of financial stability.
5   Competence of staff.
6   Understanding of your application.

7   Promptness and efficiency in dealing with you.
8   Quality of service offered.
9   Price and delivery quoted.
10   Security arrangements.
11   Provision for expansion planned in proposed system.
12   Compatibility with your other systems, if any.
13   Comments from existing customers.

Once all quotations are received you will be in a position to draw up a shortlist of potential suppliers. At this stage it is worth while seeing the representatives of the shortlisted companies to review their quotations with them so you can assure yourself that they have understood your problem. Misunderstandings and oversights by either party at this stage can lead to strained relations, additional costs and delayed delivery.

Having assessed each quotation, talked to the representatives of the bureaux and possibly taken up references with the supplier's customers you will be able to decide on a bureau or, at least, be in a position to recommend a course of action to your senior management.

Dealing with salesman

Finally a word or two about dealing with the salesman from the competing companies. A professional service bureau salesman will be genuinely interested in helping you and winning your business. He will probably already have spent considerable time with you and with others in his organisation in preparing your quotation. Remember his job is to try his best to obtain your custom so you will inevitably receive telephone calls or requests for visits urging you to decide in his company's favour.

Treat him on a professional basis by being fair and truthful. Let him know your schedule for reaching a decision. He will respect your time if you are honest with him. Evasive replies only make the good salesman more determined to keep contacting you until he gets an informative answer. Gaining the respect of your salesman can pay dividends to you later. One day you will want just that extra bit of service which is outside the terms of the official contract. A good salesman is also usually successful in persuading his colleagues within his bureau to give that favour from time to time.

Pricing and contracts

The basis of charging adopted by a bureau depends on the type of services offered and the sophistication of its equipment. The following illustrates the variety of pricing methods in existence.

Computer time   For smaller computers the price is usually quoted at a rate per hour of elapsed time taken to process the work. Higher rates are charged during the daytime than for overnight and weekend processing. The advantages is that the time is easy to record by clock but some ineffective operator time will have to be paid for. Often discounts will be given off standard rates if more than a certain number of hours a week or month are used.

Most larger computers operate with multiprogramming. The time taken to complete one job will often depend on the contention for the computer's resources by all the other jobs. Charging by elapsed time is inequitable and a more complex method is used based on a formula containing the use made of each technical feature.

Resource units   There is a move being made by several of the larger bureaux to replace the previously mentioned methods by a new basis known as 'resource unit charging'. The principle is similar, but not so precisely scientific, as the unit of charging electrical power—the kilowatt-hour. In essence usage of the different parts of the computer, such as the arithmetic unit, core storage and input equipment, are metered automatically in 'resource' units. At the completion of a job these 'resource' increments are aggregated and a quoted rate per unit applied to give the total price for the job.

Turnround scheduling   Another recent method is to quote a price according to the delay the customer is willing to accept between supplying his data and receiving his results. An application that requires an answer within seconds will be charged more than a customer who is prepared to wait, say, 12 hours for the same result. This basis of pricing will become more common in the future as remote processing develops.

Application unit charging   A common practice applied in the charging for commercial systems is that different rates are quoted for each transaction of data processed or document printed. Thus a charge may be made of, say 2p per order entry and 5p per statement printed. This method is attractive to the customer as he understands the basis of metering and, because of his knowledge of his business, can predict costs fairly accurately.

Fixed-price quotation   Some bureaux take a commercial risk by assessing a particular job and quoting a fixed annual sum to complete the necessary processing. They usually protect themselves by putting an upper limit on the quantities of documents processed but the method has the advantage for the customer that he may budget his expenditure accurately.

127

Combining initial and recurring charges

Many new customers to service bureaux are bewildered by the apparent wide variation in quotations received from different bureaux. For example, a job may be quoted by a bureau A at £5000 for initial development and £2400 a year to process. Bureau B may offer figures of £1500 initial charge and £3500 a year recurring. The differences are explained by the fact that bureau A adopts the policy of costing its software teams on a profitable basis independently of its computer. Bureau B sees its computer as its major profit centre and recovers the cost of its software team on higher processing charges over the term of the contract. In general, new users of computers do not appreciate the complexity of the work involved in preparing good software by highly skilled staff. The initial charges often seem unnecessarily high and, because they are usually treated as capital expenditure, require the approval of a board of directors. Spreading the recovery of the initial development costs over the duration of the contract encourages the customer to reach a decision to proceed and the bureau can fill its computer with work sooner.

Contracts

The nature of the contract agreed between a user and a bureau varies greatly according to the size of organisation and the kind of service provided. Often an exchange of letters setting out the main points of the deal is sufficient. With some of the larger bureaux contract documents run to six pages or more of printed legal clauses. Space does not permit an examination of all the legal eventualities of bureau operation but some of the main points to check are as follows:

1   Does the bureau agree to provide service on a specified computer? What happens is this equipment is unavailable?
2   What is the term of the contract and what period of notice is required by either party?
3   What is the basis of pricing, frequency of invoicing and terms of payment?
4   What notice is to be given by the bureau for increases in price? Is there a let-out clause?
5   Who receives title to the computer programs developed on the customer's behalf at his expense? It is usual for the bureau to retain title, so customers who want to obtain the programs at the end of the contract should establish the cost of ownership before signing the contract.
6   Who pays for reprocessing if errors are made by the bureau?

7   Is the cost of transport of data included in the price?
8   Are there any limits set down regarding assistance in training the customer's staff by the bureau?

Finally, if any amendments to the original contract are made subsequently make sure that the revisions are conformed in writing as an addendum to the contract.

Controlling implementation

Implementing a computer service is a complex operation needing careful planning and many important decisions to be taken by the user's management and the bureau staff. Unless close cooperation is maintained, misunderstandings will arise, delays occur and staff will become disenchanted with a service before it has had time to prove itself.

The following checklist indicates key points of the implementation procedure.

1   Regular meetings should be held with the user company's staff and those of the bureau to review progress, make decisions and map out future action. Meetings should be held weekly at first, then fortnightly while the system is under development and weekly again nearer the time to transfer the user's work to the computer. There should be a formal agenda and all significant facts and decisions, such as changes in specification, information to be provided, schedule revisions and assignment responsibilities, should be recorded in writing.
2   One person should be appointed in the user company to be responsible for coordinating all communications between the user and the bureau.
3   Consideration should be given to the effects the new service on staff. How and when will it be best to tell them?
4   A visit to the bureau should be arranged for staff who will be in day-to-day contact with the computer system. It is amazing the effect such a visit can have on clerical staff when they see that the computer is not some superhuman monster.
5   There should be early planning of the necessary changes to the user's internal administrative control procedures. These include form filling, preparation of batch totals and the control of data being sent to the bureau.
6   Training and trials runs should occur well before the changeover occurs. Everybody must know the part he has to play.

129

7   A comprehensive procedures manual must be prepared, written in simple english so that each clerk may refer to it at any time. Computers are unforgiving machines and several companies have suffered chaos because a clerk has left their employment with all the correct procedures in her head.

8   Requirements for special forms, needed for recording data, should be assessed. Will they be provided by the user or the bureau?

9   Requirements for special preprinted stationery for invoices, statements and so on, should be assessed. The design should be approved by the user and adequate supplies should be ordered in time to meet the start date for regular processing. Whose responsibility is it to re-order once initial supplies are nearly used up?

10 The user should establish how data is to be transported to the bureau and back to his office.

11 Special arrangements may have to be made for the initial transfer of basic record information to the computer system; for example, names, addresses, current balances on a sales ledger.

12 It is usually desirable to introduce the computer system alongside the existing system for a time. For how long is this parallel operation possible? What are the potential problems? Has the additional cost been estimated?

After installation

Inevitably some problems will arise in the early stages of implementation which will require some give and take by both parties. No matter how skilled the bureau's technical staff there will always be some unexpected event which causes a problem to occur. After three months of regular processing it is time to have a post-installation review and compare progress with the objectives that were originally set.

Are you getting the results you expected?
How are the clerical procedures being handled by your staff?
Have staff become used to the strict procedure needed to identify and correct errors in data highlighted by the computer?
Is one type of error arising more frequently? Can you identify the cause?
Are you satisfied with the accounting controls built into the system?
Do all reconciliations balance at the end of each processing run?
Is the bureau maintaining the contracted level of service?
What is the trend of charges? How do they compare with your budgeted expenditure?

Do your staff feel that the bureau understands all the day-to-day aspects of processing your application?

Are you able to check the invoices sent by the bureau?

What other areas of your company's operation could you begin to consider for further applications of computers?

PART 3

Managing the data processing function

10

Budgeting, Planning and Control of Computer Activities

Michael Thornley

The methods and techniques appropriate to budgeting, planning and control of computer activities must be designed to match the needs of the activity. The techniques and methods appropriate to a commercial bureau or time-sharing enterprise will differ from a dedicated real-time system such as a reservations system. Rather than review all the methods and techniques in their appropriate environments, which could be the subject of a book, this chapter concentrates on those appropriate for a computer activity operating within a commercial enterprise acting as a service to other departments in a company or to other companies within a group. Obviously many of the techniques, and particularly their objectives, have a wider significance. The chapter emphasises the planning and control aspects that are integrated with and fundamental to financial budgeting.

The main characteristics of a computer service department in relation to budgeting, planning and control are those resulting from serving a number of customers.

In brief terms, these characteristics are:

1   The operation of a variety of widely differing systems for departments or companies of the enterprise.
2   The development of a variety of different systems or modification of existing systems.
3   The need to meet time and date schedules for development of new systems or production of routine results for differing and independent departments or organisations that may coincide.

4   Changes in the volumes of data processed or even systems operated due to seasonal activities, changes in business patterns due to economic conditions or the businesses or industries in which the group is involved.

Need for control

The word 'control' is often misunderstood and taken in the restrictive or negative sense. In the context here control refers to the adjustment or correction that is necessary in the light of deviation from standard or a plan to achieve the standard or planned objective. The essential ingredients of the control process are:

1   Establishment of the standard or plan
2   Measurement of actual against the standard or planned performance
3   Action taken to close the 'gap' between standard and actual performance either by adjusting the resources or method to bring actual performance in line or changing the objective standard.

Realisation that control is essential to a computer activity, particularly a computer service department, is probably more important than the nature of the methods and techniques that are used. The particular characteristics of a computer activity serving differing segments of a commercial enterprise make planning and control difficult and, at the same time, more important. Inadequate planning and control of a computer activity serving a number of customers such as has been outlined could present such problems as:

1   Shortage or excess computer capacity: either not enough time to meet required production work or expensive equipment standing idle
2   Shortage or excess human resources: analysts and programmers either not available to meet work requirements or unoccupied.

Planning and control are essential to achieve the balance between the availability of man and machine resources when they are required while avoiding costly under-employment of these resources.

In planning computer activities, particularly systems analysis and programming, determination of how long a task will take is certainly difficult. It is probably a fair generalisation that the majority of major computer projects are implemented late. The time taken to devise a system and to get it accepted is subject to a series of unknowns, some of which are related to revisions, modifications and the objections of people. The time taken to produce a working program is similarly intensely difficult to predetermine and, in the extreme, can be subject to the brain waves of programmers and the possible need 'to start all over again'.

This difficulty in determining time required and therefore the resources required for planning computer work, particularly those related to human resources, must be accepted as the reason for planning and control. It follows that in computer work, deviations from standard or the plan are bound to occur relatively frequently and, consequently, that frequent adjustment or correction in the light of actual performance is necessary. The truism that the purpose of measuring actual progress against planned progress is to anticipate delay in time for action to be taken is particularly apt in computer work.

Controlled environment

The previous section outlined the reasons for careful control of a computer service department in terms of the events that could occur without control and the difficulties of planning and controlling particularly the human resources that are involved. It would seem that computer management learnt the lessons of how to control a computer department slowly and painfully. The claim that computer systems are often implemented late was, at one time, well justified. The methods and techniques of planning and control evolved with the aid of consulting companies that became exposed to the problems of late implement- ation and sometimes late realisation of the complete failure of a project.

It is now generally accepted within the industry that it is necessary to create a totally controlled environment to the extent that planning and controlling becomes the key factor around which the productive elements of the computer department revolve. Thus, the way the analyst or programmer carries out his tasks is related to units or segments of the total task which can be more accurately planned; the processes involved in each segment are defined to a uniform standard. Similarly, standards are introduced for data preparation and the operation of computing equipment so that performance can be measured, deviations identified and the control process applied. The following, in brief terms, summarises what is involved in the controlled environment for a computer service department. It should be stressed that just as the methods and techniques of control used are related to the characteristics of the department so, in turn, should the extent by which the enviroment is controlled.

Management and organisation

Leaving aside the obvious factors of strong and capable management and the aspects of technical knowledge, the management of the computer department must be trained and capable of managing the department as a formally structured and disciplined unit. The practice of management must be based on a well-defined organisation structure, terms of reference and procedures and disciplined planning and control.

Terms of reference

Each of the functional areas—systems analysis, programming, operations, systems programming, and planning—should have clearly defined responsibility and the senior staff should have written terms of reference stating their areas of responsibility and authority.

Documentation standards

All documentation, particularly relating to systems, programs and operations, should be standardised to obtain relative uniformity throughout the unit.

Programming standards

The programming language or languages used and the specific version of these should be standardised and, where more than one language is in use, there should be rules covering the circumstances under which each should be used.

To simplify the programming and program testing tasks and also to provide a means of planning and control, the programming task should be broken down to controllable units or modules. A variety of modular programming techniques exist, all of which, in simple terms, aim at reducing each program to a series of modules or controllable units. The Diebold system, which restricts modules to a maximum size of ten program statements, was one of the first approaches to modular programming. A number of equipment manufacturers and other consulting companies supply both modular programming systems and test programs.

Procedures

Specified procedures should exist for the main activities of the department of which the following is a representative list.

1   Providing quotations of costs and date schedules for requested projects to companies or departments served.

2   Arranging and agreeing new or modified schedules for the produc-
    tion of results involving computing and data preparation equipment.
3   The transfer of projects between departments as the preparatory
    work progresses through the development stages of systems,
    programming and implementation.
4   Short- and long-term planning of human and machine resources.
5   Purchasing of equipment and supplies.
6   Project control.
7   Recruitment, training and staff development.

Planning

This section explains a series of techniques that are applicable for planning the
activities of a computer service department with particular reference to
computing, allied equipment and the human resources concerned with systems,
programming and machine operating. The techniques described are appropriate
for an on-going situation and aspects such as accommodation and the
installation of new major equiment are omitted.

Time planning unit

The primary element of planning for both human and machine resources is that
of time and it is necessary to identify a unit of time that can be used for planning
purposes. Of the various alternatives appropriate for human resources—man-
days, man-weeks, or man-hours—the unit found most acceptable is the half day.
This unit allows adoption of the decimal system since there are ten half days in
the five-day working week and thus twenty-five units represent two weeks and
five half days or two and one-half weeks. For planning of machine resources,
hours and minutes are customary and adequate for most planning purposes.

Long-term planning

For most purposes, the computer service department is concerned with detailed
planning for one year ahead and the staffing and equipment required during that
period.

Manpower   For systems and programming staff, following the approach that
has been described, the objective is to identify the resources that are required
and to design a system which provides for measuring the utilisation and

productivity of these resources against the plan. The process of calculating the resources required and their utilisation is carried out by adding together those required on the known systems and programming projects, estimating those projects not yet identified and combining the result of these calculations with:

Administration	National holidays
Supervision	Annual holidays
Sickness	Training

In this way, a staff establishment of the systems and programming staff for the year is calculated together with an analysis of how the resources will be consumed. A Gantt chart setting out the analysis of how the resources are allocated in terms of percentages can be prepared. A specimen Gantt chart setting out the allocation of resources is given in Figure 10:1. This Figure demonstrates the value of the planning process and the proportion of time the analysts and programmers can be reasonably expected to be engaged in

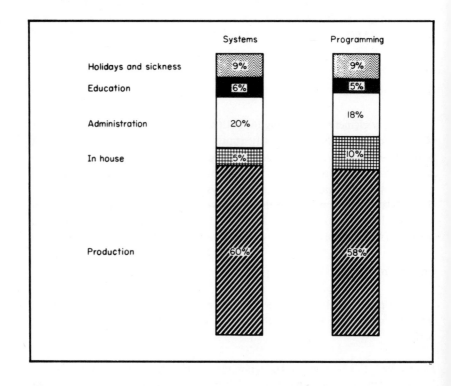

Figure 10:1   Resource planning standards

productive work. On the example shown, analysts and programmers are respectively productive for only 60 and 58 per cent of their time.

For machine operators of both computing and data preparation equipment the number of staff required can be calculated rather more precisely on the basis of equipment planned to be installed and the time or shifts that are planned to be operated. As for planning systems and programming resources, allowance should be made for holidays, etc. and standards established for the allocation of operators' time against which actual performance can be measured.

Equipment Equipment planning must essentially be a continuous process of determining future requirements of new systems to be applied to the equipment in terms of workload and the technical capability that is involved in running the work of the department. An essential procedure of the department must be to adjust future equipment loading plans in the light of new systems to be applied to the equipment, changes in volumes of data handled and in the equipment installed. Care will be necessary to avoid overloading, for example, if testing of new programs coincides with the introduction of new equipment.

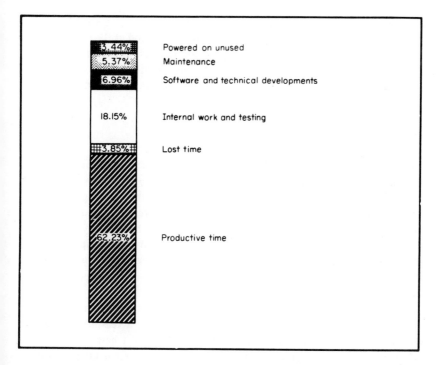

Figure 10:2 Resource planning: computer equipment

A satisfactory means of planning the equipment that is required and its scheduled load over a planning period of a year is the creation of a graph, plotting time on the x-axis and load in terms of hours on the y-axis. On the same chart, equipment or other changes, such as software involving changes to multi-programming techniques, can be marked in.

On similar lines to that described for human resources, standards can be prepared for the utilisation of computer equipment and portrayed in Gantt chart form. A representative chart showing the projected analysis of computer equipment utilisation is set out in Figure 10:2. The analysis is under the following headings:

1   Productive time—in respect of users of the department
2   Lost time—due to causes under the departments' responsibility
3   Time spent in development of computer department's software or other technical developments
4   Maintenance
5   Unused time—switched on but not used.

Planning of data preparation equipment requirements is a straightforward process based on the number of key depressions required in the preparation of the data. It is usual to apply a 'weighting' factor to punching speeds based on the clarity and standard of the basic document. This 'weighting' factor may be used as a basis for a grading or bonus payment system for data preparation staff.

Project planning

The nature of the service provided by the computer service department is the development (that is, systems analysis and programming) of new or modified systems and their implementation as on-going procedures involving the user and the computing equipment installed. To calculate the resources required by the department and to identify and meet date schedules required by users of the department, each new task (or project) undertaken by the computer department must be carefully planned. The difficulty of achieving an accurate forecast of the resources required has already been acknowledged and explained as one of the primary reasons for planning.

At the time the project plan is developed, the computer department will have carried out an initial survey and, for larger projects, a feasibility study, to determine the economic justification and viability of a new system. Some calculations of the resources required will therefore be carried out at the survey stage.

The quantity of resources required for systems, programming and equipment should be determined by, or in consultation with, the line managers concerned. Each manager, knowing his commitments and the resources he has, or has authority for, determines the quantity that will be required and the date schedule that he can reasonably meet.

A project accepted in terms of costs and dates by the user and undertaken by the computer department should have a documented plan setting out:

1   Project number
2   'Customer' name
3   Systems department:
     (a)   Date of commencement
     (b)   Number of units of time (half days) allocated
     (c)   Scheduled completion date
4   Programming department
     (a)   Date of commencement
     (b)   Number of units of time allocated for preparation of programs
     (c)   Machine time required for program testing
5   Operating departments
     (a)   Details of data preparation resources allocated
     (b)   Machine time allocated for operational running
     (c)   Details of production deadlines.

Controlling

As already explained, controlling is the process of adjustment or correction in the light of deviations from plan or standard so that objectives or standards are maintained. The primary element of controlling is the feedback of actual performance or progress which is compared with the standard or plan. In a computer service department, control is necessary so that:

1   Schedules for the implementation of new systems and the production of required results from the computing equipment are met
2   The consumption of human and machine resources is in line with plans
3   Quality standards of the department are maintained
4   Productivity standards of the department are maintained
5   Operations can be within cost budgets.

This section describes methods of controlling these five types of objectives. With the exception of cost, which is dealt with independently, the method of control that is explained involves a procedure for reporting actual performance against which comparison with plans is made.

Performance reporting

Reporting actual performance is best carried out by the line managers in respect of the functions for which they are responsible. The less desirable alternative is to have progress reports produced by a planning or administrative department. The last section showed that project plans should be formulated by or in consultation with the line managers and, in particular, that they should be involved in determining date schedules.

The performance reports produced by the systems and programming departments are identical in format. Two reports are produced each month: the project progress report (Figure 10:3) and department productivity report (Figure 10:4). The project progress report contains information relating to each project and is produced by analysis of time records kept by each analyst and programmer. It contains the following information for each project:

1   Project number
2   Project name
3   Name of user department
4   Total planned units (half days) for the project
5   Total units consumed (or spent) to last month
6   Units consumed (or spent) this month
7   Latest best estimate of units of work required to complete the project
8   Scheduled project completion date
9   The words 'on schedule' or 'late'
10   Number of units forecast to be under- or over-consumed on the basis of the latest estimate compared with the original plan.

The productivity report is produced by further analysis of the time records maintained by each analyst and programmer and is produced in Gantt chart form identical to that shown in Figure 10:1. To permit ease of comparison, the Gantt chart report of the current month's performance is shown adjacent to the standard. Figure 10:4 shows an example of a productivity report for a systems department setting out the utilisation of resources and the standard in terms of percentages analysed under the following headings:

1   Productive work on projects
2   In-house work—in respect of internal technical or systems changes
3   Administration

| | | | SYSTEMS DEPARTMENT | | | | | | PERIOD NUMBER | | ENDING |
Project Number	Project Title	Division/Department	Total planned units	Units spent to last month	Units spent to this month	Estimated units to Completion	Completion deadline	On schedule or late	Completed units over/under those planned	Improvement deterioration over the last period	Comments
Q232	Vehicle Scheduling (initial investigation)	–	600	243	317	283	31.1.71	On schedule	0	–	
Q233	Stock control	–	60	15	26	34	Under Review		0	–	Live on schedule—to be handed over.
Q244	Payment of pensioners	–	56	50	52	9	1.12.70	On schedule	Over 5	Imp. 5	
Q245	Stocktaking amendments	–	34	31	33	0	6.10.70	Complete	Under 1	Imp. 1	
Q252	Annual stocktaking	–	64	27	27	37	1.2.71	On schedule	0	–	
Q256	BOMP development	–	80	32	39	26			Under 15	–	
Q266	Cost of sales	–	14	16	27	2	1.12.70	3 weeks late	Over 15	Det. 11	
Q268	Revised trial balance	–	3	2	2	0	21.11.70	Complete	Under 1	Imp. 1	Change of management in department concerned. Requirements being reviewed.
Q274	Hamburg—post-implementation	–	80	54	70	0	25.12.70	Complete	Under 10	–	Awaiting programs for systems test.
Q284	Managers' salaries	–	6	5	6	0	13.11.70	Late	0	–	
Q291	Material processing File listing	–	4	0	0	2	20.2.70	On schedule	Under 2	–	
Q297	Vehicle costing amendments	–	16	1	1	15	15.2.71	On schedule	0	–	
Q298	Selected model analysis	–	3	2	3	1	1.1.71	On schedule	Over 1	Det. 1	

Figure 10:3 Project progress report

4   Education
5   Holidays and sickness

Similar performance reports are produced for the operational departments and that produced for the computer operating department analyses time under the following headings:

1   Productive time—occupied in processing information for users of the computer department
2   Lost time caused by errors by:
     (a) Operators
     (b) Data preparation

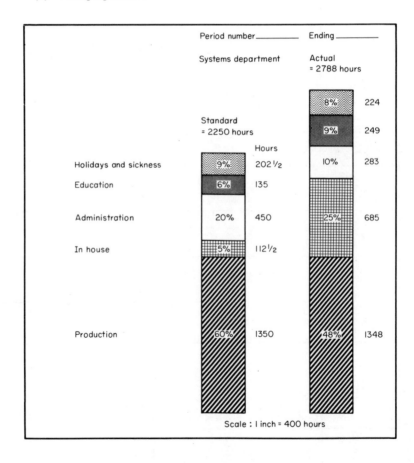

Figure 10:4   Productivity report

(c) Control
(d) Systems
(e) Programming
3   Computer time occupied in computer department internal work, for example a costing and charging system
4   Computer time occupied in development of the department's software or other technical developments or changes
5   Maintenance and repair
6   Time during which the equipment was switched on but unused.

The total time during which the equipment was switched on and the standard or planned 'switch-on time' is also shown. The number of sets of printed results dispatched to users behind schedule (late) is shown as additional information.

Performance reports in respect of data preparation are based on the number of key depressions per operator-hour against the standard rate.

Control to meet systems implementation schedules and production of results from the computing equipment.

Project progress reports are the primary means of controlling progress of projects during development phases. It will be noted that the report is designed to highlight anticipated delay at the time that it can be first identified by the column headed 'on-schedule or late' and in indicating the quantity of resources projected to be consumed against those that were planned.

The project progress report could be augmented by introducing the 'module element' if modular programming techniques are employed.

Control of consumption of human and machine resources

The project progress report provides control information on the consumption of systems analysis and programming resources against those planned. The productivity reports provide control information relating to the operational departments and, specifically, machine resources. As a further control, information can be produced setting out the time taken on each job run on the computer and the standard time.

Control of quality

Control of the quality of the work of the computer department is largely dependent on adherence to the standards for documentation, programming and procedures. Maintenance of the necessary high quality is best carried out by regular review of the work of the department—perhaps reviewing the documentation of a number of projects each month to ensure that standards are being adhered to.

Control of productivity

The productivity reports provide information to control the productivity of the department and the project progress report provides some means of identifying low performance of individual staff, by highlighting excess time spent in systems analysis or in preparing programs. Normal supervision by line management should further identify poor performance.

Control of costs

The integration of financial budgeting with the planning and control of human and equipment resources is dealt with in the next section.

Budgeting, charging and recovery of costs

A computer service department's budgets should be based on the long-term plans described in previous sections covering staffing and equipment. Actual salary rates and equipment costs should be applied to the plans and combined with accommodation costs, consumables and travel and other expenses to produce the annual expenditure budgets. To facilitate comparison of actual expenditure with budgets, the budget should be broken down to months or accounting periods and the same careful control procedures involving com parison of actual performance with budgets applied. In addition, to cope with the quite significant variations in costs that may arise, and which relate to the difficulty in forming accurate plans for a computer service department, forward projections of the budget for the year should be made each month so that, again, action can be taken to control deviations.

While the normal accounting practices and procedures should be applied to a computer activity, there are several aspects in which some departures from these may be necessary. Examples are:

1   Just as financial justification for investment in equipment should be based on the life of use of the equipment in the department, so the annual rate of depreciation should be geared to write off the total costs over those years. This may depart from standard practices of the company or group and is caused by the need to take advantage of technological developments that are beneficial in the short term.

2   Investments in the form of purchase of software or systems packages and in development of special software may rightly be treated as capital expenditure. With these exceptions, it is normal to write off systems and programming as they occur. Similarly, costs of training, even those involved with change of programming language which may be significant, are probably best treated as revenue expenditure. The technology has been moving too fast to relate this type of expenditure to the years ahead.

The form of the budgets and financial records of the department depend on whether the costs of the computer department are charged to its users and also whether the department is required to make a profit. It is normal, and probably most effective from the aspect of management control, for the department to charge its users on a basis related to the resources they have used (see Chapter 11). The question of whether the objective should be to charge competitive market rates and thus make a profit need not be debated here. There may be contradiction in objectives that combine the provision of a service and the creation of a profit. However, the budgets of computer service departments that charge for their services must obviously include income received and there is need to control the revenue earning activities of the department. The productivity reports and the project progress reports produced each month contain all the required information, with the addition of cost information, to carry out adequate control of both the recovery of charges for specific projects and the rates that are charged to users. Project progress information indicates the accuracy of quotations and consequently whether there may be over- or under-recovery of costs on each project. Productivity reports provide means of controlling the rates charged to users of the computer department and determine whether or not the proportion of chargeable work is sufficient to recover the costs of each section of the computer department and the department as a whole.

It is a matter of policy whether a computer service department should attempt to fully recover systems and programming costs that are incurred or whether it permits some subsidy by inflating charges for processing data on the computer once systems are fully in operation. Certainly commercial bureaux practice some flexibility in recovering their costs in their charges. For the computer service department, it is generally advisable to aim at full recovery of each category of service provided—systems analysis, programming and 'systems operating'. The practice is certainly appropriate if the computer department is organised as a cost centre but some flexibility is advisable if the department is required to make a profit.

Rates charged to user departments should be calculated on the basis of the costs of each type of service provided by the department which are generally:

1   Systems analysis and design

2   Programming

3   Data preparation including control

4   Computer processing and associated stationery handling and communications.

To the direct costs of each section of the department, calculated in drawing up budgets, an equitable share of management and overheads must be added. The rates charged to users of the computer department can be calculated by reference to the standards for productivity which have been prepared in Gantt chart form and which show the proportion of resources occupied in 'chargeable' work.

The monthly productivity reports can be used to control the revenue earning performance of each section of the department.

11

Computer Operations Management

Bill Brooks

The job of computer operations management, like any other senior management task, consists of making decisions about the efficient utilisation of resources. Computer managers have a fixed resource with a known capacity, a budget of men and money, a workload of company systems producing information required by other managers to perform a function, and a responsibility to contribute to the overall company effectiveness, efficiency and profit.

Control—the secret of successful computer operations management

Before any computer operations manager can begin to be successful, he must learn how to control the resources which are available to him. The introduction of workable controls marks the acceptance of the fact that there is no secret technique known only to computer operations management. Workable control over a resource is the mark of any well-managed business function whether it be in the workshop, the office or administration. Walking into a business function which is being managed with effective controls is an experience that is easily recognised. Everyone seems to know his job, work moves smoothly and there is a quiet air of self-confidence in all members of the group from the manager to the lowest clerk.

Gaining control

The computer operations manager must be solely responsible for control within his area. He cannot entirely delegate this responsibility. The pressures which quickly build up within the operations area require the operations manager to be a very strong individual, otherwise he will be pushed one way and then another. It seems to be an accepted fact that all systems analysts and programmers look upon the computer as their personal machine and resent any work other than their own being done. This leads to them pressuring the operating staff to do their work ahead of others, whether that be production work or not.

In order to gain control it is obvious that the computer operations manager must have the final say on what work is done, when it will be done and how it will be done within the presented systems definition. Therefore, he must be made a part of all system design work at an early stage and be actively involved right up to the introduction of the system. Only in this way can a full understanding of the user's requirement and timing be obtained. Matching of user requirements against the available computer resources can be done only by the person ultimately responsible for meeting the agreed output. It is also obvious that the operations manager must be the only person to accept a new system into the production stage. He is then fully responsible for agreeing that all necessary documentation, controls and so on are available and that the system can then be run regularly with confidence. If he is willing to accept work which does not conform to the necessary controls then he alone is responsible for any failures on the operations side.

Control of time

The one single factor which best measures the resource of the computer is time. Time is a familiar form of measurement to all computer people. The daily conversation is constantly filled with references to time, in terms of years, months, weeks, days, hours, minutes and seconds, and each person in the computer operations section accepts that time is a real and pressing resource. Time, once lost, cannot be retrieved and it is the only resource where this is true, so for that reason alone all attempts at establishing control within computer operations must make use of time as the primary source of control.

Need to know where time goes

Once it is accepted that control will be established and that it will be based upon time, the next step is to begin to collect data showing where the present computer day goes. Starting on a very basic analysis Figure 11:1 shows the sort of time breakdown which will be required for each week.

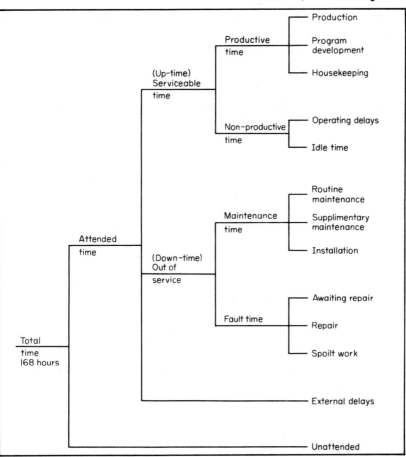

Figure 11:1 Computer time analysis

Total time. The computer is a costly resource and should be running as close to the maximum time available as it possibly can. It is therefore necessary to account for 168 hours each week.

Attended time. This is the actual amount of time that the computer is switched on during the week. It can vary from running one 40-hour shift to three shifts a day for seven days. It provides a measure of the present usage in terms of hours run each week.

Unattended time. This represents the difference between 168 hours each week and the total attended time. In essence, this represents available capacity of the computer.

Within *attended time* it is necessary to provide a detailed analysis of where and how this time is used.

Serviceable time. (Sometimes referred to as *downtime.*) This is a measure of the time the machine was not available for productive work because it was being worked on or awaiting an engineer to repair it. This is an extremely useful figure to keep an eye on as it shows whether the machine is meeting the desired reliability standard.

Within *serviceable time* it is necessary to provide a detailed analysis of where and how this time is used as it represents the major reason for having a computer.

Production time. This is split into segments showing the amount of time spent on *production, program development and testing, housekeeping* and *miscellaneous.*
Non-production time. This is split showing *idle time* and *operating delays.*

Within *out-of-service time*, it is necessary to provide a detailed analysis of where and how this time is spent.

Maintenance time. This is split between *routine maintenance, supplementary maintenance* and *installation.*
Fault time. This is split between *awaiting repair, repair* and *spoilt work time.*

There are two further categories which should be included but used as seldom as possible.

Debatable time. This is used to account for those items whose real reason is obscure and not readily identifiable.
External delays. This is used to record the time lost through *power failure* or *air conditioning fault.*

Having once established the categories into which the time is to be shown, it is then possible to quickly complete a history of the past by having a clerical analysis made of computer logs. A report summarising these figures is then prepared and used as the basis for further study and control of specific factors.

In setting up such a record-keeping procedure it should be emphasised that unless there is going to be a consistent review and follow-up of these figures it should never be started.

The computer operations manager should be the sole judge of where to allocate time in this analysis and when there is a dispute over the proper assignment, his word is final.

Involving user departments in control systems

As a clear picture begins to develop of where the time within the computer area is spent, there will emerge some situations which will require a re-examination of agreed output or input deadlines. This then leads to a series of long discussions with systems analysts and user departments in attempting to persuade them to agree to a change. If it is at all possible, an attempt should be made to involve systems analysts and user departments as soon as the time analysis begins to be available. In this way, the problems can be identified early and, because of their involvement, the user departments may well be able to offer revised dates and times without needing the pressure of senior management. Involving user departments in trying to determine problem areas as well as solutions is usually an effective way of gaining respect and acceptance of the control system. It is always easier to catch flies with honey than it is with vinegar!

Efficient layout of computer room

Before the computer operations manager can begin to examine all of the various activities under his control he should sit down and carefully examine the layout of entire work area of his responsibility as shown in Figure 11:2.

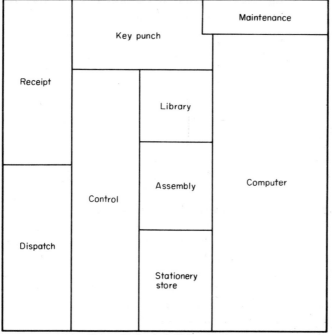

Figure 11:2   Installation layout

Having looked at the installation layout it may well be possible to decide that some one function is located in the wrong position for a smooth flow of work. Probably this sort of information will not be very evident without a detailed study on the part of qualified work study engineers or O & M practitioners. Nevertheless, the computer operations manager should take the time to physically follow one or more jobs through the various functions. Once he has done this, his understanding of the importance of control of all of the work functions should be increased. He will then be able to ask for the technical help he needs in solving the problem of efficient work flow within the layout of his area.

It may well follow that the entire area should be reorganised since far too often the ancillary areas of a computer installation became literally the 'poor relation'. If a fair amount of money is spent on building a computer room to show off the newest acquisition then there tends to be a belated penny-pinching attitude on the part of senior management so that virtually no money is left for all the other functions. This results in them being tucked into areas not always suited for their job. Poor surroundings and an unattractive environment probably result in more staff turnover than any other single factor.

One other factor, which must be recognised in the examination of the work area layout and the work flow, is the need to design a system which will help to provide a series of checks to ensure the security of information as it flows around. This topic is commanding more and more attention on the part of senior management. The need to be able to guarantee that there will be no area of security of data left to chance again requires an intimate knowledge of how and where all work goes while under the responsibility of the computer operations management.

Data control

The examination of the layout, the work flow and the problems of control of work movement and responsibility for data security will probably result in the realisation that the job is a major one and that a specific organisation, a data control group, should be set up to cope with it. In small installations it may well be only one man while in large installations it may be a group.

The function of data control (sometimes called production control) in any computer operations area is quite easily defined. It is responsible for the coordination of the workload between control offices in the user departments and in the data processing area. It also receives, records and controls requests to the operations group for all data processing It must also schedule the completion of accepted work in conformity with agreed output dates, priorities and the availability of the equipment. The data control function is also responsible for seeing that all work received and distributed meets the required quality standards.

Figure 11:3 illustrates the various activities of data control.

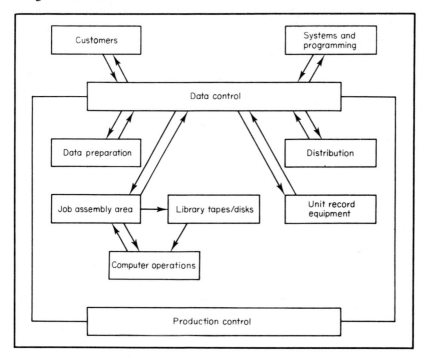

Figure 11:3 Functions of data control

The personnel chosen to operate the data control function must possess the ability to follow prescribed procedures and yet have sufficient initiative to take independent action to overcome late receipt of data, late delivery of output and all the many related problems. They must be tactful yet firm, polite yet aggressive, agreeable but capable of being disagreeable. It has been suggested that this type of work suits people with a military background. This is probably because it requires a dedication to seeing that there is a plan for everything and that everything follows its plan.

Controlling flow of data through operations area

Perhaps the largest single area of responsibility for data control is to set up and maintain an accurate record of the flow of user department data through the operations area. In order to do this a simple manual system will probably suffice in most installations.

157

The basic record for control is the data control file. This is a set of index cards maintained on a weekly basis. The source of information for these cards is the workload list of production requirements on the monthly master production schedule. The data control clerk completes a data control card for each job which the operations group is required to process. Figure 11:4 illustrates this card. It shows the job number, the function and the scheduled date and time the job is due in and/or out.

Job Punch mare tickets					
User Production control					
Job #	Task	Scheduled		Actual	
		Date	Time	Date	Time
PC 45	KP –1	21· 7 · 71	09 .30	21· 7 · 71	09 . 45

Figure 11:4   Data control card

Where the job consists of multiple input batches, one file card is created listing each batch and the time it is expected in. A second card is created for the job giving all the information normally recorded commencing with the receipt of the final batch. This card is marked with a red indicator to alert the data control clerk to check the individual data batches.

For jobs which are required to be processed and which are not part of the regular schedule, data control cards are created as the jobs are received.

As each card is prepared it is filed between tab cards according to the date and time at which the first check should be made (see Figure 11:5). This first check should be before the first scheduled time as shown on the card. The amount of this lead time depends upon the function, the job priority and the scheduled output time.

Once cards are set up for each job to be processed they then become a flexible timetable of data checkpoints for the entire week. As each checkpoint is reached (four times each shift) the data control clerk takes out all cards in the file for that quarter of the shift and checks the progress of the data on the jobs.

If data is late, missing or incomplete, follow-up action is immediately taken.

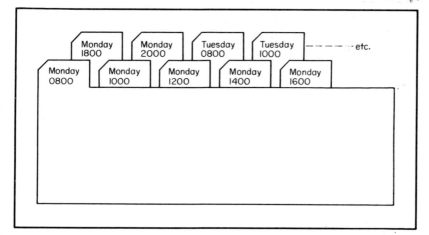

Figure 11:5 Data control file

If the work has been completed, the clerk records the actual date and time. The card is then replaced in the data control file according to the time the next check is required. When the job is successfully completed, the card is removed and stored for one month as a record of completion and for any historical reference which may be required.

Using this system, the chances of data being lost or late can be reasonably expected to be quite low. No system can ever ensure 100 per cent control where people are concerned.

Budgetary control

Without exception, computer operations must have a budget in order to assess the overall running costs of the function. Depending upon the installation and the company, this budget may vary from being part of a large management services department budget to a specific operating group budget. It will also vary depending upon the primary purpose for the installation. If, for example, it is a bureau, budget details are more exacting because they form the basis of the rate charged to customers. On the other hand, an installation which is part of a company or group of companies is an overhead group whose budget is included in the cost of doing business. In either case, a close examination will be made of all items included in the budget and the results throughout the year will be closely monitored.

Preparing the budget

Budgeting as a resource control has been a management technique for a great

159

many years, it is relatively new only to computer operations management. Since budgets have been around for some years the rules governing what is included, how it is arrived at, and so on, are all well established. Most companies have already set up a budgeting group either as part of or in conjunction with the accounting function. Computer operations management becoming involved with budgets for the first time will find a great deal of help from the budgetary control people.

Most budgets tend to follow a fixed pattern on what items of cost are included. Figure 11:6 illustrates the form of a typical budget preparation sheet listing the general items which computer operations management have some control over.

Training costs. This item reflects the amount included in the budget to cover the cost of department staff going on courses and being trained. It includes only course fees and travel since salary is included elsewhere.

Data processing salary—monthly. The annual salary for all members of the department on monthly staff. Includes holidays, etc.

Data processing salary—weekly. The annual salary for those members of the department on weekly staff. Includes holidays, etc.

Overtime—monthly and weekly. The estimated amount of overtime premium to be paid to all staff.

Night-shift allowance. The amount to be paid to those members of the department who are paid an allowance for working on shifts.

Office equipment-rental. The annual cost of hiring calculators, typewriters, tape recorders, etc.

Office equipment—service. The annual cost of service agreements for office equipment in the department.

Computer rental/associated costs. The annual rental or leasing costs of the existing computer configuration plus any expected changes in the coming year. In some cases where the computer has been purchased, the maintenance cost and depreciation allowance is shown here.

Computer supplies. The cost of printer ribbons, magnetic tapes, disk packs, etc.

Data processing stationery. The total estimated costs of computer paper, forms and punch cards.

Office stationery. The annual cost of supplying the normal office needs: pens, paper, pencils etc.

Technical society subscriptions. The cost of approved membership in computer technical societies.

Technical magazine subscriptions. Annual subscription costs to approved technical computer magazines.

Travelling expenses. The expected expenditure to cover the cost of members of the department travelling to courses or on company business.

Department name _____ Date prepared _____

Department number_____ Date approved _____

Overhead account number	Description	Budget amount required	Budget amount approved
001	Training costs	_____	_____
002	Data processing salary-monthly	_____	_____
003	Data processing salary-weekly	_____	_____
004	Overtime - monthly	_____	_____
005	Overtime - weekly	_____	_____
006	Night shift allowance	_____	_____
011	Office equipment-rental	_____	_____
012	Office equipment-service	_____	_____
013	Computer rental / assoc. costs	_____	_____
021	Computer supplies	_____	_____
022	Data processing stationery	_____	_____
023	Office stationery	_____	_____
031	Technical society subs.	_____	_____
032	Technical magazine subs.	_____	_____
041	Travelling expense	_____	_____
042	Entertaining expense	_____	_____
05.	Consulting charges	_____	_____
061	Protective clothing	_____	_____
071	Miscellaneous charges	_____	_____

Occupancy costs

_____ . Per square foot

_____ . Square feet occupied   _____

Administration costs   _____

Total _____   _____

Figure 11:6   Budget preparation sheet

161

Entertaining expenses. The amount for expected entertaining of visitors, etc.

Consulting charges. Consultants or other outside professional assistance brought in for specific assignments, or on an annual retainer or contract.

Protective clothing. The amount for providing some form of protective clothing to be worn by employees performing work such as decollating where carbon could damage clothing.

Miscellaneous charges. The usual catch-all for those items which do not fit into one of the above listed items.

Occupancy costs. This figure is prepared by the accounts department and represents rates, rent, heat, light, power, etc., for the entire company building. The allocation is based upon the square footage each group or department occupies.

Additional administration costs. Prepared by the accounts department, this is a percentage figure applied to the wages portion of the budget to compensate for fringe benefits and senior management salary.

Controlling the budget throughout the year

It must be obvious that if a real attempt is to be made at controlling the money resource a feedback showing how the actual performance compares with the estimated should be provided. Figure 11:7 illustrates a form of reporting on the budget position. It can be provided monthly or weekly and shows amount spent during the current month/period, the cumulative amount spent to this month/period and also the total amount budgeted for the year. The lower part of the form provides space for the computer operations manager to explain the reasons for under- or over-spending. From a budgetary control point of view it is equally important to explain underspending as it is to explain overspending. The need to provide this detailed explanation should be tempered by the 'rule of reason' that the amount of over- or under-spending should be considered before launching onto a detailed explanation. Normally, an explanation is only required when the amount exceeds plus or minus 5 per cent.

By plotting each month's spending it is often possible to detect a trend toward over- or under-spending before the time it actually occurs. This in turn allows for a detailed examination to be made so that the reasons are clearly identified and action taken to correct the problem.

Budgets for user departments

Budgets for computer operations managers should provide an opportunity to exercise not only good managerial control of this resource but more importantly to advise user departments of what expenditure is involved in producing their work.

Department name _Computer Operations_   Report for ~~period~~/month _August_
Department number _500_

Overhead account number	Description	Spend this ~~period~~/month	Cumulative spend year to date	Approved annual budget
001	Training costs	120	945*	1,040
002	Data processing salary - monthly	5,020	39,530	59,080
003	Data processing salary - weekly	860	7,050	10,520
004	Overtime - monthly	—	250*	970
005	Overtime - weekly	15	121	180
006	Night shift allowance	40	308	460
011	Office equipment - rental	10	84	120
012	Office equipment - service	—	—*	36
013	Computer rental / assoc. costs	12,200	96,600	138,000
021	Computer supplies	106	835	1,200
022	Data processing stationery	847	6,700	9,700
023	Office stationery	8	65	100
031	Technical society subs.	30	125*	75
032	Technical magazine subs.	4	35	50
041	Travelling expenses	110	740	1,200
042	Entertaining expenses	3	25	50
051	Consulting charges	—	—	—
061	Protective clothing	—	—*	25
071	Miscellaneous charges	7	53	75

Explanation of over/underspends

Account number	Description	Over/ underspend	Reason
001	Training costs	Overspend	Special courses - programmers
004	Overtime - monthly	Underspend.	Holidays - less overtime
012	Office equip. - service	Underspend	Invoices not due until Sept.
031	Tech. society subs.	Overspend	Two added memberships approved D.P.M.A.
061	Protective clothing	Underspend	Replacement due Nov.

Prepared by ___g.R. Cross___   Date ___5-9-71___

Figure 11:7   Budget performance report

It has generally been accepted by accounts departments that there is little to be gained by charging user departments for the services of an overhead facility since it only adds to the cost and does nothing to control or reduce the facility. This is true of most computer installations within a company or group of companies. However, unless some form of control on user department demands can be set up, the computer operations group will always be faced with demands for processing time which will quickly exceed the available capacity.

Many computer operations managers as well as senior managers are trying various ways of preventing this continuous creep of user department demands. One method which has worked quite well is to control the amount of computer hours available to any system or department as a budget. Figure 11:8 shows the basic information as it is produced for reporting purposes. The past usage of computer time for a system or department is determined at the end of the year, then this figure plus any allowed factor for normal company growth or for any already agreed increases in the coming year is presented to the user department management in the form of a graph. The graph shows the cumulative total from week 1 to week 52. It can be altered or adjusted as required, provided that some agreement or control exists whereby the head of the user department agrees to the alteration and carries the case to senior management. In this way, computer operations management start each year with an agreed workload that the various user departments have accepted. Throughout the year any changes or alterations are not incorporated until senior management agrees to the user department's request.

Reporting on user department budgets

At agreed intervals, say of four or six weeks, the computer operations manager collects from his computer log and other sources the total amount of time worked by the computer on a particular system or department's work. This figure, by weeks, is manually added to produce a cumulative total which in turn is posted to the graph. Figure 11:9 illustrates how the cumulative effect of the actual total hours is shown. Copies of the graph are sent to the head of the user department. Again the value of this form of budgetary control lies in both the user department and computer operations manager being able to detect trends before they are a problem. The result of such a trend analysis as shown in Figure 11:9 is action on the part of the user management to obtain an official agreement to alter the budget line of hours available for the system.

Benefits from user budgets

Perhaps the most impressive benefit of these user department budgets based upon hours, lies in the ease with which they can be accepted. The cost in actual

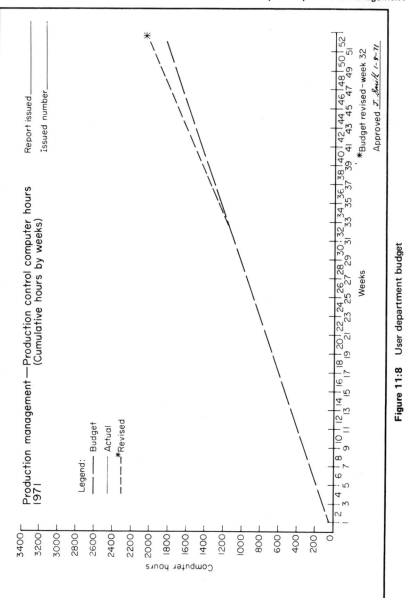

Figure 11:8 User department budget

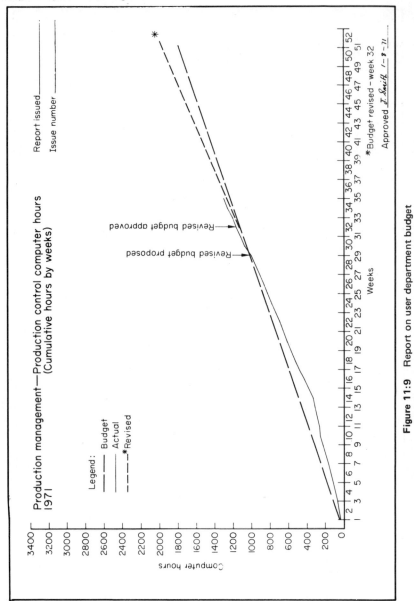

Figure 11:9 Report on user department budget

money seems to lack the necessary powers of deterring unrestrained growth of the computer facility yet the impact of the expected growth when translated to hours and presented graphically seems to be very strong. Since the budget and the reporting is done in computer hours it also tends to reduce friction over how the cost represents 'living in splendid comfort at our expense'.

Before any control on user requirements will be effective, senior management must adopt a hard line that no expansion to existing workloads in the computer area will be permitted unless the department requesting the expansion is prepared to prove that it is absolutely necessary. If this is followed, senior management will be able to personally control the expansion of the computer facility and thus relieve computer operations management of the blame for rising computer costs within a company.

The control method outlined above can also be very effective in reducing or holding expenses for special forms or increased printouts by setting a budget in boxes or sheets and doing the same sort of control graph, obtaining user department management agreement and insisting that alterations or revisions must be approved by senior management.

12

Control and Management Standards

David Tebbs

The implementation of complex data processing applications has called for an ever increasing range of skills in the data processing profession, despite the advent of such aids as high-level languages and operating systems. However, experience with installations and projects continues to show that 'success' in data processing is as much a function of the management skills and disciplines that are applied as it is of the intellectual skills and technical capabilities of computer staff. 'Data processing standards' is the expression normally used to describe the pertinent disciplines which might otherwise be called 'techniques for effective data processing management'. Standards are, therefore, concerned both with establishing methods for the way in which computer staff will do their work and with controlling the performance and productivity of the data processing department.

Need for standards

The youth and dramatic expansion of data processing have not allowed time for the standards that have developed through years of practice in the older professions and trades to be established on an industry basis. The result is a wide range of data processing productivity from organisation to organisation. The gap is so wide that where one installation may plan on a programmer producing 300 Cobol statements per month another can expect between two and three thousand a month in ideal circumstances. Low productivity means high costs or delayed systems. Standards aim to improve productivity.

Equally, there are installations where tens of thousands of pounds have been expended on computer systems development and where only the sketchiest documentation of this work is maintained. Consequently such installations are dependent on retaining the staff that originally developed the systems, to enable modifications to be introduced in systems which have become essential to the actual continuance of the business. Standards aim to eliminate this dependence and secure computer systems as real business assets. This chapter is concerned with a consideration of what types of standards are required in an installation together with a review of the alternative methods that can be adopted in developing suitable standards manuals. The purpose of standards will vary between installations, but certain fundamentals are now becoming accepted.

In most cases standards should be effective on three levels: progress, reactive and retrospective.

Progressive   Well-organised work and staff are the best environment for high productivity. Standards should therefore set a framework for efficient work by the staff.

Computers are beset by jargon and complexities. A disciplined approach to formal documents eases communication not only between data processing personnel but also between them and their end users of the computer system.

Reactive   Project and quality control are essential for effective management of the data processing activity. Standards should, therefore, not only provide a recognised procedure for that control—at all levels down to the individual computer programmer—but also the very methods necessary for efficient work and should provide a convenient framework to check progress and quality. Because of the high development content of its work, any installation is subject to problems where key staff are removed from a project, whether because of illness, leaving the organisation, or even temporary transfer to high-priority maintenance work. In any case, formalised recording of systems development in proper working documentation makes it more straightforward for others to take over rapidly.

Retrospective   Most installations have faced the problem of modifying an operational system whose aims and detailed computer program were badly documented. Formal documentation of computer systems is as important as method engineering, production directives and parts breakdowns are important to an engineering company. Historically, standards have too frequently been limited to formal documentation.

Thus standards need to cover:

1   All stages of system development from conception to production planning

2   Standards in methods including working documentation
3   Standards in formal documentation
4   Obligatory techniques
5   Standards in optional techniques
6   An approach to project control related to the basic standards for
     methods

This chapter is not concerned with setting a snapshot set of standards, but rather with giving a picture of the important elements and structure of a standards manual and the approach to a standards project, and thus starting to answer the questions: what is a comprehensive set of standards? and how do we implement them in our installation?

Having determined the need for standards it is necessary to consider their form. Basically, they need to be incorporated in a manual that clearly sets down the standard procedures, documentation, controls and so on. However, the danger of any comprehensive manual is that it will gather dust on the shelf. Presentation therefore plays an important part of manual design. Standards must be reviewed and taught as part of the regular training plan for data processing staff, including beginners, experienced recruits from outside, and experienced staff.

Standards development programme

Today most installations will start with standards at some level and therefore a standards development project will often consist of partial redevelopment. The last section of this chapter looks at the standards manual that may be developed during the project. However, the first problem is how to organise the standards project to get the right standards, economically and in a manner acceptable and easily implemented.

Project Staffing

The average user installation has a number of choices:

1   Take relevant standards off the shelf from: friends, manufacturers,
     consultancies
2   Develop standards to meet the specific local requirements, internally
3   Call in consultants to do the work
4   Call in a consultancy to do the work in conjunction with user staff.

Many standards have failed because the first line was taken and not related to the particular installation. The other three choices are but a variation on project staffing and in each case the amount of original working (tailoring) to adapt past experience and reference material is very dependent on the particular situation. Experience shows the last approach (mix of user staff and consultants) is most effective because'

1   The consultancy will have wide experience in different standards and the organisation of a standards project.
2   The consultancy should have much reference material not readily available to the user, such as past project documentation and library material built up over the years.
3   The consultant is not biased on internal matters
4   The user staff on the team have the best knowledge of particular ways of the installation. The consultant can recognise what are *real* needs
5   The user can provide resources for elements of the standards manual from idle time on other work
6   The consultancy can have experience of a new area for the installation, for example, using high-level language in real-time systems
7   The user will thoroughly understand the philosophy behind the final manual, thus making training and later modification straightforward

Certainly this approach has been the most effective in getting good standards well implemented.

Project organisation

Proper organisation of the standards project—like any other task—leads to an improved project. Three essential groups of people are concerned: the standards review committee, the project team and experts who are called in to assist.

Standards review committee   This committee will consist of senior members of the department whose sections are covered by the standards project. The purpose of the committee is to interact with the project team, with two aims:

1   To get the committee involved so that they feel the standards are theirs
2   To ensure that they can feed policy into the manual.

The committee will meet the project team no more frequently than once a month, and will have the opportunity to read and comment on all drafts. The review committee should never take executive responsibility for the project, although the responsible executive will be on that committee.

Project team   At least one full-time member, or more appropriately two—one user, one consultant—will be on this team. The project team will be responsible for the standards project, the bulk of the work, the plan, and the format of the manual.

Assistance   Either as an additional resource or to cover special skills, other staff from either user or consultant will be assigned specific set tasks within the project. For example, the senior most experienced Cobol programmer may draft Cobol language conventions.

Project steps

The standards project falls into a number of steps common to most installations. Such steps fall into four phases, and will include:

1   Plan project and establish the philosophy of the approach to projects and standards; draw up table of contents of standards manual and draft sample standards
2   Develop standards
3   Production, installation and training
4   Maintenance and reviews

Project plan   The first step is to agree the basic philosophy to guide the standards project and then set an initial overall plan. This will cover such aspects as the fundamental breakdown of computer projects, staff responsibilities, etc.

Table of contents for standards manual   The table of contents (first draft) for the standards manual defines in some detail the areas to be covered. Explanatory expansions of titles are necessary at this point, as is a basis for format and presentation. All reference material needs to be gathered as appropriate.

Sample standards   To set an example for other areas, one or two initial standards are developed in draft form. These embody the philosophy set at the beginning and act as guidelines for anyone drafting (or tailoring) the various later elements of the standards manual.

Development   This is when drafts are developed for each standard area. The bulk of the work is done at this time. Drafts need to be reviewed if possible outside the project team. A consultancy can provide extra support to this activity. This stage is complete when all sections of the standards manual covered by the project have been drafted and edited for content. Many of the less used techniques that one might like to have covered by standards can be excluded from the project, but slotted in at a later date when developed. Obviously, the manual needs to be structured to permit such items to be added easily.

Production The production process consists of detailed text and cross-reference editing; decisions on final format and presentation; and printing. Procedures need to be established for the later amendment and updating of standards. Certainly amendment can be simplified by the maintenance of a master copy, probably including extra material such as back-references to any cross-references.

Installation and training Once the manual is complete, standards have to be installed before they can be of value. A number of recommendations arise from experience in this area:

1   Standards are best applied at the start of a new phase. One need not wait for a new project
2   Formal in-house courses are valuable in introducing standards
3   Some aspects of project control and time recording need to be brought in across the board by a fixed date
4   Over a period of six months management needs to make special efforts to ensure that standards are followed
5   Pressure of work must never be an excuse to avoid standards; otherwise standards will soon drop out of use
6   Quality control procedures need to include checks that standards are being applied
7   Once installed, standards training should become the norm for staff training, both on recruitment and on staff development (in-house) courses. If external courses are used, then brief internal courses should follow up to relate to the standards manual.
8   A post-project review should take place some six months after initial installation.

Maintenance A regular budget of about one man-week per year for each major standards area should be allocated for standards review and maintenance. If the manual includes estimated standards for systems and programming work, these should be updated at least annually on the basis of actual performance. Comparison of such quantitative standards with those published from time to time and from other organisations can be helpful yardsticks, providing account is taken of important working differences.

Standards and organisation structure

It is important to relate standards to the personnel structure in the installation. Regrettably it is not uncommon to find standards that become inaccurate once the installation structure or personnel responsibilities are changed, and hence fall rapidly out of date and out of use. The main problem here is that standards are too often expressed in terms of the personnel structure and staff titles. This is not necessary, especially if the development process is broken down to a number of phases, such as:

1 Feasibility study
2 System summary
3 System analysis and specification
4 System design or engineering
5 Program specification and writing
6 Programming

Each phase can then have its standards written in terms of 'staff on this phase', 'team leader', and so on, and not 'programmers', 'analysts', and so on. Elements of the standards manual concerned with staff structure and job description will then relate to these phases by setting up (explicitly or implicitly) a matrix relating staff to phase, for example:

SECTION/PHASE	ANALYSIS	DESIGN	PROGRAM SPECIFICATION
O & M	A	—	—
Analysts	R/W	R/W	A
Programmer	—	W	R/W

where
R = section responsible for the phase
W = section will contribute to work on this phase
A = section may assist on this phase

Many installations assign responsibilities for the various stages of systems development to different sections in the data processing department; such responsibilities must be related to standards. If the phase concept of project development, introduced above, is used, then handover is best related to a phase boundary. However, it is important to recognise that the point of handover of responsibility does not necessarily relate to the end or start of a section's work on that project. Let us consider an installation simply divided between analysts and programmers under separate managers. Say the analysts hand over to the programmers once the suite has been designed and, further, say the user is responsible for the acceptance of a system as defined in user terms by the analyst. In this environment the following might apply:

1   The systems analysis and specification phase ends with the production and acceptance of a systems specification. Responsibility for development—analysts. Responsibility for acceptance—user departments. The final document will include:
    (a) System specification—definition in user terms
    (b) Definitive additions to the specification to make it clear for programming
    (c) Appendix describing *possible* suite structure.
    The appendix would be checked by programmers to ensure that the principles inferred by the system were sound. However, the appendix would in no way be a specification.
2 The analyst on the project will design the system in terms of suite structure, outline program descriptions and detailed file design. All input/output will be frozen. Depending on his machine-dependent backround, he will call upon senior programming support as necessary (planned from the start of the project). The design document plus the system specification will then be the definite document produced at the end of the system design and handed over to the programming section for program specification writing to programming.
3 The programming section takes over the system for the purpose of developing a working suite of programs. The analyst may be called upon for advice or against a request for changes in specifications.
4 The analyst will accept back proven program for later system testing assisted by programmers.

Structure of the manual

Experience in standards development shows that it is difficult to establish the balance between sufficient and excessive material. Excessive in this sense can mean that few staff read the standards properly and hence do not follow them. It is found that careful structuring of the manual in a modular and hierarchical manner greatly eases this problem.

The manual may initially be divided thus:

Volume 1   DP department background

	Hardware/software structure
	Administration standards
	Department structure/terms of reference
Volume 2	Basic methods and documentation
Volume 3	Mandatory and optional techniques
Volume 4+	Examples of well-documented projects

Other divisions may be by development phase so that staff need only consult one area at a time. The core of the above approach to a standards manual (different volumes need not necessarily need different physical storage) is volume 2, which is the bible of day-to-day activity for the staff.

The first step in structuring volume 2 is to divide the systems development process into the selected steps or phases. (Although such phases are in practice partially parallel activities, it is often convenient for the purpose of standards manuals to consider them as serial.) The volume would then be divided into chapters, one per phase, plus some general chapters on such subjects as project control. If we consider each phase, one can often detect a structure common to all phases, in such subjects as: mandatory methodology (and use of techniques), working documentation, formal documentation and real-time variations.

Clarity can be added to the manual if each phase is now developed with the same structure, even if this means some vacant slots: for example, each chapter in volume 2 will have the following sections:

1   Introduction to the phase
2   Methods standards
3   Formal documentation.

Methods section of the manual

The purpose of the methods section is to set down the explicit steps, both control and technical, that staff are to follow in each phase of systems development. The problem at this level is to decide what material should be relegated to techniques (volume 3) in order to keep methodology short, sharp, but complete. If clear techniques are required, then an appropriate statement in context might be 'Flowchart at macro level using standard flowcharting techniques—see volume 4'. That is, all the standards for symbols, layouts, paper, and so on, for flowcharts would be defined in the appropriate techniques section of volume 4, not in the middle of the methods standards.

This approach is particularly useful for techniques, such as flow charting as used in the example above, which naturally apply to a number of places in the standards manual and therefore do not readily fit one area of the methodology.

Some techniques or methodology may not be easy to express in a precise

177

form (for example the suite design process). If such material is needed or considered constructive, then it can and should be related to techniques with a reference such as 'Design file structure taking into account the main points to be kept in mind during this process as covered in volume 4, section n the preferred file structures as defined in volume 4, section m.'

The advantage of this approach is that any new member of staff assigned to a specific task need read only the relevant section of the manual without having to skip other material selectively (with the danger of skipping too much intermediate material). However, standards manuals often err both ways, missing an ideal opportunity to set standards for the obvious. For example, many installations have had trouble because an analyst considered 'numeric' to include 'spaces' and the programmer rejected 'spaces' as he considered 'numeric' only included the digits 0 to 9. There is a long list of standards of this type that can be built up in time in volume 3, with the aim of increasing clarity of expression, and which should include such elements as:

1   Meaning of field definitions
2   Standard controls—system, program
3   Standard program structures (eg line of balance)
4   Specific programming conventions for selected languages
5   Installation standards on check digits
6   Rules for justification

Documentation section of the manual

Documentation needs to cover four topics:

1   Formal documentation format and content
2   Formal documentation standard forms
3   Working documentation:
    (a) Whether completed freehand or typed,
    (b) How stored/filed *during* the project,
4   Working documentation—standard forms.

Most installations are weak at filing even simple documentation during the development process, for example:

1   Interview notes,
2   Initial suite designs,
3   Flow charts,
4   Listings,
5   Parameter lists.

However it is vital to know where these documents are when there is an unexpected absence of key staff.

Project control

A project control system may be designed to fulfil the following functions:

1   An aid to estimating for project planning and justification at a total project level
2   An overall date processing management tool to control commitments made on budget, cost and timescale
3   An estimating method to make phase control effective
4   A control system to aid team leaders to carry out specific elements (phases) of the project in the most timely and least costly way given the actual circumstances as well as the targets set by early estimates.

The potential conflict of functions especially between a corporate target and the current practical situation relating to phase control can best be solved by recognising the differences between overall project planning and control and the planning and control necessary to carry out a 'phase of development'. The state of the art of systems development is still such that although there are people who can set a maximum cost (and then spend it), estimates made at the beginning of a project are likely to be very imprecise, despite, the variety of formulae that have been developed. However, at the beginning of a phase, as defined above, estimates can be reasonably accurate. An analysis of the late projects will often show that a major factor in 'how late' was the fact that once slippage was detected then ill-advised attempts were made to meet old deadlines, thus causing extra problems and delays, for example because of:

1   Short cuts—that fail
2   Mixing systems and program testing—that confuse and delay debugging
3   Panic or excessive pressure—that lead to further error.

Any control system needs to recognise that a late project can only be redeemed by hard work to the standards originally set. After all, these standards were set to achieve efficiency. Experience shows that phase-level control under a broadly based project-level control has several advantages:

1   The team leader can have a realistic medium-term target
2   The work can be broken down into targets with a sufficiently short time horizon to be meaningful to individual team members

179

3   The team gains enthusiasm from involvement in phase control
4   Local replanning can be made without necessarily affecting an overall plan
5   Clashes between reality and targets are highlighted.

This does not advocate defeatism. Realism and hard work are the best ways to win.

Quality control

Quality control standards need to be set both in their own right and also as clearly defined steps in basic methodology and project control procedures. The prime aim of quality control in this context is to check dynamically the validity and quality of work on a spot check, selective sample, or total cover basis. Standards need to relate to constructive work within a project plan rather than after the event, and in general will involve a second party checking the work. This second party may be the team leader, another team member, or a second party outside the mainstream of the project. What is important is the establishment of basic procedures.

Presentation of the manual

Apart from content the next most important aspect of the standards manual is its level and clarity of presentation. By definition the manual is the major guideline to newcomers and a reminder to older members of the department. Therefore if it is to have impact, that impact must start with presentation. Scruffy binders and quickly duplicated write-ups are only useful for a short-term stopgap. When the material is ready, consider:

1   Some form of hard-cover binder with binding that allows the document to be read (will it lie open at the required page?)
2   Standard paper for manual—make it the standard manual
3   Set a standard format for the manual:
    (a) Headings
    (b) Layout
    (c) Contents pages
    (d) Structure
    (e) Numbering system
4   Have it printed on good-quality paper, using a process that provides a smart finish. The cost of printing will always be small when compared with

(a) The cost of producing the final draft
(b) The total data processing budget

5 *But* avoid losing the text in too much heading and indexing

Standards for other areas

Standards generally concentrate on the popular tasks—programming, system analysis, and so on. However, the other areas necessary to a successful installation should not be forgotten:

1 O & M procedures
2 Data preparation
3 Machine operation
4 User manual priorities
5 Recruitment.

13

Staffing and Job Specifications

M. H. Sturt (1973)

We are probably tired of hearing that the quality of the data processing department's output depends on the quality of its people and the skill with which they are managed, that the money spent on the people will approximate to that spent on the hardware and should we not therefore take more time and trouble on selecting them or keeping them happy? The difficulty lies not in gaining acceptance for these propositions but in doing something about the underlying difficulties; that good staff are hard to get, quick to leave and hard to make productive during their stay in the data processing department. The purpose of this chapter is to suggest personnel policies which will reduce these difficulties and to give some of the factual background in the hope that it will help data processing and personnel managers to devise policies and programmes of their own.

In comparison with the physical sciences, psychology is underdeveloped territory and the occupational psychology of computer professionals is almost *terra incognita*. The most significant pioneering work has been done by people like Robert Reinstedt in the US and a number of other members of the Special Interest Group of the Association for Computing Machinery. In the United Kingdom we have seen projects from Enid Mumford and Philip Sadler and we have some material from opinion surveys carried out by IBM among its employees. While relying, gratefully, on the published (and some unpublished) data, the bulk of the chapter that follows is of necessity a personal interpretation based on experience, and makes no claim to be authoritative or non-contentious.

Organisation

Organisation structures serve a number of purposes: they group together people doing similar tasks; they define boundaries of authority and responsibility; they provide a chain of command and a channel for information to go up and down; they enable the man at the top to initiate and control; they provide training for performance and for succession; they provide a career ladder for individuals; they may group people with differing skills together temporarily for projects.

Size is a very significant factor. As the number employed increases it becomes easier to afford specialist functions and there are more layers of management. Both these consequences carry their own problems: the more specialists there are the more communication links there must be. Communication takes time and introduces noise into the system in the form of distortions or misunderstandings. A similar effect can be seen with multiple layers of management, and for similar reasons. The more complex the work the more concentrated, generally speaking, must be the supervision. In a large and complex computer installation you have a high proportion of managers to the managed and, with a traditional hierarchical structure, several layers of management.

The large installation has advantages for its staff. They can work on large-scale configurations with advanced operating systems and high-level languages. They can progress through a number of specialisations each of which may be practised at a high level of sophistication. They are more likely to be able to take time off for training than are members of small installations.

The large installation is rather more likely to preserve the traditional organisational split between the systems and the programming function. It is also more likely to be able to afford the headcount needed to provide what Dick Brandon called the problem analyst—the person with some computer training well versed in company and user department systems who acts as definer and interpreter of company requirements to the systems analyst. The separation of systems analysis and programming leads to the development of the respective skills of each funtion at the cost of fragmenting project responsibility.

The alternative, which is gaining ground but which was always prevalent in the small installation, is the combined analyst/programmer working in project teams under a project leader, or under a systems and programming manager. Responsibility for project development is clearly vested in a single person, the project leader, or systems and programming manager as he might be in a small installation; the natural evolution of the programmer into systems analyst is facilitated but at the risk of the individual not acquiring skill in depth of either function. The latter point is often made by those who stress the essential difference between the systems and programming tasks and therefore between the types of people best suited to perform each. In some companies the project team is an ad hoc gathering of specialist analysts and programmers under the leadership of an individual with appropriate experience in each function. The danger in this approach is that the individual analyst or programmer is likely to have a series of bosses none of whom has any responsibility for his long-term development. He is perpetually on assignment to one project leader or another. Two skeleton organisation charts are given in Figures 13: 1 and 13: 2. These show the major alternatives. Organisation is not an easy task for the data processing manager as he needs to control functions which differ from each other in fundamental ways, No one else in the company structure, other than the Managing Director, needs to control planning, research and development, and production functions, and to ensure that all work together to meet the required deadlines. Until comparatively recently he had at least one additional difficulty peculiar to himself; his people have worked in a seller's employment market and found little difficulty in moving when they were dissatisfied.

Characteristics of data processing personnel

What sort of people comprise a computer installation? For detailed job descriptions see the IBM booklet, *Organizing The Data Processing Installation* (C20-1622-0) or *Staff Titles and Job Descriptions in Commercial Data Processing* (HMSO, 1967).

The personal attributes needed by those occupying these positions cover a wide spectrum. Operating and operations management are production activities requiring organising ability, thoroughness, conscientiousness, intelligence and educational achievement at the 'O' and 'A' level in terms of the British educational system.

Programming is a highly specialised activity without any obvious similarities with other occupations and requires intelligence, logical power and perseverance of a high order. The activity does not in itself require advanced education but in practice in Western societies programmers are normally drawn from the ranks of those who leave school at around 18 or from graduates.

Systems analysts are usually drawn from those with programming experience but they need to have a number of additional attributes: an understanding of the problem area to which the computer will be applied (or an ability to acquire such an understanding very quickly), an ability to communicate with and influence people, an ability to devise solutions to problems in computer terms (which itself requires a knowledge of hardware characteristics).

The management tasks in the development areas (systems analysis and programming) share the difficulties of all technological development, in particular how to estimate and control time and cost for projects. Innovation and economy are uneasy bedfellows; people who are good at both are rare.

185

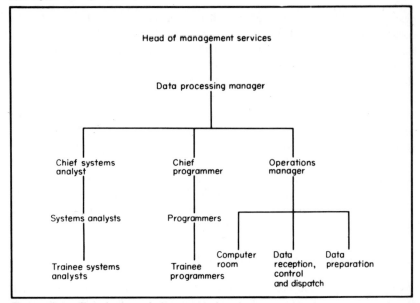

Figure 13:1 Organisation of data processing department with systems analysis and programming separated

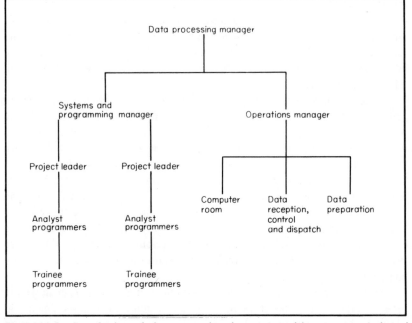

Figure 13:2 Organisation of data processing department with systems analysis and programming combined

Recruitment

Manpower supply for the information processing industry comes direct from the education system and from other types of employment. A survey carried out in 1970 among British undergraduates showed that no less than 69 per cent regarded computers as being the industry with the greatest growth potential.

Thus although the industry has a high requirement for graduates the supply appears to be ample, particularly as it is augmented by a steady stream of graduates who wish to make the switch from other occupations.

The advantage of using as trainees those with experience in other occupations is that they will have a closer acquaintance with the problem areas and they will be older, which makes them more acceptable than direct entrants from the educational system as systems analysts. Programmers, on the other hand, can be taken satisfactorily direct from school or university.

Unfortunately the long time interval required to turn a trainee into a productive business data processing professional has caused users to try to fulfil their needs by taking trained prople from outside. In turn computer professionals have looked to changes of employer to provide advancement in their knowledge. If a user has a machine configuration, programming language and operating system which changes little over a period of, say, seven years, he runs a danger of losing his staff through boredom or fear of technical obsolescence.

Thus it is prudent to take in annually a batch of trainees so that when the inevitable losses occur they can be replaced internally. New users have a more serious problem: if they start off primarily with trainees who have been internally recruited they have an ample supply of people who know the business and have good links with user departments. Additionally career opportunities are provided which will help to gain acceptance for the innovative process and tolerance for the pains which go with it.

On the other hand users staffed largely with trainees will have long development lead times and the experienced leaders that they bring in from outside will be used in a training role, which they may not welcome and for which they may not be suited.

Thus a balance has to be struck by using a mixture of internally recruited trainees (plus a few external trainees if internal resources are inadequate), experienced people from outside brought in on permanent staff, and possibly consultants and/or contract analysts and programmers. Another possibility (see Chapter 7) is facilities management.

In the sixties we became used to an unusual recruitment market in data processing with a difficult manpower supply situation caused by the explosive growth of the industry. In most Western countries the period of fastest growth is now over and losses from the profession through retirement or desertion are still very small. In these circumstances one must expect maturity to increase and recruiting difficulties to reduce.

However, staff at the leading edge of the profession will continue to be difficult to obtain as, during periods of rapidly evolving technology, they will be in demand as an original source of know how and will wish to keep their knowledge up to date by concentrating on advanced projects. This kind of motivation is typical among the better date processing professionals and as a consequence they will tend to find jobs in manufacturers, major software houses, or in users with large-scale applications which incorporate advanced concepts.

Thus those users who qualify in the latter category will tend to sell their jobs as a technological challenge. Others may have to concentrate on other advantages such as management opportunities.

The advertisement in the national weekly or daily papers or in the data processing weeklies still remains a good method of recruiting in the UK. Consultants can also be helpful in saving time and spreading the net wider, provided that they are specialists and can provide valid technical vetting. Specialist consultants have the additional virtue of providing a trickle of recruits who constitute fall-out from other clients' advertisements or who have visited them for career advice. Agencies and registers may also be effective for lower-level appointments.

The data processing manager should have a long-range manpower plan to provide a mix of skills, management succession, a career path for individuals and a good distribution of his people by length of computer experience. A measure of success will be the ease with which he can replace losses without hurried recruiting or without having to recruit experienced people. He will not achieve this without a long-term plan and without very careful attention to the hiring mix. Obviously the more versatile his raw material the fewer difficulties he will face. When recruiting trainee programmers he will need to strike a careful balance between those who will become specialist programmers and those who will evolve later into systems analysts.

The recruiting process must be efficient if it is intended to recruit experienced people from outside. Once the quarry has decided to move he is likely to make up his mind quickly, to approach more than one potential employer simultaneously and to conclude, in the absence of evidence to the contrary, that a firm which cannot manage recruiting cannot manage anything—rough justice we may think but not unfair. Thus recruiting must be carefully planned, the telephone must be used to the full, the people who will carry out the interviewing must be present and prepared and the deal must be clinched as soon as the decision is made. All of this seems so elementary as to be not worth mentioning, but the firms which achieve it will certainly be in a successful minority.

It is helpful to devise a specialised application form which asks for information on experience with programming languages, operating systems, hardware configurations and applications or techniques experience. A variety of gummed or stapled printed panels can be used for this purpose in conjunction with the standard application form.

Aptitude tests should normally be used only for those without computer experience and treated with circumspection as one among a number of items of evidence. Experienced programmers can properly be exposed to practical problems based on the language in which they claim proficiency and/or to one of the few available proficiency tests or evaluation devices. (A comprehensive study of the available testing instruments available up to 1968 was made by David Mayer of IBM and Ashford Stalnaker of the Georgia Institute of Technology and published in the Proceedings of the 1968 ACM National Conference.) Aptitude tests have a better record for predicting success in training than success in programming.

There is not at the moment, and probably never will be, a substitute for the interview as the principle selection device and it is normally necessary to use it as a pointer to professional ability as well as to personal qualities. This requires that the interviewer himself is personally experienced in the intended work areas of the applicant. Unfortunately technically trained people do not necessarily make good interviewers. The tendency to reminisce over mutual acquaintances is strong; the ability to cover relevant ground in a methodical way is often weak. However, people can be trained in interviewing—a good way is by two-man interviewing with one being a skilled personnel specialist. As soon as a sufficiency of interviewing skill has been attained by the technical man he should operate solo. He should always remember that the interview is a medium for communication as well as assessment, and show consideration for the applicant's need for enough information to be able to decide whether to try for the job or whether to accept it if offered.

The personnel function should contribute its experience to the drafting and placing of advertisements and to the inculcating of interviewing skills. After the applicants come in personnel should make it their business to give them a brief picture of the nature of the company and its conditions of employment so that the technical interviewers can devote their time to their principal task.

Motivation and retention

Professional computer staff have professional motivations. They want to learn, to improve their skills, to keep up to date by working with intelligent colleagues on advanced problems. The potential for job satisfaction and positive motivation is therefore high but so too is the expectation of satisfaction and, in normal circumstances, the ease of movement to another employer if these expectations are not met. From the point of view of personnel management there are probably only two differences between the computer professional and any other kind of employee: one is the freedom of movement mentioned above, and the other is his high level of intelligence and a consequent sensitivity to antiquated personnel attitudes or phony motivational programmes.

Opinion survey material in IBM tends to confirm the Herzberg motivational theory (see Herzberg's article *'One more time: How do you motivate employees* ?' in *Harvard Business Review* January-February 1968) both as regards the positive motivators like job interest, achievement, advancement and recognition, and the dissatisfiers like poor pay, maladministration, insecurity or bad personal relationships. In a survey carried out in 1969 among analysts and programmers in IBM Data Centres in the United Kingdom very strong correlations (chi-square figures ranging from 33.3 to 48) were established between intentions to remain with the company or leave within certain defined periods and degree of satisfaction with the following factors, in order of significance:

1   Sense of accomplishment
2   Satisfaction with earnings related to outside
3   Confidence in immediate manager
4   Freedom to adopt own approach
5   Extent of use of skills
6   Satisfaction with past advances in earnings
7   Opportunities for advancement.

A study of this list gives quite a good indication of the kind of personnel environment and management style which will be appropriate and effective in retaining and motivating professional data processing staff.

Salary policy should aim to achieve the difficult task of reconciling internal equity, obtained by job evaluation, with a reasonably competitive market standing. In so far as this is successful a potential dissatisfaction can be avoided. External market standing is best identified by clubbing together with other like-minded employers in a salary survey, which should include regular job-matching visits. Another method is to use an external proprietary salary survey. In either case a target relationship to outside should be established and monitored at least annually.

Overlapping salary brackets should be fixed and attributed to grades which themselves will be arranged to provide a promotion ladder for all classes of employee. A useful extension of the principle is to make progress through salary bracket dependent on performance in relation to the requirements of the job. One such system is portrayed diagrammatically in Figure 13:3.

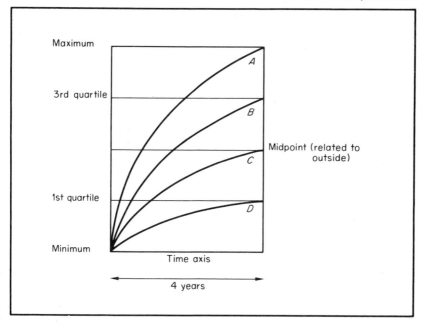

Figure 13:3 Progress through salary bracket for performers with four different merit ratings

In this system, salary progression is obtained by the use of a grid containing percentage increase figures depending both on merit rating and on the bracket quarter in which the individual being reviewed is at the time of the review. Maximum flexibility is obtained by allowing the manager to award an increase at any time but increases at less than annual intervals are reduced by one-twelfth for each month short of a year since the last increase. A cost-of-living-increase element may be added to the merit review simultaneously or separately.

The system depends on acceptable merit appraisal and it is suggested that this is based on performance against mutually agreed objectives. Formal reviews should take place at least once a year in which employee and manager sit down and discuss the past and agree objectives, training needs and career moves in the future.

Annually agreed (not set!) objectives in no way replace the normal process of project control in which tasks with deadlines are allocated by the manager. Project control can of course be linked with objective setting in that performance on projects can be one of the criteria of assessment. However, the objectives should go much further and cover subjects such as personal knowledge or skills development, housekeeping and relationships with users or other departments.

How does the manager measure his own skills in personnel management? An opinion survey programme is a useful aid. In this employees answer an anonymous questionnaire asking about attitudes to the company, the job, the management, salaries, workload, administration and the like. Summaries of the data should be fed back to the employees and explanations given of remedial action intended. The disadvantage of this kind of programme is that expectations of change will be aroused if serious problems are revealed. There must, therefore, be some degree of commitment to the possibility of change and a willingness during feedback sessions to be frank about reasons for not changing. Willingness to listen to and to be open with employees is, I think, a factor of the first importance, whether this is expressed through appraisal and counselling meetings, opinion surveys, suggestion schemes or other personnel programmes.

The discontented employee will, of course, vote with his feet by leaving the organisation. The data processing manager would be well advised to get a sympathetic person outside his own department to interview leavers before they go. Often the departure will be for valid and unavoidable reasons. If it is not then things must be put right. A good consultative manager can learn a lot from a disgruntled employee if he has ears to listen. Data processing professionals as a group tend to have intelligence and creativity which can be powerful aids to the manager who can harness them.

14

Training for Data Processing

S. J. Macoustra

The shortage of suitably qualified and experienced data processing staff, high staff turnover rates, and suggested misuse of many computer installations, are all indicative of a need for training both in professional data processing skills and in a wider understanding of computer advantages and limitations.

The time will shortly come when nobody can expect to get into top management without an understanding of computer usage any more than one can get into top management without a substantial understanding of business financing. One might say that responsibility for the wider aspects of data processing is too important to be handed over to the data processing department, but in practice there are too many cases of abdication of this responsibility by the upper management. To be fair, this is not helped by the common inability of data processing staff to talk in English rather than computerese jargon. To be a specialist does much for the ego. As managers need computer education, so computer staff need company education.

Computers have made such an impact that it is all too easy to forget how recent the technology is. The first models produced for general, as distinct from laboratory use, date from about 1960. Thus it is only relatively recently that computer workers were pioneering. Formal education cannot be established until the technology stabilises enough to enable the training needed to be accurately assessed. If this stage has been reached in computer training, then it has only been reached recently. The difficulties are not entirely explicable in terms of newness. Computers are all-penetrating in that they appear to have capabilities, or at least potentialities, for almost all aspects of commercial and industrial work. Computer technology can never become a closed shop in the way that some professions can become a closed shop. The training requirement can be compared to that in financial training. Finance, like computers, has a part to play in almost all parts of the company, and in financial training there coexists both professional accountancy qualifications and a range of financial courses for managers whose responsibilities require some basic training in financial techniques.

Areas of training

Computer training therefore consists of two distinct areas. A professional area for those who are thinking in terms of a data processing career, and 'intelligent involvement' area for people to whose work the computer makes some contribution.

The first of these areas is the one developing, as accountancy has developed, into formal training schemes and national qualifications. The second area does not lend itself to easy formal definition.

Data processing work is usually defined as three, sometimes four, major functions. First computer operations. The work here is similar to that of a highly automated factory. The notion that a computer is some kind of elaborate information-processing machine tool is quite an accurate one. Operators need training in handling the input and output equipment and media. The supervisors and managers are faced with problems which are essentially those of keeping a manufacturing plant going at full capacity. Most current installations are 'batch processing' and have problems of the same type as a small batch factory. They are concerned with meeting delivery deadlines, with machine utilisation, with scheduling. They are perhaps spared the stock control problems of most batch manufacturing plants, but against this are faced with problems of information security and those of a service department serving several masters.

Secondly, programming. For many outsiders this has always been something of a mystery, for which perhaps early manufacturers' publicity must carry some blame. The fact is that programming, certainly conventional commercial programming, is rapidly becoming a semi-clerical job. The only mystery about programming is what all these programmers did in pre-computer days.

The job certainly requires a sense of logic combined with a rigorous attention to detail, but some programming capability is within the reach of any intelligent person who cares to try it. As a result it is usually seen as a first step into computing and such training as is required is usually provided by the manufacturer.

Thirdly, systems analysis. At this point it should be said that the description 'programmer' and 'systems analyst' do not, by any means, carry the same implication in all data processing departments. Only computer operations work can be said to require a distinctly separate set of skills. The rest are somewhat intermingled, there being no generally recognised sharp borderline between systems analysis and programming. The confusion arises over two principal points. The function of 'systems design' that is, determining the principle features of a computer program, is sometimes organised as part of programming and sometimes as part of the systems analysis department. The second point is a variation in the responsibilities at the user interface or in the problem investigation area of systems analysis. Traditionally this belongs to the data processing department, but there is a discernable increase in the number of organisations who regard this as a user department function. It is inevitable that as computer skills become more widely known, user departments will feel increasingly competent to make their own decisions. Thus the 'systems cycle' of problem investigation, systems design, and programming are liable to be organised in differing fashions in different organisations, and indeed within the same organisation as computer knowledge slowly spreads.

A further complication in training occurs at the supervisory or management level in systems/programming work where organisation can be based on one of two basic principles; either 'functional' or 'project' oriented. Functional organisation gives departments containing similar skills. This would commonly be an 'analysis' department and a 'programming' department. 'Project' orientation puts all skills required to complete a particular job under one department. The differences clearly seem to imply differing requirements in training. It seems, therefore, that even in the professional area of computer training the situation is far from static. None of this is in any way to decry the excellent efforts of the British Computer Society and the National Computing Centre in attempting to formalise the professional training area, but it seems sensible to suppose that the rate of change is still liable to be high. An example of this continuing evolution is the relatively recent discovery that the problems of systems analysis are sometimes at their severest in the area of human relations.

The 'intelligent involvement' area of data processing training can perhaps now be seen in a more accurate light. It is not so much 'involvement' but part of the 'problem investigation' phase of systems analysis. Until quite recently there was a great vogue for the 'computer appreciation' type of course for non data processing staff. Strictly speaking, there should be no such thing. One trains to give a skill, or educates to change an attitude. 'Computer appreciation' should be—indeed may already have become—a definition of user responsibilities as recognition grows that data processing skills should not be locked inside the data processing department, but belong increasingly to the user department. To summarise, we are seeing perhaps the beginning of formal training and additionally the beginnings of an understanding that responsibilities outside the data processing department need training in at least some aspects of systems analysis. The situation seems far from stable but some major training areas can be defined. These are: computer operations, programming, systems design, systems analysis (here used to mean 'problem investigation') and supervisory/management training for all these areas.

Which courses?

The climate created by the training boards' levy/grant schemes resulted in a boom in training services generally. In data processing, as in other areas, there exists a bewildering number of organisations claiming to be trainers. Almost every university provides computing courses either leading to a degree or at least as a component of a degree course in other disciplines. Together with technical colleges they provide a wide range of full-time, part-time, and sandwich courses. This type of training is particularly suitable for those intending to become involved in the scientific/engineering environment. The British Computer Society has established examinations of a similarly high professional level.

For most commercial data processing departments, these levels are too advanced and the National Computing Centre (NCC) has developed a range of more suitable courses. Consultancies and colleges are licensed to present these 'packaged' courses. The well-known NCC six-week systems analysis course leads to a nationally recognised certificate. Manufacturers commonly have substantial training establishments for training based on their own product lines. For the principal manufacturers this can be a most profitable sideline.

In addition to all this, most major data processing users run their own training establishments covering, at least, basic training.

Faced with this massive variety in choice, and a substantial variation in requirement, it is hardly surprising that there have been difficulties. Just how difficult depends in part on the size of the company concerned. Companies vary widely in their personnel policies, which in turn, produce a variety of training polices. The larger, more stable companies, especially where top management see themselves as heavily dependent on the quality of their staff, tend to develop the full panoply of job descriptions, appraisal schemes, graded salary structures and, perhaps, manpower planning. The effect of all this, particularly of a highly developed appraisal system, is to identify clearly training needs. Given a clear statement of training needs, the problems reduce, in principle, to finding courses whose objectives correspond to the needs established and of determining whether the demand is high enough to justify a company training capability or so low that external courses are sensible.

Smaller companies who cannot justify the overheads that such elaborate personnel schemes imply have bigger problems. If they cannot identify their training needs what can they sensibly do? This is an area in which one would think training boards should concentrate. The big organisation is, or should be, able to accurately determine its own needs, the smaller organisation often simply cannot afford it.

How then does the organisation whose data processing involvement is not on a large enough scale to justify having its own training capability choose its training? Superficially it might seem to have the choice of doing none, but this implies a continuing high staff turnover—the great fear of data processing staff is technical obsolescence—in which case staff loyalties will remain obstinately to data processing technology rather that to the company. Additionally, hiring new staff as a continuing policy, is expensive in executive time and far from error-free.

The choice then, is not whether or not to train, but how to do it.

Course evaluation

The evaluation of course suitability has two basic components. What are the course's objectives, and how well does it achieve them? A set of course objectives define rigorously, or should define rigorously, what a suitable attendee will be able to do as a result of attending. The commonly published 'syllabus' is a poor substitute, certainly for the skills training area. Syllabuses are perhaps a more acceptable approach in the educative type of course, where the teaching problem is one of attitude changing, but, for skills training, objectives are by far the best guide.

The second problem, that of how well a course attains its objectives is rather more difficult.

In practice decisions are often made on the basis of word of mouth or attendees' reports. A commercial service based on the latter exists. No doubt this is all useful and should certainly be an element in any assessment of how well a course meets its objectives, but it is not enough. Attendee reports are essentially amateur judgements, influenced by social factors as much as by teaching ones. Judgements by attendees' managers on improved performance are better, but really there is no substitute for the judgement of a competent training officer.

Encouragingly the training officer function has arrived to stay. It is estimated that over 25 per cent of personnel staff are concerned with training, where twenty years ago training officers were an almost unknown species. One only hopes that they function as influences for effective training and not merely as training grant maximisers.

Length of courses is a much-discussed item. There are really two extremes which should be avoided. If a course is too short, it makes little impact, and what is learnt is liable to be rapidly forgotten on returning to one's normal working environment. If a course is too long, the chances of using all which has been taught on return to work are slim. The most efficient arrangement is to train for a specified range of skills and to use those skills immediately on return to work. This 'modular' approach maximises the usefulness of training. The ideal picture is, therefore, to give training in relatively short, say five-day, concentrated courses, spaced out as the job allows the trained skill to be used. This ties in ideally with modern personnel thinking on career structures, most of these being based on the idea of a continual progression, or enrichment, of employee's jobs. To consider the problem of choosing courses is therefore an over-simplification. The problem is rather to establish an integrated series of courses suitably spaced to allow practical usage of skills taught and reinforcement before continuing to the next step.

No career-strucured training scheme should be bureaucratically rigid. As one learns, one's ideas and future ambitions are liable to alter. Optional paths should always be left in any scheme. Such schemes, even quite primitive versions, have other advantages. Constant enrichment creates a frame of mind which minimises parochialism, and parochialism in data processing—essentially a company-wide service—ought to be regarded as the ultimate crime. Another spin-off is the removal of some pressure on salaries. Without some type of progression, staff will find their own and salaries are a natural target. Employees need some measure of their success and a planned training progression comes cheaper than most.

A reasonable guide to the effectiveness of courses in achieving their objectives is the type of teaching method used. It is often said that attendees remember 20 per cent of what is said and 30 per cent of what is seen, but 50 per cent of what is both seen and heard. A lecture has been described as 'a process by which information passes from the notes of the instructor to the notes of the student without passing through the mind of either'. Visualisation is, therefore, a basic item. Further, attendees need to accept reponsibility for their own learning. Learning is not a passive occupation. Involvement is the keynote. Guided discussions are helpful, particularly in attitude changing. Case studies are even better. Not only do they provide involvement, but there are additional advantages of increased confidence in overcoming difficulties to obtain an acceptable solution. For systems analysis work especially, social awareness is a not unimportant factor and syndicate case work can give training in this area also.

Future of computer training

For the future of computer training, one must first establish the framework of future usage. Brief though computer history is, there are a number of identifiable stages. There is the stage establishing how to engineer the hardware; the stage of high-level programming languages which simplified programming— and the stage of redesigning hardware systems to give multi-programming as the speed of electronics outstripped the speed of the peripherals. On might argue that this ended the preliminary establishment of the technology. Further developments—like the recognition of systems analysis as a separate function— are more concerned with the use of computers than concerned with the technology.

These latter developments are far from finished. If one assumes that data processing knowledge will gradually become widespread and that user departments will gradually take over more and more data processing functions, then the data processing department is left with a computer and little else. There is, however, another major factor.

Many installations have computerised most of their organisation's basic requirements and now need to integrate the separate programs and stored information into what is sometimes called a data base. This implies two capabilities. A capability of ensuring the computer system is a 'technically' sensible integration, and a capability of maintaining a management structure aimed at ensuring cooperation between user departments with competing claims on the data base. The data processing department of the future would therefore seem to consist of three elements: the computer itself and associated operating staff, a centralised system design function and a coordinating function.

Training then polarises clearly into two distinct requirements. The data processing specialist will use formal institutional training leading to nationally recognised qualifications. The 'users', by doing their own systems analysis and quite possibly their own programming, will use training not to acquire qualifications but to give them enough skill to get their own work done efficiently. The current widespread rethinking of the role of many computer installations may lead to this quite rapidly.

There are many indications that the role of computers in business environments needs this rethinking. Most authorities point to lack of communication as the major reason for unsatisfactory performance. This can be expressed in many ways: as lack of understanding of business by data processing staff, or lack of understanding of data processing by business management. In either event it indicates lack of training.

15

Installation Audits

M. J. B. Naughton

Writing in the *Harvard Business Review* in 1969, John Diebold observed: 'By the mid-1970s corporate success will be determined by the effectiveness of computer applications at all levels and in all areas of business activity.'

This is already evident. Some companies are using advanced information processing methods and seeing significant benefits, ranging from shortened delivery times to reduced inventory.

Others are spending heavily on computers and achieving longer delivery dates and frequent stock-outs.

This chapter, therefore, is not primarily concerned with methods for improving computer operations or ensuring accurate payrolls. These can be controlled by a series of checks which will be listed later. The aim of the *management* audit of the installation is to ensure that the computer department is in sound condition for the increasingly vital part which it must play in the company's activities in the future.

The auditor

Obviously the audit of both the technical function—computing—and its present and future interaction with the company demands a rather special breed of man. He will need a knowledge of the company and of its corporate plans. He needs management accounting expertise in order to balance objectively computing costs against benefits. He must be aware of good computing practise and of the h ardware and software facilities available. As a person he needs to be able to cut through waffle and jargon, to be inventive enough to devise his own crosschecks on actual as opposed to alleged facts and yet be one who is manifestly anxious to aid the computer department, not a 'management spy'. Lastly, he must have enough strength of character to avoid being swayed by emotive arguments about hard work in the past or the need to maintain morale. He will be making criticisms and will thus need to achieve the 'integration of viewpoints' which Mary Parker Follett saw as the source of new and effective ideas when disagreement exists. A thoughtful line manager or well-briefed management consultant will often have these skills.

Planning the audit

In the same way as care must be taken in choosing the man, so also must the audit itself be carefully planned. An audit is expensive in time and manpower, both of the auditor and those audited; an audit that is not clearly defined both in scope and timetable can degenerate into a vague consultancy operation.

The area of the company's operations which can be covered by a computer audit is very large and it is possible that only segments of the work discussed here will be covered in any one audit assignment. These segments must be clearly specified at an early stage. Terms of reference will be determined. The willing agreement to them of the line management to whom the computer department reports is essential; that of the computer department itself, desirable. Initial meetings will be held to determine the plan for the project. Normal project control techniques are desirable, especially if the audit is being done by a team rather than by one man. For this, the tasks proposed and the areas to be examined must be listed, the estimated time needed for each determined, a timetable drawn up into which the tasks are slotted, and a monitoring system of achievement against the timetable established.

The normal ancillary preparations for an audit will be made: the creation of questionnaires, checklists and standard forms for logging, recording and acknowledging interviews. An additional aid in the case of a large audit might be a computer program which would analyse basic data concerning installation costs, performance, file sizes and volumes submitted to it, and extract meaningful information.

What does management think of the computer department?

The man has been chosen and, in conjunction with the main board director and the local management, a controlled plan of audit has been developed.

The first area to which attention may be turned is that of the same local management. It is an axiom that the sucess or otherwise of computing in a company is directly related to the degree of management participation.

'Does the local management take account of the views of the computer services manager in their five-year forward plan?' the auditor will ask.

Have they a five-year forward plan?

If not, what is the sense in creating computer systems of any breadth which, in general, need to run for five years to be viable?

What is the mandate developed for the computer department by the local management? Do they feel that the computer installation has interpreted their mandate well or badly since it was given? Has the department any terms of reference? Is it restricted by artificial boundaries such that applications on the computer stop when they get to 'accounts' or to 'engineering'? Has the essential nature of successful computer applications been recognised, namely that they ignore existing departmental splits and concentrate on the *real* flow of information and action across a company?

The auditor will continue to examine the environment in which the computer department works by discussing with users their ideas on what the computer should be doing. Were existing applications forced on them by enthusiastic but ill-informed top management? What do they regard as the activity most central to their work? What plans are in hand for the computerisation of this activity? Are existing applications mere clerical automation or do they significantly improve efficiency? In general, is the computer department a valuable partner in improving profitability—or is it an unwanted overhead?

Systems development: the crucial area

Having gained a feel for the environment, the auditor may now turn to the computer department itself. Here the area most crucial to success or failure is the systems development function. These are the personnel responsible for the overall design of the computer systems, in liaison with the user departments. Their vision and experience will make or break the company by 1980

But how do new systems projects start? Who initiates them? Who decides what resources will be allocated to what project? Are there defined levels of authorisation, as for any other capital expenditure, above which the approval of the next level of management must be sought? Is there a standard format for a development proposal? Is it sufficiently searching in its questions about costs to be incurred and alleged benefits to be obtained? Is a checklist in existence, listing points to be considered when submitting a proposal, ranging from: 'Has another company in the group a similar system already in existence?' to. 'Has the group capacity analysis department been informed of the proposal?'

Is the systems work done on time?

Once the development of a system has been approved, it must be controlled. The auditor will ensure that the project is broken down for control purposes into standard, identifiable tasks and sub-tasks, that an estimate of time and costs is made for each and that a monitoring system which rapidly reflects variances from budget and schedule purposes and for monitoring staff performance.

Staffing and organisation

Staff must be scheduled into the future like any other expensive resource and matched against future workloads. Has this been done and does it agree with the computer department's financial projections? The auditor will check the user department's views on the proposed future projects and compare them with the installation's plans. Under- or over-staffing in future months may be indicated. What plans have been made to deal with this situation, whether by recruitment or by redundancies? Does the training programme reflect these future needs?

What is the staff turnover percentage? Is it rising or falling? How is this related to salary levels, and how do salary levels relate to national figures? How do the individual members of the staff view their future? In discussion with them the auditor will form an opinion of their morale and their suitability for the work, a task which must be done with extreme tact.

How is the department organised? Is there over-specialisation such that poor planning allocates those with special skills to fire-fighting computerisation jobs? Is the sytems effort centralised under a systems manager or decentralised to the users? How effective is the form of organisation chosen, and has increasing skill specialisation made it unsuitable for present-day conditions?

The question which the auditor will constantly ask himself in this phase of the audit will be: 'Is the systems function well managed?'

Systems: where is the company going?

The study of the overall philosophy of the systems department should be a study of the corporate plans of the company as a whole. The auditor will ensure that there is liaison between the plans of line management and those of the systems department. Is there a policy of designing all systems such that they will eventually link into the corporate data base? Are the projects visualised for the future those which management agree are central to the profitability of the company? Is there a clear differentiation between long-term planning by the systems department in which very senior user management will participate, and short-term projects in which more junior management play a greater role?

In long-term planning are the effects of the centralisation of information on the structure of the company being borne in mind?

Two systems diseases

Systems departments often suffer from two diseases: the first is omniscience, the second is NIH.

Omniscience shows itself in the belief that a nodding acquaintance with for instance, linear programming empowers the possessor to change a company's entire operating procedures.

NIH, or 'not invented here', is the belief that the problems of one's own company are so special that experience gained elsewhere is of little use. Packaged computer systems or programs bought 'off the shelf' are, in consequence, rejected in favour of 'hand-made' systems.

The cure: standards

A sound systems philosophy, embodied in well-written departmental standards, can go a long way towards curing both these diseases.

Standards of methodology may be studied first. These should lay down, for the guidance of all members of the systems department, the phases of a systems investigation and how they will be carried out. Feasibility study, systems survey, systems analysis, systems design, program specification—these are all identifiable and necessary phases in the work of developing systems. Does the spirit of cooperation with user departments, of *joint* efforts to find systems solutions, breath through the pages of these procedures? Do the procedures ensure that users participate at every stage on a project, from authorising the information requirements contained in the systems analysis stage up to checking test data? Are the standards adhered to?

Standard techniques should also be in existence to ensure that a common approach to problems is maintained. The subjects covered will be as diverse as when to use batch control to guidance on video screen layouts.

Views on the use of software or preprogrammed aids to the design of systems will also appear in an effective techniques manual. These will range from decision table processors to generalised file handling suites such as a bill of material processor. The auditor will satisfy himself that knowledge of or access to appropriate O & M and OR techniques is available to the systems departments. This may cover statistical methods, principles of work study, procedure analysis, inventory control theory, network analysis, linear programming, and queuing theory.

The auditor will ensure that there is liaison between the systems teams and those responsible for providing the computer hardware. Are the implications of the rapidly falling cost of direct—access devices appreciated in terms of their implications for corporate data bases? Communications-based or real-time systems can add significantly to an organisation's effectiveness and will be economical on a wide scale in the very near future. Does the systems department realise this, or are they hidebound by a batch systems mentality?

Programming

An effective audit of the programming function can be especially valuable to management as it is often regarded as a black art into which finance directors or chief engineers are unwise to pry.

As for the systems function, the basic *methodology* by which the programming function goes about its work and the manner in which it is organised will be studied first.

When work is received for programming, it will be conceptually broken down into a series of tasks ranging from flow-charting or designing the logic, through coding, 'dry' or off-computer testing, then testing using the computer and, lastly, documentation. The auditor will satisfy himself that this is being done and that estimates for each task are incorporated into a project plan.

A *monitoring* system should be in operation to ensure that variances in elapsed time or cost are rapidly brought to the attention of the programming management. In programming, the work done at any one stage is often difficult to quantify as it consists of interrelated logical statements which may or may not form the basis of a working program. An essential control feature which the auditor will look for is a personal check of each programmer's logic by a senior member of the programming team before the completion of that stage is signalled to the project control.

The auditor will next study the programming department's published standards. These will specify the manner in which each programming task is to be undertaken; such as rules for drawing flowcharts, obligatory modularisation of programs above a certain size, and the way in which a working program is to be documented for future reference.

Another management control on programming for which the auditor will search will be the maintenance of skill/performance history records for each programmer, in order to isolate those who are consistently under- or over-performing against their standard. Histories of actual programmer time and machine time needed to complete each task of programs written, together with details of the complexity and number of lines of code in the program, should also be maintained in order to refine progressively the estimating techniques discussed above.

As with the systems function, the *organisation* of the programming department will be studied. Are programmers engaged on writing new programs frequently called away to maintain old programs? Are specialists on operating systems being committed to normal programming to the detriment of the installation's overall performance? What is the projected future programming workload, broken down by system, maintenance and software? How do the manpower and training plans reflect this?

Programming techniques

In terms of generating working programs, a good and experienced programmer can be ten or more times as efficient as an untutored one.

Much of the difference is accounted for by the use of established programming techniques. The programming department should, therefore, have published guidelines for its staff outlining these techniques and where they may best be used. The auditor should satisfy himself that this has been done and that junior programmers are instructed in them. Examples of such techniques are balance line (a standardised file updating mechanism), binary search (a method of looking up tables in core) and core sorts. An example of the usefulness of having such techniques widely known in the installation is seen in the case of a program run on the very large computer of a major oil company, which originally took an hour to run. When the table look-up in this program was converted to a binary search method, the running time fell to three minutes.

The auditor will look for awareness of the need to disseminate time-saving techniques such as these, but will also satisfy himself that excessive man-hours are not wasted in programming elegantly for the sake of elegance.

The audit of programming techniques is an opportunity to review the installation's computer language policy. The auditor will ensure that the company language policy—which may insist on COBOL or FORTRAN, for example—is being observed, and that use of assembler or other languages is only made where necessary. He may well investigate the suitability of the company standard language to the installation. Is it possible, for example, that the interface between scientific work and data processing is such that a language of the PL/1 type, which can handle both, is now more suitable than the company standards?

Operational systems

It is now time to examine more closely the systems actually on the computer. The statistics of the computer workload will be studied and, in conjunction with the computer department management, those systems most significant in terms of computer time, plus those considered most valuable to the organisation, plus some selected at random, will be brought out into the light of day.

Computer systems can be divided into a series of subsystems and each of these will be examined.

The *input* will be studied in terms of the volume originally planned against the actual volume of cards, source documents and video transactions now prevailing. When the system was first set up, schedules will have been established for submission of data by the users. The auditor will check whether or not these are being adhered to.

The control over input will also be examined, to ensure that the batching or hash totalling originally planned is still being carried out, and that its purpose is still being achieved: namely, ensuring that there is no loss of data between user and computer. The auditor will satisfy himself that where data transmission or tele-processing is involved, checks are built in, either electronically (such as cyclic check character generation) or clerically (such as mailing batch totals). Lastly, discussions will be held with the user at clerical or shopfloor level to check that the input documents are easy to complete, do not impose an excessive workload, and are still relevant to current conditions.

The *output* subsystem will be examined in a similar manner to the input in terms of volumes planned and actually encountered. The planned schedule for delivering processed results to the user is compared with that actually achieved. The controls built into the original system for ensuring by means of check totals and external registers that data has been processed according to program within the computer will be reviewed.

At this stage the auditor is examining the systems from the viewpoint of performance rather than their value to the organisation. So when he discusses the usefulness of the output with the user at this stage, it is looked at as a document—stock re-order schedule, for example—not as part of a system which may, or may not, be of value to the company. Armed, therefore, with specimen printouts, the auditor will again visit the users' departments. Who gets the printout? What do they do with it? Who is it passed to? How rapidly? Are too few or too many copies being produced? Is it too late to be of any use to anyone? Or is it, in the light of changing user requirements, being produced unnecessarily early? What problems are the users finding in understanding or using the information displayed on the output? Is the computer system being altogether bypassed by the user; such as in a production control system where progress documents are sent to the computer installation only occasionally and well after the event, production control having degenerated into progress chasing?

Still in the process of examining the operational systems, the auditor will now focus more sharply on the computer department. To what extent is each system studied effective *as a suite of computer programs*? Are there excessive tape changing or other set-up problems relative to the processing time? Has the suite collected in the course of its life a large number of adhoc programs, which are tagged on to the end of processing rather than integrated with the suite as a whole? The auditor will watch the suite being run— probably at a personally inconvenient time—and check whether its operating documentation and console error messages permit the operators to do their work effectively. What does the shift leader think of the suite? Is full use being made of opportunities for parallel processing —for example, printing the results of an earlier run while calculating the next? Which programs take longest to run? If they are processor-bound, that is they make lengthy use of the computer itself rather than the card-reader or disks, is this caused by poor programming or genuinely complex computing?

At this stage the auditor may consider the use of hardware or software monitors. These consist of either electronic devices of special programs which analyse the use which each operational system is making of the computer. Startling improvements have sometimes followed the use of these devices and expensive computer enhancements have been avoided by reprogramming. Their utility must be balanced, however, against their cost, and an experienced man can often obtain the same results by observing a program in action.

The auditor will examine the program amendment register in relation to the suite. Are frequent *changes* being called for? Is this caused by poor analysis in the first place, by poor programming, or by genuine changes in requirements?

Is the *audit trial* still meaningful after program changes? Is it used by the company's internal auditors? Have the procedures in the computer department changed such that an operator could tamper with the programs without disturbing the controls?

Lastly, each operational system should be examined *vis-à-vis* its *future* characteristics. The auditor will have ascertained in his data-gathering phase the likely growth rates and changes in the system visualised by the user. Do these agree with the computer department's estimates, and what forward planning exists to deal with these changes?

Are the systems profitable?

The auditor will now look at the operational systems from the point of view of *cost justification*. What were the original estimates of systems and programming effort, machine time and user support to develop the suite? How much did it actually cost and how long did it take? Why did it overrun estimates? Where did the overspending occur—analysis, programming, systems testing?

What were the justifications for developing the system, whether tangible and easily measurable (staff savings), tangible but not easily measurable (work-in-progress reductions), or intangible (better customer service)?

Have the aims been achieved? What are the comparable figures, before and after the introduction of the system, for stock turnover, stock as a percentage of sales, late delivery ratio, staff per thousand invoices handled, or whatever other control figure may have been devised?

The problem of ascertaining the true running costs of a system will be discussed later, but at this point the installation's own figures may be accepted. How do these compare with the estimated running costs? And with actual current benefits, difficult as these are to quantify?

Is the system, then, running at a profit for the company? Or at a loss?

The data processing factory

Throughout the earlier phases of the audit, the computer equipment itself and the staff who operate it have, for the most part, been treated independently of the development of the information processing systems of the company. This is reasonable. In the early days of computing, when a few mathematicians struggled to get the sales ledger operational, the computer and the systems function were closely interdependent. This situation changed with the advent of standardised, interchangeable ranges of computers, with the spread of bureaux, and the development of data-transmission techniques.

Today, the computer installation may be regarded as a data processing factory, subject to the same criteria of efficiency as any other factory—equipment utilisation, costs, delivery, production control

When studying equipment utilisation the first requirement of the auditor is the compilation of representative statistics of machine usage. The auditor will check that computer time is booked accurately, whether automatically or by the operators completing a log. Once satisfied that the figures are meaningful, he will call for the statistics of a day, a month, or randomly selected periods, according to the type of work carried out.

These will be analysed under a series of headings, typically:

1   Hours spent on production work—that is, useful work—by suite and by program.
2   Testing—by suite and by program
3   Program maintenance—by suite and by program
4   Rerunning of programs, broken down by cause:

    (a)   Operator error
    (b)   Program error
    (c)   Hardware errors
    (d)   Defective tapes, cards, etc.

5   Under, or awaiting, repair

6   Development of own software.
7   Software maintenance, such as generating new operating systems or
    disk reorganisation.
8   Idle, or awaiting work
9   Not switched on

The time wasted through the installation's own shortcomings, compared to total time switched on will be examined and a decision made on whether or not it is acceptable or whether further investigation is called for.

The percentage time wasted by defective hardware will be similarly studied. The figures will be compared with the manufacturer's own records of downtime. The manufacturer's records of extra use will also provide a check on the usage times submitted.

What does the sales ledger system really cost?

Parallel to this investigation, a study will be mounted of the costs of the computer installation. Cost directly attributable to computer operations— operators' wages, machine rental, purchase of tapes—together with overheads— such as a percentage of management salaries, company administration charges, software support—will be collected together. These will be divided by productive hours in order to establish the cost per hour. In some installations a full standard costing system already exists and this can be extremely valuable in analysing costs where the computer load and thus recovery of overheads is constantly varying. A further refinement is to calculate the cost per hour per hardware unit, for example, printer or disk drive.

The actual cost of each application will now be calculated and compared with those charged to users, and with the amounts incorporated in the users' budgets.

This is valuable from two aspects. It is a check on the validity of the data supplied, and it is an indication of any distortions in the charging policy. It should be ascertained whether or not these distortions are acceptable to management.

The costs will now be expressed, if this is not already done, in terms of units handled—for example, stock bins controlled, items scheduled, staff paid. These costs may now be compared with those prevailing in outside bureaux, other computer centres within the group, or other companies' figures. If the costs are roughly comparable in terms of work done, the figures may be accepted. If significantly higher or lower, a more detailed investigation must be made. The suites under examination may provide significantly more or less information than those with which they are being compared. The program development costs may need to be added to obtain comparable figures. Control services provided by the computer installation must be costed. The auditor will examine past years' performances and check whether unit costs are rising or falling and at what rate.

Is the second printer really needed?

The utilisation of the other equipment associated with the installation may be examined in a similar manner. If data transmission is in operation, whether by Post Office line or by private transport, its costs may be extracted. The utilisation of hardware units and certain types of storage media may be studied, but not by asking for monthly statistics by application which, unless such figures are recorded automatically, could be an astronomical task. Such figures must be built up by the selected timings of the most frequently used programs, but can be extremely valuable once available. In conjunction with the operational systems audit discussed above, it may be discovered that the configuration has bottlenecks in some places and unsuspected slack in others; that, for instance, an unbuffered printer is demanding excessive channel time which is slowing down disk accesses. Disk packs are expensive (typically £200 upwards) and, if carelessly organised files can consume vast area of disk space. What is the percentage utilisation, or characters stored per pack divided by character capacity?

The costs of data preparation should also be studied. True costs, both direct and indirect, may be calculated and the cost per numeric and alphabetic keystroke, punched and verified, determined. This again should be compared with other installations in the Group, in similar companies, and in outside bureaux. The key depressions per operator-hour will be compared with the standard obtained by other users. The actual cost should be compared with those charged to users.

Is it a well-run factory?

Having examined the installation from a primarily financial and statistical aspect, the auditor will now examine it as an efficiently run organisation. Work should be scheduled ahead in normal production control manner—that is to say in broad loading patterns for several months into the future, in finer detail for several weeks, and with extreme accuracy for several hours. The auditor will examine this planning and ensure that there is close liaison between the work of the systems department and the department responsible for running the installation. The procedure by which tapes, disks and cards are marshalled by the computer librarian for submission to each operating shift will be studied. If an automatic or programmed job-scheduling system is an operation, the auditor will study its effectiveness. If one is not being used, he will ask why this is so.

The published *standards for methods of operating* in the computer room will be examined, and the auditor will compare these with what actually happens. These standards will cover items as diverse as the procedures to be followed if a program fails, down to a prohibition against smoking in the computer room.

In this context the auditor will study the quality of the documentation supplied to the operators with each program to enable them to carry out their work. Are the instructions clear and unambiguous? Are the possible messages which could appear on the operator's console fully explained? Are the instructions modified immediately there is a change in the system?

Security will be studied. This ranges from the procedures to be taken in case of fire or in case of severe machine breakdown, to the security of processing *vis-à-vis* the operators themselves. Are any of the operators trained programmers? Are such operators ever in a position to alter files and cover up such alterations? If passwords are used to prevent unauthorised access to computer files, who has access to the passwords? When were they last changed? Are all documents date-stamped after punching? Can data preparation operators change control totals? What happens to punch cards after use? (They represent valuable scrap.) Is there a standard notification form for submission to the manager when serious delays occur?

The concept of overall organisation was briefly touched on above in mentioning the separation of duties between those who compile check totals and those who process them. The auditor must now examine the *organisation and workflow* of the installation in detail. An organisation chart and details of job specifications will be requested. Areas of clerical overload and underload will be noted. The manpower will be compared with that of other installations having similar workloads and with figures supplied by experienced personnel outside the installation. The flow of work through the installation from initial receipt of data to the return of output to the user will be examined for security and efficiency, using procedure analysis techniques.

The forward plans of the data processing factory will now be studied. The base for this will be the financial projections for two to three years ahead in terms of estimated growth of existing systems and new work planned by the systems department. These projections will be compared with the user departments' financial plans. Using true processing costs, these will be translated back into machine load. What plans have been made in terms of upgrading the equipment to meet this load? Are they overoptimistic in that the installation is planning for a load that will not materialise? Or underoptimistic in that there is a danger of the existing equipment being swamped with work faster than new equipment can be delivered? What plans are in hand to move on to a different operating system or to handle multiprogramming?

What plans are in hand for ensuring a supply of trained operators to handle the new systems? If the system department foresees a tele-processing requirement, are negotiations in hand with the Post Office, bearing in mind that lines and modems may take eighteen months to become available?

The examination of the operations function is the last of the major area to be studied.

The auditor will now begin to consolidate his working papers, progress any outstanding questionnaires, review the results of any computer analysis programs used, and evaluate the installation as a whole, cross checking his figures from each function within it. He may then move to the last stage in his audit.

Report and action

A company-wide standard should exist for installation audit reports. The very existence of such a predefined format is valuable. It will make systems designers wary when describing the benefits to be gained from their proposals if they know that their claims are to be analysed after the event to discover whether or not they materialised. It will remind user managements that the staff reductions they promised to achieve will be looked for as an automatic procedure. Computer operations management will keep the control ratios discussed above in the forefront of their minds, if they know that they will be judged on them.

Much of the report will consist of quantitative data presented in a standard company format; staff numbers by category, details of applications and computer utilisation figures, although lengthy schedules will appear as appendices.

The main use of the report, however, is as a tool to improve management. Management here means primarily the local management whose work has been audited. Drucker has shown the ineffectiveness of management auditors who report in secret back to top management. In the data-processing field, hampered already by novelty and suspicion, such a practice will ensure in a short time that the auditor is met with hostility and suppression of information at all levels. The local management must know from the outset that they will have an opportunity to see and discuss the report before it goes higher. This does not necessarily mean that the auditor will change his views. But it does mean that errors of fact or interpretation not appreciated by the auditor at the time can be brought out and, if thought relevant, incorporated in the report.

In commenting on the data-processing situation in the area under review, the auditor will take an objective viewpoint, avoiding censure as much as lavish praise. He will indicate the strengths and weaknesses found in each of the sectors of the data-processing organisation examined. He will pay particular attention to the operational systems and those planned for the future. He will point out, for instance, that no plans exist for computerising conveyor belt control, the central problem, let us say, of the company, even though detailed proposals exist for improving the sales ledger. The auditor may indicate that the true running costs of a stock-control system greatly exceed the expenses that would be incurred if it was handled manually. The true costs of the computerised payroll in the installation under examination may be far higher than those c harged by a local computer bureau: the auditor may well recommend that the payroll be transferred to that bureax, with a magnetic tape being received back regularly for cost-allocation purposes.

As well as local recommendations, however, the auditor will draw general conclusions of value for other parts of the company or for the future. Why did the production control system, for example, take such a short time to get working? What characterised the systems team which did it? Did they use any particular techniques in designing the system, such as file management packages? If so, should such knowledge be spread more widely in the company, perhaps by specialised training? A real-time engineering design information system has, the auditor finds, had an abnormally short payback period. Have real-time information systems a similar potential elsewhere in the company, in say inventory or cash control? The dissemination of lessons such as these into company practices and standards manuals can be one of the most valuable features of the computer audit.

Lastly the report is printed in company report format, submitted to local management and the main board, and its formal acceptance negotiated. A schedule for the implementation of its recommendations in an agreed priority sequence will be prepared and using a project control monitoring system similar to that used to control the audit, implementation will be carried out.

If the auditor has done his work well, not only will implementation be rapid and thorough, but a date set for a second audit, perhaps a couple of years in the future will be welcomed by both the local line and computer management.

16

Security of the Computer Installation

Eric Oliver and John Wilson

This chapter will deal with the protection of the computer installation in detail from the planning of a new site. Most of the chapter will describe the methods of protection from fire and other environmental hazards that can cause enormous damage if records are destroyed or if there is a prolonged shutdown.

By comparison with the consequential loss from a shutdown, potential losses from fraudulent operation are relatively minor and the probability of their occurrence more remote, though less so than formerly, possibly due to the amount of sensational publicity which has been accorded to them. While incidents have occurred in this country, the bulk of reported frauds continue in the USA. Nevertheless systems analysts, programmers and computer operators have increased in accordance with the law of supply and demand, which has brought in its train high wages and excellent prospects. It is too much to expect that the criminal percentage of the community will not have due representation among these. Sooner or later frauds will be perpetrated—if they are not already in being, but undetected due to the expertise of the practitioners. Fortunately, publicity has also brought precautions which make their task more difficult— these are mentioned hereafter.

Standby facilities

A first consideration when installing a computer is a rather surprising and pessimistic one, but one which the manager has to bear in mind from the outset—it is that of ensuring alternative suitable facilities in the event of a break-down from fire, supply failure, or any other cause. In many concerns such a break-down can cause utter confusion in an otherwise well-organised regime because of the degree to which the computer has been integrated into the firm's activity.

Standby arrangements should be explored from the outset on a mutual-aid basis with owners of like machines within reasonable distances. This could have a bearing on which of two equally acceptable machines is selected for purchase in that an identical standby for one of them may be immediately to hand. There is little doubt that full cooperation will be extended, though it might be advisable to avoid potential competitors in making the arrangements!

The manual or detailed instructions kept in the computer room should contain as a minimum of information:

1   The exact specification of each standby computer contact with details of time availability.
2   The identity and means of contacting those personnel at the other installations who can authorise use of the machines
3   A list of contacts in order of preference to minimise delays in the event of the first choice being unusable.
4   The precise location of each contact with instructions how to reach it.
5   A checklist of the minimum software, stationery and other equipment needed together with any particular personnel to be called out.

All senior personnel should be accessible by telephone at their homes and detailed instructions should be laid down for action in the event of a failure.

Hazards to be guarded against

Environmental disaster   Fire, explosion and flooding can destroy not only the building fabric and the machine itself but also computer programmes, information, data and records stored on magnetic media. Card and paper tape input, printed output and supplies of special paper are also at risk in this context.

Machine failure   New generations of computers should have increasingly greater degrees of reliability with their improved technology, but they are still pieces of equipment subject to mechanical failure and dependent on external power supplies which can fail.

Deliberate or accidental loss of information held on computer files This is an area of human involvement and covers all those aspects outside environmental damage. The loss can arise from errors and acts of negligence on the part of the operating staff, faults in programmes, the consequences of unauthorised persons or visitors gaining access to the computer room—or deliberate acts of sabotage.

Misappropriation of company funds and assets The areas which effectively provide the best opportunity of using the computer resources for this purpose are those of programming and operations—they will be dealt with later.

Fire

It would be thought that the construction and usage of modern computers made fire a minimal risk; this has been effectively disproved by several disastrous fires which have originated in the computer rooms themselves and resulted in almost total destruction. Where a central computer processes information from ancillary 'slaves' in essential component factories, even a minor outbreak might have consequences affecting the whole production schedule. Preventive precautions must therefore be designed to detect and control fire at the earliest possible stage. The means of doing so must be built into the installation during construction, and the environment in which the computer is situated must not be neglected as a source of potential danger.

Housing of computer

Although computers are usually inserted into existing buildings, the amount of work entailed may render this a false economy when all the requirements of the insurers have been complied with. It is better in every way to house it in separate purpose-designed premises. If this is not feasible, the whole computer should be enclosed in a fire-resistant compartment, protected both from horizontal and vertical spread—and from potential water damage if other parts are affected. •

The isolation of the central area containing the vital computer equipment is most important. Here the devices for detection and protection must have maximum effectiveness. Segregation from the surrounding areas of data processing and ancillary offices must be by fire-resisting partitioning or solid walls. If other offices are sited above, the roof of the computer room must be fully resistant to water as well as fire. It must not be perforated by openings whether for lighting, ventilation or any other reason. Rooms below are equally important and their occupancy should be limited to purposes which entail the least possible fire risk. There are advantages in locating the room at ground level.

These steps of segregation will meet a further essential purpose in that a reception area can be constructed to stop casual entry into the central rooms.

Contents of the central area

It is elementary that all furniture and fittings in the central area should be of metal or at least of materials which are not readily combustible. This must be remembered during the ordering stage of such items when the thoughts of the senior personnel, being consulted on their requirements, may be more concerned with comfort or possibly even prestige.

Tapes, cards, plans or files should be restricted to those needed for immediate use, fire-resisting cabinets should be available for their temporary storage. Any bins or containers for waste paper should likewise be of metal and regularly emptied. Smoking should be prohibited within the computer room and the ban extended to the stationery stores where it is even more important. Consideration should be given to incorporating a rest room where smoking would be allowed as this might limit abuse of the rule where it mattered.

Floor and roof voids: ventilation and wiring

Temperature and humidity have to be controlled between relatively narrow limits. Extensive fluctuations adversely affect the computer and its tapes, and could cause operating failures. There must, therefore, be a full and reliable air-conditioning system with extensive ducting which, with the huge amount of wiring, has to be housed in roof and floor voids. A false floor is preferable to cable trenches in the structural floor as, among other advantages, it allows a construction whereby computer equipment can be easily rearranged or added to. The floor itself should be of prefabricated panels of fire-proofed timber or metal, individual panels of which can be lifted by suction pads to give access to the services beneath; all such removable panels should be clearly marked. It is conventional for the false floor to be at the same level as the rest of the building, the void beneath it will then become a potential water trap in the event of flooding or fire in other parts of the building, causing danger from the presence of live cables. It is therefore advisable to fit a sill across the threshold of any door leading onto a false floor.

It is important to eliminate combustible materials as far as possible from these voids, materials for suspension units and brackets, insulation, sound and waterproofing panels, and ducting must be considered with this in mind, ducting in fact should be of metal. A fire in these areas may not be immediately perceived and could be difficult of access for portable fire extinguishers. Detection devices in these voids are essential and they should be coupled to an automatic fire-extinguishing system.

The extensive ducting of the air-conditioning system provides an avenue of entry for heat and smoke, particularly if the computer room shares a ventilating system with the rest of a building. Sampling of the airflow is necessary to ascertain combustion and smoke content by means of probes and detectors, fire dampers held open by fusible links or electrically operated should be built into the ducts to stop smoke or hot gases reaching areas where they could cause damage. A manual means of operation should also be incorporated.

In addition to normal detectors, heat-sensitive cables can be laid among the wiring runs to detect abnormal temperatures before they reach the stage of creating smoke or flame.

Doors, hatches and windows

In the computer room, partitions, doors, hatches and glazing should generally have a fire resistance of at least half an hour. The offices surrounding the computer room can be treated as a 'buffer' zone for fire defence purposes between it and the rest of the building by giving them a high degree of protection, though not equal to that of the central installation. Sprinklers could be used in the main areas of the building if there was no danger of water damage to the computer installation but smoke/heat detectors should be installed in the adjacent offices and hand appliances made available.

Doors in the rooms around the installation should be self-closing to function as 'smoke stops' and fitted with sills where required. Doors to the computer and plant rooms are especially important; substantial five-lever mortise locks should be fitted on these and strict control kept of keys. If these doors open internally into the rest of the building then they must be further shielded by self-closing four-hour fire-proof doors operated by fusible links. This is a normal requirement of insurance companies and fire protection officers, which is only relaxed, and then to two-hour doors, when the rest of the building is office accommodation of negligible risk.

Where 'borrowed' lights are needed they should be of wired glass and fixed shut, any sliding or drop hatches should be self-closing and of fire-resistant wired glass if vision is required. If a viewing window is desired from the reception area into the computer room it must be expected that a solid fire-resistant, drop panel will be required as an emergency shield. This viewing window is a good idea since it permits visitors to be shown something of the computer at work whilst keeping them at sufficient distance to preclude damage or seeing restricted material. It also provides an opportunity for patrolling security officers to inspect the interior without entering—for the same purpose, doors in the installation offices should have clear, wired-glass panels. Having regard to the importance of the data held, this is an ideal situation for fitting special security locks under a master key system to all doors.

Fire detection and extinguishing equipment

Limitation of direct and consequential loss rests on the prompt detection of abnormal conditions such as may be caused by insulation failure and overheating. Detectors must be linked with a method of audible and visual warning and be capable of setting off an automatic extinguishing installation after a predetermined interval. The warning system should be linked to a repeater unit at a point which is permanently manned—either a security gate office, or a fire station in a similar manner to which a burlar alarm is linked to a police station.

The area surrounding the computer itself must have complete space protection. The usual practice is to halve the normal coverage which is allocated to a detector to double the certainty of immediate recognition of a fire source. Smoke-sampling detectors are recommended for general purposes and those of the ionisation type are particularly suitable in underfloor spaces and for airflow sampling in probe units. The computer room, underfloor and ceiling voids should be covered by separate groups of detectors so as to define the fire area immediately. The detection circuit must be so wired as to be capable of automatically shutting down the ventilation system and activating a damper unit in the duct into the computer area to stop the inward spread of smoke and heated air; it should also automatically cut off all power supplies to the computer itself. An unnecessary automatic shutdown could cause serious consequential loss—hence the need of alternative manual operation when the computer is in use. Switches or buttons for this purpose should be located near the operator's console and the exit doors. A clear visual indicator is needed to show whether the system is on 'automatic' or 'manual'.

The extinguishing agent is provided by separate banks of gas cylinders for the plant and computer rooms. These are usually housed in the plant room with interconnecting delivery piping. Carbon dioxide is commonly used but vaporising liquids of the BCF variety are tending to supplant it since they are less likely to cause the thermal shock to the computer which results from the cooling effect of a massive CO_2 release in a confined space. For testing purposes, a cut-off switch or mechanism for the bank of cylinders must be incorporated; this must have a prominent warning light or buzzer to ensure it is not left in the 'off' position leaving the cylinders inoperative after the test.

A predetermined delay on 'automatic' before release has a positive value in that it allows an opportunity, albeit brief, for an immediate investigation to stop the sequence if the danger is one easily contained or the functioning is accidental. This could happen with a circuit fault on changing from manual operation.

In addition to the large fixed installation, adequate hand-operated extinguishers of the CO_2 or similar type should be readily to hand in the computer room to deal with minor incidents. While water extinguishers should be available to attack carbonaceous fires in outer offices, they should not be put in the inner rooms where water could be an embarrassment. Prompt and knowledgeable action with hand appliances can avoid problems caused by the use of gas in a preventive flooding of the area.

The recommended minimum for the computer room is

   2 x 5 kg (10 lb) CO_2 extinguishers
   2 x 2.5 kg (5 lb) CO_2 extinguishers
   2 x Asbestos cloths 1.4 m (4½ feet) square.

Humidity Warning

The damage that can result from substantial humidity or heat changes has already been mentioned; the suppliers of the air-conditioning system must build in adequate temperature controls but it is advisable to have a separate form of warning for dangerous humidity fluctuations. This can be equipment showing conditions in the form of a graph in the computer room itself, with linkage to an indicator unit in either the gate office or some other permanently manned point to show when a state of dangerous humidity is being neared. This unit should incorporate a means of showing that the equipment and link is in order.

Indicator panels, manual buttons and switches

The main panel should be sited in an open position adjacent to the central area and in clear view to everyone. By means of coloured lights appropriately labelled—or something similar which is obvious in meaning—it should show at a glance

1   Whether the power supply is operative.
2   The location of a fire—with separate lights for computer room, roof void, floor void or plant room (these could be extended to other parts if desired).
3   The presence of a fault in any of the sections of the installation.
4   By separate lights, whether the gas cylinders are set to operate manually, automatically or have 'discharged'.

A push button or switch should be fitted into the panel to stop the alarms with manual operating buttons for computer and plant rooms to be used in emergency.

Other manual buttons should be sited inside the computer room itself, preferably beside the exit doors; a distinctive audible warning buzzer should also be there. Both CO_2 and BCF are said to be non-toxic, but in fire extinguishing concentrations the staff must get out at once. There are obvious advantages in having the buzzer of a different variety to that which functions when a fire warning is given for parts of the building outside the computer area.

Manual buttons

Apart from entailing expensive refilling of gas cylinders, inadvertent discharge will cause time loss, potential damage and the displeasure of insurers if replacement cylinders are not readily to hand. The buttons should be such that the chance of accidental firing is at a minimum; glass fronted alarm boxes are suitable but the buttons must not be spring loaded to fire on the glass being broken. Each of these buttons should be tested at specified intervals and the test recorded.

Manual/automatic switch

While staff are engaged in the computer room, the presence of a fire condition should make its presence known to them at least as soon as the detector equipment picks it up and it would be invidious if some inadvertent action by any of them caused the system to fire while they were there. This can be obviated by coupling the alternator control which activates the computer to the release system, so that switching on the computer effects the change from automatic to manual operation and the reverse happens when the computer is closed down as staff leave.

Repeater panels

The remote panels in the security office need not be as comprehensive as the main indicator. It would suffice if the 'manual' and 'automatic' conditions were shown, together with 'fault' and 'fire'. Similarly, the humidity repeater need only consist of red and green lights. A test switch to check the circuit should be incorporated in each repeater and regularly used.

Action in the event of fire

All staff must be given instruction and have drill in fire prevention and the use of the hand appliances that are available for fire fighting. They must know exactly how the fixed installation functions, who to contact in the event of faults developing, and their own sequence to follow when leaving the premises, or when a fire occurs.

A notice should be displayed in the computer room on the following lines:

In the event of fire

1   Turn off master switches for machines, ventilation and ancillary plant.
2   Inform telephone operator who will call fire brigade.
3   Attack the fire with apparatus to hand (gas cylinder on electrical apparatus, asbestos blankets on waste bins etc.)

A checklist of action to be taken when leaving the premises normally should be displayed beside the departure door. An example is:

Check

1   All doors and hatches between rooms are closed.
2   All waste paper has been removed.
3   Any soldering irons or heating appliances have been unplugged from sockets.
4   All master switches have been turned off.
5   Security office notified you are leaving.

From the outset of building a computer installation, the local fire brigade should be kept in close liaison and their advice sought on any matters of difficulty; it is not enough to decide on a series of structural measures and then ask their approval, they should be consulted at the draft plan stage when their suggestions may save time, inconvenience and money later. This liaison will pay off in their intimate knowledge of the premises if they have to attend an actual outbreak in or adjacent to the installation.

The Ministry of Technology has published a useful booklet, called *Computer Installations: Accommodation and Fire Precautions,* obtainable from HM Stationery Office, price 19p.

Safeguarding the installation

If the installation is sited in a part of premises away from immediate surveillance or in buildings unoccupied and unsupervised outside normal working hours, serious consideration should be given to incorporating an effective burglar alarm installation. The contents have little value to thieves, unless they are expert to the degree of being interested in the data content of the records, but the damage a frustrated intruder can perpetrate among that kind of equipment is frightening.

In other instances, patrols should visit and inspect the main indicator panel regularly, the first occasion soon after the staff have vacated. Lights should be left on in the computer room and approach passages to deter the unauthorised interloper.

Insurance cover

Apart from structural and equipment loss from any cause, that of consequential loss might reach monumental proportions and could be induced by a simple prolonged power failure. The risk is almost impossible to assess, the extent of coverage is a matter for experts and will be related to the degree to which the firm's activities have become reliant on the computer. One thing that is certain is that the insurers will insist on all the aforementioned precautions as a minimum requirement.

The Fire Offices Committee has issued a Pamphlet, *Recommendations for the Protection of Computer Installations Against Fire.*

Duplication of records

The information stored on magnetic media, such as programs, master records or data for future reference, is more valuable by far than the media. Its loss or the cost of recreation could be a serious matter. It is conventional for all master file records on magnetic tape to be kept on the 'grandfather, father and son' principle. Master files on disk are usually duplicated on tape. The hierachical system works on the basis that 'grandfather' tape contains master records updated two processings before the current updated master file—the 'son'. The 'father' tape is that immediately before it. Both these preceding tapes, and the duplicated master record copies, should be kept in a purpose-built cabinet-type safe which in itself is thoroughly fireproof and away from any fire risks likely to affect the central area.

The compiled tape and disk programs will have source program-card packs backing them; these packs should also be separately and securely housed in a different part of the building, to be used if necessary to recreate the programs.

Fraudulent manipulation of computers

The worst problem for companies is not deliberate fraudulent action but simply ordinary human error. There is no evidence to suggest that deliberate f raud is prevalent but odd instances could well lie unrecognised amongst the human errors which are regarded somewhat philosophically.

We feel that the methods whereby frauds can be carried out have already received more than adequate publicity, sufficient perhaps to influence those who are easily tempted. We do not therefore propose to deal with means whereby they are perpetrated but to concentrate on preventive measures. Fortunately, professional institutions are setting high standards of ability and behaviour for data processing personnel which should help to ensure trustworthiness.

Operators and programmers have the best opportunity to defraud and the precautions that can be taken will to some extent be dependent on the number of computer staff involved. If working is continuous with operators on the rotating shift basis, there is less chance of collusion because the job mix will change weekly and give little opportunity of an individual running one job as a permanent basis; operators thereby acting as automatic checks on each other. In writing programs, the work can be organised so that no one programmer is employed in writing a complete suite for a system. A commonsense checklist in accordance with normal usage is suggested.

1   A library should be established for the safekeeping of programs and magnetic tape files. The librarian should keep an accurate record of usage and should not be a member of the computer operating staff; programmers should not have unsupervised access to the library.

2   There should be prior authorisation of all computer usage by a senior operations officer. A tight control should be exercised on computer time; the job sheet for a program should be endorsed with the estimated running time; a run of unexpectedly long duration should be queried and an analysis of computer use should be made periodically.

3   A formal standard manual should be laid down and supervisors must see that its standards are maintained.

4   No operator should be allowed to work the computer alone, a second operator should sign the log book which should contain times of starting, stopping and reasons for any delays.

5   Programmers should not be allowed to operate the computer.

6   When amendments are made to a program in use, it should then be tested by an independent person. Program documentation should include a list of all changes.

7   Operators should not be involved in the preparation of any operational programs, nor should they be allowed to alter input data.

8   In the punch room, punching and verification of data should not be carried out by the same person; the work should be batched and controlled so that unauthorised batches cannot be inserted.

9   A log of all errors should be kept with a note of the remedial action and a copy of the print-out.

10   With a main application to banks, master files should be printed out periodically and checked for accuracy, any changes in information on them should be handled so far as possible by personnel other than those handling day-to-day transactions.

Theft: 'industrial espionage'

There have been occasions where computers have featured in this context. A magnetic tape containing the entire name and address list of a company's accounts could be removed under a coat or in a briefcase: alternatively it could contain confidential records of a company's financial position or a set of computer programs. Such records could be of considerable importance to a competitor and at takeover times would be invaluable to anyone interested in stock manipulation.

File security under computer conditions is likely to be more effective than under normal manual systems. However, a computer program represents a huge assembly of information which can be rapidly copied and used to advantage. Moreover junior staff in systems and programming will have access in the compiling. Thus in selecting and training staff, apart from ability, due consideration must be given to qualities of loyalty and honesty. If an employee does intend to pass on information from matter he handles daily, it is almost impossible to prevent, but steps can be taken to reduce the opportunities of deliberate damage or theft.

1   A reception area should be created and manned at the entrance of the computer area.

2   Visitors, except with high-level authorisation, should not be allowed in the computer room.

3   Unknown engineers, cleaners or others who might legitimately claim access should be asked for the credentials in reception.

4   Mutilated copies of print-out should be destroyed and not disposed of with the ordinary waste paper.

5   Duplicating paper used in print-outs must be destroyed by shredding or burning.

6   Staff who are discharged for any reason, or give notice under a cloud, should be paid off immediately in lieu of working notice. Consideration should be given to applying this rule to all leavers.

If the last suggestion would appear to be detrimental to an employee's interests, remember that a disgruntled programmer has been known to wipe off a complete program and at least one individual leaving for another position has taken all details of his employer's current research with him.

Where a firm takes advantage of time-sharing on a large commercial multi-access computer and has matter to feed which is vital to its functions it should query what controls are incorporated to ensure that other users have no access. Elaborate password systems are now commonplace and can be supplemented by other measures.

PART 4

Applications of computers in business

17

Computers for Planning and Control

J. U. M. Smith

In many areas of business, management decisions can be assisted and improved by the use of mathematical or logical models run on computers. This chapter describes the nature of these models, how they are used and the benefits that may be derived.

The idea underlying the modelling approach is that if a firm's operations, or some important aspect of them, can be described in mathematical and/or logical terms then a computer can be programmed to study alternative methods of carrying out the operations so that management can see the consequences of different courses of action in advance. The term 'model' is used because the mathematical or logical description can be regarded as an abstract representation of the real-life operations described. In many cases the model can be used to calculate within the computer the optimum course of action to take to achieve a specified management goal.

The variables that enter into these models represent factors that may or may not be within the control of management. Those representing controllable factors can be regarded as 'decision variables', whose optimum values are sought by management. Those representing uncontrollable factors can be regarded as the constraints within which management must operate, at least for the moment. The model collects all these variables and their mutual interactions together into a single self-contained system, which can be used to study how changes to one part affect other parts.

Variables may be continuous or discrete. For instance, management may wish to study the optimum level of production in a factory, in which case a continuous variable would be used in the model to represent possible production levels. On the other hand, the problem may be to decide whether to invest in a new piece of machinery or not, in which case a discrete variable would be used with two allowable values only: standing for the two possible decisions that can be taken—to invest or not to invest.

Of course no model can describe reality with absolute precision. Inevitably there is some degree of uncertainty concerning the relationship and factors included. This is specially true if external influences are represented. How can such uncertainty be recognised and accounted for? There are two ways. First, the model itself can be regarded as a completely accurate representation, and a series of runs can be performed to test the sensitivity of the outputs to variations in the doubtful factors. Alternatively, the model can be regarded as an incomplete representation with some factors specified in terms of probability distributions rather than single values. In this case the outputs are also given in terms of probability distributions rather than single values. In the first approach the model is said to be *deterministic* and in the second *stochastic*.

Another distinction that can be made is between optimising and non-optimising models. Non-optimising models are purely descriptive of the real-life system, and are used to show how certain cause-effect relationships work within the system. Optimising models, on the other hand, have, in addition to a description of the real-life system, a built-in method of optimising the system so described. These models, in other words, prescribe as well as describe. The distinction is really a question of how the decision variables are treated. In a descriptive model, the decision-variables are varied usually one at a time outside the model. The 'optimum' values are found by inspecting and comparing the results of successive runs. In a prescriptive model, the decision variables are varied within the model and the optimum values, when found, are printed out at the end of the run.

Simulation models

Non-optimising models are chiefly used when it is desired to study the time-dependent behaviour of some system, or where unpredictable effects or factors are at work, or both. To study time-dependent behaviour, a set of variables that describe the state of the system is stored in the computer. Transformation rules incorporated in the computer as program instructions are then used to determine how the system moves from one state to the next. A run of the model is initiated by setting up appropriate starting conditions and then allowing the program to take over control and run the system through the series of consequent states. When a sufficient period has been simulated in this way, the run is terminated.

To study the effect of unpredictable factors, frequency distributions representing the probabilities of different outcomes are stored in the computer. In a run of the model, when a given type of random event is due, a value from the appropriate outcome distribution is selected at random. In the course of a run, a large number of such random selections are made, so that the full effect of the unpredictable factor on the final outcome is adequately represented. Several such factors may be included in the model, in which case their mutual interactions will be described. A run of such a model is usually known as a Monte Carlo simulation—simulation because the state variables of the model mimic the behaviour of the real-life system, and Monte Carlo because of the random sampling process incorporated.

As can be seen, the simulation approach is quite general. In consequence a great variety of operations can be modelled. In addition much detail can be included. It is a mistake, however, to try to represent real-life operations in too much detail as this makes the model complex, difficult to formulate without logical inconsistencies and lengthy to run on the computer.

Optimisation

From the user's point of view the main disadvantage of simulation—the purely descriptive approach—is that it does not give any indication of where improvements to the real-life operation can be found. The user has to present his own ideas to the model; by comparing the computer outputs, the best of these can be determined. But the onus is on the user to provide the ideas. There is no systematic method of advancing from the simulation of one set of conditions to the simulation of an improved set, although a careful study of the results often suggests a possible line of advance.

The optimising type of model does not suffer from this deficiency. A built-in set of mathematical decision rules—an optimising algorithm—enables successively better solutions to be obtained from a given starting position. The optimising algorithm used depends on the way in which the real-life system is described mathematically. This description has to be reasonably simple otherwise there is no guarantee that the algorithm will work.

The most widely used model is the *linear programming model*. This consists of a set of mathematical equations in the decision variables and a criterion to be optimised, the *objective funtion*, which is expressed as a linear combination of the decision variables.

The process of finding the optimum proceeds in steps from an initial starting point provided by the user. At each step a subset of the total set of decision variables is retained, the values of the retained variables being chosen so as to satisfy all the equations of the model. For the next step the

235

optimising algorithm seeks a variable not currently retained that will provide an improvement to the objective function. Then this variable is substituted for one of the members of the current best subset, values of variables being adjusted as necessary to remain consistent with the constraint equations, and the search process starts again. Eventually no further improvement can be found by further substitutions whereupon the process terminates with a print-out of the solution obtained in the form of the optimum found for the objective function and the values of the variables which yield this optimum.

The linear programming model can be applied if the following requirements are satisfied:

1 The decision (controllable) variables can be regarded as continuous quantities
2 The objective function can be expressed as a linear combination of the variables
3 All constraints or other factors to be included can be expressed as linear equality or inequality relationships among the decision variables.

While there are a great many situations meeting the above conditions, it is clear that there are many that do not do so. In these cases it may still be possible to use an optimising model, but of another type. If requirement 1 is not met, some of the decision variables being discontinuous (discrete), it may be possible to use *integer programming*. This is a relatively new technique and often involves prohibitive computer time, but rapid advances are being made. The following is the usual method employed to obtain a solution.

First a transformation of variables is made to turn the problem into one whose discontinuous variables can only take the values zero or one. Then a feasible solution to this new form of the problem is obtained by using ordinary linear programming and adding additional constraints as required to force each discontinuous variable to take one or other of the allowed values of zero or one. A search is then made to find improved solutions, by varying one at a time the constraints imposed in the first stage. To explore all combinations of constraints in a problem with more than a few zero-one variables would require prohibitive computer time even with fast machines. But by careful design of the search strategy, making use of the properties of the solution as it develops, many combinations can be eliminated as being less good than the current best solution. It is often possible to obtain the overall optimum fairly quickly. Even if not, the computer run can be terminated to yield an intermediate solution which is very close to the optimum.

Having discussed the situation if the continuity requirement is not met, the next few paragraphs will consider what happens if the second and third requirements fail, that is to say if the objective function or the constraints cannot be expressed in terms of a linear combination of the decision variables.

If it is possible to express the objective function, or constraints, as *non-linear* combinations of decision variables, a variant of linear programming known as *separable programming* can often be used. The non-linearities are approximated by a series of straight-line segments, and the solution constrained to move from one segment to an adjacent one. It should be noted, however, that this method does not necessarily give an overall optimum, but may yield only a local optimum which although better than the initial solution is not the best possible.

A completely different approach which can often be used where the above methods cannot be applied is provided by the technique of *dynamic programming*. The optimisation process is regarded as a multi-stage process in which a set of best-solutions-so-far is carried forward from one stage to the next, sub-optimal solutions being rejected as the solution progresses. At the last stage the overall optimum is selected from the set of best-solutions-so-far remaining in play. Dynamic programming can only be applied if the problem can be formulated in terms of independent decision stages, with no constraint relationships spanning all stages. Problems with an explicit time element lend themselves rather well to such a formulation, because a series of time periods can be used as the decision stages and all relationships among variables can be reduced to equations between variables in consecutive time periods.

Other than the above requirements there are no restrictions on the type of objective function or constraints that may be used. Complex, non-linear, functions are allowable, and variables may be discrete. Computer time may, however, prove excessive if there are many possible values of the variable (system states) to be considered at each decision stage in the process. Then a dynamic programming formulation, theoretically attractive, often proves infeasible in practice because of the computer time needed.

Model building

Before the stage of computer running can be reached much effort is needed to formulate the problem, decide on objectives and collect suitable data.

The first task is to decide what areas of the business to model. While it is difficult to give any definite guidance, the following rules may be useful. Suitable areas to consider are where decision situations occur in much the same form over and over again. Preferably, a fairly simple objective should be definable, and the effect of decisions on this objective should be fairly straightforward to predict and quantify. Unpredictable human influences should be absent as far as possible. If similar situations elsewhere have been modelled successfully, so much the better.

The feasibility of model building in a given area should be carefully judged against the above criteria by line management assisted by a specialist in modelling techniques. Potential savings in terms of improvements to the objectives and other intangibles (see final section) should be balanced against development effort and cost, and the likely costs of computer running time for the completed model. At this stage success cannot be guaranteed and a decision to go ahead must be attended by a certain degree of risk. In order to reap the potential gains, however, management must be prepared to accept this risk; a decision to go ahead must be made in the knowledge that there may be some false starts and failures. It may even turn out that no model of sufficient accuracy can be constructed because of the influence of unpredictable elements, or that no optimising method can be found that yields adequate improvements in the objective function defined.

Once it has been decided to start modelling, the next step is to select the most suitable type of model to employ, unless this has already been decided when considering the feasibility of modelling. A useful starting point is to ask: Is the system to be modelled sufficiently predictable to allow the use of a deterministic model? Can the decision problem be expressed in a simple enough way to permit the use of one of the optimising techniques mentioned in the previous section? To answer these questions a detailed study will usually be necessary, based if possible on statistical records. This will normally be undertaken by modelling specialists calling on local line management for assistance as necessary.

The next step is to formulate the rules of the model, where these are not obvious; to isolate the variables that enter into the decision process; to discover other factors that influence the outcome but are not controllable, or not required to be changed; and to list any other constraints that must be taken notice of. The appropriate level of detail for the model must be considered, including the size of time unit to be used, if the model is a multi-period one. Then the objective function, or measures of performance, have to be determined. Unlike the other items, this last can only be arrived at by discussions with, and agreement of, the management commissioning the model-building activity.

Sample data are now collected. If the objective is to minimise costs, care should be taken to obtain only the true variable costs that apply. Computer programming is undertaken where necessary. In some cases, the programming task is eased by the existence of standard routines. The most notable example is the case of linear programming which is available as a standard program package with most machines. For any particular problem it is only necessary to prepare a suitable input and output routine to fit this standard program.

The same is true of integer and separable programming.

The other types of model do not lend themselves easily to the standard package approach; the user normally has to write his own program. The use of a special programming language sometimes helps, particularly in simulation. Otherwise a general-purpose mathematical language such as FORTRAN or ALGOL with appropriate subroutines if available is recommended.

The program, with all its input and output routines, is now assembled and run with specially prepared test data to check logic or other errors in the program.

The model is now ready for use. But before proceeding, it is necessary to check that the model represents reality with sufficient accuracy. A series of validation trials is called for. Sample data are collected over a typical period of operation of the plant or other system being modelled. The model is run and its outputs are compared with the corresponding performance measures experienced in real life. Significant mis-matches must be explained. In the case of a simulation model, the transformation rules often need modifying in the light of validation runs. In the case of an optimising model, extra constraints are often required to account for real-life effects not obvious at the time of model building. Confronting management with the first results of optimisation usually invokes the response, 'a very fine solution we agree, but unfortunately we cannot implement it because of such and such'. 'But you did not tell us about that factor,' the model builder replies, 'however, I can easily introduce an extra constraint to represent the effect.'

When sufficient runs have been made to prove the adequacy of the model, 'production' runs can commence using data collected for the purpose. The process of production running a model usually contains an element of exploration about it. It is rare for the user to be able to specify all the decision variables in advance, nor all the constraints or operating rules and conditions. In use, therefore, optimising models are not so dissimilar from simulation models. The user does not look for a cut-and-dried optimum from the model; he seeks, rather, the effect on the computed best result of altering the constraints and other 'fixed' factors in the model. This exploratory nature of modelling can be best illustrated with a flow diagram, see Figure 17:1.

Outputs and results from each run of the model are considered from the point of view both of feasibility—can the suggested improvements be implemented—and optimality—can a better solution be obtained if some hitherto constraining factor is relaxed, or some hitherto constant factor is changed to a new value? These questions usually suggest a new run to test some further possibilities. The cycle then repeats itself. Ultimately, solutions are obtained which are regarded as satisfactory from all points of view. Recommendations for action can then be made to management. The process

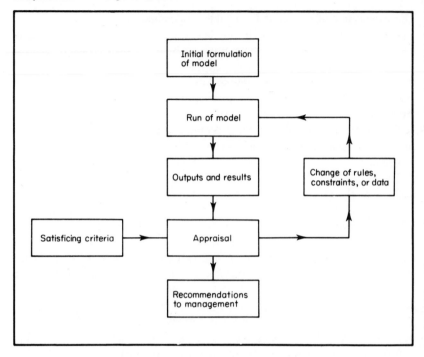

Figure 17:1   Use of models to find solutions

is thus more correctly thought of in terms of 'satisficing' than in terms of optimising. Certain criteria of acceptability, 'satisficing criteria', not explicit, are applied to model results. If the results do not satisfy these criteria, ways of improving the model performance are sought, and the model is rerun, until acceptable results are eventually obtained.

Application areas

Most areas of business have proved amenable to modelling techniques. The following gives a brief account of some of the applications known to me. It should not be taken as an exhaustive list. The intention is only to suggest and illustrate by examples some of the types of application that are possible and have been found to give satisfactory results.

Production

Production is considered first because this area has probably received more attention than any other.

The basic *operational* decision problem is how much to make of which items on which pieces of equipment, and when. It is common to have a fluctuating, say seasonal, sales demand to meet using equipment and a labour force of which the capacity is essentially fixed. What is the best way of smoothing the workflow on the factory floor? This is a problem that can be studied with the aid of an optimising model using either linear or dynamic programming. It is first necessary to define the options to be considered by the model. Can work be subcontracted out? Can temporary labour be engaged to cope with peak loads? Then it is necessary to define the constraints. Can any number of finished items be stored, or is there a store capacity limit to be taken into account? Lastly it is necessary to obtain all relevant costs. These are likely to be as follows.

1   Unit production cost. This will vary according to the amount of overtime worked, etc. A figure is therefore needed for each possible production level.
2   Any cost associated with a change in the level of production, as distinct from the level itself. For example, advertising and administrative charges might be incurred if extra staff have to be engaged to permit production increases. Or costs of arranging contracts might be incurred if work is to be subcontracted to meet increased requirements.
3   Storage cost. The cost of storing finished units before sale, and raw material before production.

With a knowledge of these costs the mathematical model can be formulated as follows. The planning period is divided up into a series of sub-periods (typically monthly) and within each a constant production rate is assumed rate. The decision variables are the production levels in each sub-period. Constraints are of the form: production in any period plus items in store must be sufficient to meet the demand predicted for the next period. Other constraints may be necessary to confine production levels within reasonable limits, or to set a maximum storage capacity. The objective of the model is to find the set of production levels that meets the specified demand at the least overall cost.

While this method can, if required, take into account capacity constraints on individual machines and processes within the factory, it cannot include sequencing and precedence rules of the form 'operation A must always precede operation B on any given workpiece', or 'workpiece A must always precede workpiece B if both are waiting for a given machine'. To introduce such rules, zero-one variables must be used and the size of the model greatly expanded. Optimisation has been found to be extremely difficult when more than a few machines and processes are present.

241

In this situation the alternative approach of simulation can be used to advantage. Any given production plan can be input to the model. The required precedence rules, programmed into the model, can then be used to simulate the flow of workpieces through the factory from process to process. The throughput time of workpieces can be evaluated, as well as machine utilisation and statistics on work-in-progress. On the basis of these outputs the feasibility and cost of any given production plan can be assessed. By running a series of alternative plans through, improvements can be found. In addition the effect of alterations to plant configuration and operating rules can be tested.

This approach was successfully used in the finishing department of a tube mill where a variety of finishes were being applied to a few basic raw tube batches. Runs of the simulation model showed that bottlenecks were not where management had thought them to be, and problems of intermediate storage not so intractable. A changed manning arrangement on some of the machines was tried out and found to be feasible within the constraint of the plant. With this scheme, throughout could be significantly increased, saving the cost of processing elsewhere in the company. Further details are given in *Computer Simulation Models* by John Smith (Griffin, 1968).

Purchasing and supply

When ordering raw materials, management may have a range of possibilities to choose from. For instance in petroleum refining, several crude oils can be used singly or in combination to give the product or products desired. Each crude has a different price and a different chemical make-up. Management must choose the most appropriate mix of crudes to buy to support production in the next period.

This type of problem can often be set up in linear programming terms as follows. The decision variables are taken to be the amounts of each raw material to purchase. The quantity and quality of the finished product are expressed as linear combinations of these variables. Then the following constraint can be written down.

1   Quantity of finished product must not be less than the quantity required
2   Quality of finished product must lie within specified, acceptable limits.

The objective function is taken to be the total cost of all the new material in the plan. The model is thus set up to find the minimum-cost method of meeting production requirements for the next production period, from the choice of raw materials available.

Whether a purchasing problem can be modelled in this way is largely a question of whether the properties of the finished product can be related to the raw material mix in a simple mathematical way. It so happens that in the petroleum refining industry this can be done with a high degree of accuracy. The choice of crude mix can therefore be optimised for each production period, taking account of the most recent information on crude prices and availabilities.

The process of converting mineral ores into iron and steel can also be modelled in this way. There have been several successful applications at major steel-producing works in the UK. In one case the problem was made more complicated by the fact that there were two steel works in the company at different sites and a proportion of the ore had to be preprocessed in a sinter plant. Decision variables therefore included the production level of the sinter plant and the mix of ores for sintering as well as the ore-sinter mix, or burden, for the furnaces. Constraints were the physical, chemical and market limitations on the burden; fuel requirements, production rate and other furnace limitations. Due to the non-linear nature of some of the mathematical relationships, separable programming had to be used.

One of the by-products of the model was the ability to study the economics of the sinter works in relation to the operation as a whole. In particular the relative advantages of on the one hand increasing sintering capacity, and on the other buying in more sinter, could be assessed.

So far, this section has discussed 'one-period', or static, problems in which the time element is absent. If demand, or other factors, are known to be changing with time, a multi-period or dynamic approach is more suitable. In fact a changing demand situation is very common as we have observed when discussing manufacturing applications. There may be a seasonal factor influencing the final demand for a firm's output, or there may be a predictable build-up of demand for a particular raw material or part caused by the winning of several large orders for a final product.

In this situation the problem is when to buy, and how much. Quantity discounts and price breaks complicate the decisions that have to be taken. The advantage of lower unit costs for quantity should be weighed against the costs of extra stockholding. Possible effects on future decisions should be considered when making current decisions. This type of problem lends itself rather well to a dynamic-programming approach. From a mathematical point of view the problem is in fact very similar to that encountered in manufacturing as discussed in the previous section. Those were concerned with decisions to make; these are decisions to buy. More precisely the decision variables are quantities to buy (possibly zero) in each period. The constraints are that, for each period, quantity bought plus stock must at least equal quantity required for production. The objective function is the total cost of the buying programme.

The number of periods to include in the model will be determined by the accuracy with which future demand can be forecast and in some cases the risk of obsolescence of parts bought too far in advance of production needs.

Physical distribution

Purchasing problems and production problems have been discussed. But the product still has to reach the customer. Transport arrangements must therefore be made, depots and warehouses established and retail outlets found. This is another field in which mathematical models may be used to advantage.

Consider, for example, the situation of a manufacturer who has several factories supplying several warehouses, from which final deliveries are made. Which factories should supply which warehouses? Within the capacity constraints of the factories, there may be many different answers, some of which may not have occurred to management, used to a particular way of doing things found to work well in the past. Each distribution pattern will have its own cost, and there will be one which is cheaper than all the others. If the relevant transport costs are known for each factory warehouse pair, and can be assumed to be proportional to quantity shipped, this least-cost pattern can be found either by straightforward linear programming or, more efficiently, by a special form of it known as the *transportation method*. The decision variables are the quantities to be sent from each factory to each warehouse. The constraints are the quantities produced by each factory, and the quantities required by each warehouse.

This type of problem affects shipping companies serving the oil industry. Their task is to transport crude oil from several sources to refineries in several parts of the world.

When calculating the optimum pattern, constraints due to the finite size of ships as well as their current location and other attributes must be taken into account. The solution cannot therefore be obtained directly from a 'transportation' calculation as described above because this might give a transport pattern incompatible with the current fleet disposition. But such a calculation often provides a good starting point for the necessary planning and scheduling of the ship movements.

A somewhat different type of problem faced a shipping company engaged in the oil and bulk-cargo trades. Their ships sailed on ocean routes throughout the world carrying crude oil, mineral ores, wheat and other homogeneous commodities from primary producing areas, mostly in the Southern Hemisphere, to the industrial regions in the North. The company's business was conducted on the basis of long-term contracts for shipments at regular intervals. In addition, however, single voyages could be sold for ad-hoc 'opportunity cargoes' appearing at short notice in the chartering market. Management had to ensure, however, that by accepting such voyages the regular business of the company on long-term contract work was not put at risk. Sometimes extra shipping capacity could be made available for short-term opportunities by subletting the contracted cargoes to other companies.

The optimisation problem was thus seen in terms of the need to make the maximum profit from the fleet of ships owned by the company, bearing in mind the actual geographical distribution of the ships at the beginning of the planning period, the need to fulfil contracted commitments, and the existence of sources of extra revenue available in the market. Integer programming was used to ensure that solutions came out in terms of whole numbers of ship voyages consistent with certain required timing constraints.

First production runs of the model showed the interesting result that it was often more profitable to keep a ship idle, awaiting the availability of a cargo at a port, than to send it in ballast to pick up another cargo already available elsewhere. This surprised management who would not normally have considered keeping a ship stationary in port when there was work for it at other points in the route network. But the computed solution saved the cost of empty positioning voyages that would have been necessary to pick up the remote cargoes, which were allocated by the model to ships nearer at hand. To give an idea of the scope for savings in this area, every productive ship-day gained was worth about £1000 to the company.

With road vehicles, somewhat similar problems of scheduling and routing occur. Costs per vehicle are much less but fleets may be much larger, so that the scope for improvements may be of a similar order of magnitude. Where a regular fixed pattern of deliveries is required by, or arranged with, customers, considerable savings may be achieved by optimising the routes followed by drivers and the sequence of calls made.

Unfortunately none of the standard optimising techniques described in this chapter can usually be directly applied to these scheduling problems because of the integer nature of the variables and the many special constraints that must be taken into account. A formulation in integer programming terms would be extremely cumbersome, and solution times would be excessive. Instead, special-purpose algorithms have been developed based on common-sense rules for combining deliveries into vehicle loads to minimise the number of vehicle trips and vehicle miles involved. Some of these methods start with a continuous linear programming run to allocate vehicles to delivery areas. Others select the final schedule from a partial enumeration of all possible trips for each vehicle. For a good account of developments in this field, see *The Impact of Computer Techniques on Road Transport Planning* by W. E. Norman (National Computing Centre, 1969).

It has already been pointed out that a model once set up to optimise a particular operation can be used to advantage to study larger policy questions affecting the running of the operation. A vehicle-scheduling model is no exception. For instance, the effect of depot location, fleet composition and customer delivery constraints on the optimum trip pattern and its associated cost can be evaluated by running the model with the particular parameter or parameters of interest set at various different levels, and comparing the results. Useful information on the costs of different distribution and delivery strategies can be obtained in this way.

Advertising

Although there is, as yet, no exact science of human behaviour, quantitative methods have been and are being used to predict and explain the response of potential customers to advertising and sales promotion activities. Both simulation and optimising models have been used, but the former have been favoured.

Several types of problem have been studied. At the lowest level of decision, the advertising budget is assumed as given and the problem is seen as that of choosing the best schedule of advertisements to use within the overall budget constraint. In this context a 'schedule' can be thought of as a list of press publications in which advertisements of stated size and colour are placed and/or a list of television regions, days and times for commercials of a stated length. 'Best' is interpreted in terms of maximising either the number of people who see at least one advertisement (coverage) or the number of advertisements seen weighted by a function of the number of times each advertisement is seen by the same person (exposure). A simulation model can be used to predict either the coverage or the exposure (or both) given a schedule and data on readership, viewing, etc., from consumer-panel surveys. A simulated 'panel' is set up in the computer to represent a sample of the target population. The effect of the schedule on each member of the sample is then estimated. If certain simplifying assumptions are made, it may be possible to perform an optimisation calculation to find the best schedule. However, the objective function is usually non-linear and optimisation is often not possible by conventional mathematical programming techniques.

Special methods are needed and overall optima cannot usually be guaranteed. Failing optimisation, different schedules can be tried, and the most promising selected. By making many runs of the model, a feel for good schedules can be developed.

A possible disadvantage of the above methods is that effectiveness as measured by either coverage or exposure is not directly convertible into sales. A given increase in effectiveness cannot therefore be quantified in money terms. It is not therefore possible to go on from this calculation to ask if the budget constraint itself is optimal. To ask, in other words, if this level of expenditure

246

gives the best return per advertising pound spent. For this a further step must be taken. Effectiveness must be turned into customer purchasing behaviour by a further set of mathematical equations. Work has been done along these lines using learning theory as developed by psychologists to explain behavioural conditioning.

Models of several areas

Decisions in one functional area of a business, divided off from other areas for administrative convenience, may well have repercussions elsewhere in the business. From the point of view of optimising the results of the firm as a whole such repercussions should be taken into account. In many cases it is possible to construct a model of several functional areas and include their mutual interactions. As an example, the purchasing and production activities may be modelled simultaneously. If manufacturing is carried out in several stages at different locations, internal transport operations may be included as well. Decision variables are then the decisions to buy, make and move different work items of materials in each of several time periods. Constraints are availabilities of raw materials, capacities of manufacture, transport and storage, and demand for final product in each period. The objective is to minimise cost. If sales decisions affecting sales volumes can also be modelled, then the higher-level objective of maximising profit can be used instead.

Several models of this general type have been formulated and successfully run by some of the largest companies in the UK and elsewhere. But few details have been published, probably because of their confidential nature.

A decade has now elapsed since general-purpose computers began to be introduced into business firms in large numbers, making the application of mathematical models practicable. In this period, how successful has the modelling approach been? Some of the wilder claims originally made have not been justified by results. But in many cases it has been found that real benefits can be obtained.

In the early days some people thought that many, if not all, aspects of management would become automated with the advent of large computers and mathematical methods. Sobering experience has shown that, on the contrary, management functions, especially at the higher levels, are likely to remain a predominantly human province. The activities of setting objectives, and searching for possible solutions in unstructured problem situations, do not seem readily amenable to quantitative methods, at present.

The role of mathematical models seems to lie in providing relevant, but not necessarily complete, information on tactical decisions in well-structured problem situations where objectives, constraints, and management's options can be specified in advance. In fact it can be said that the success of modelling varies in proportion to the degree to which the problem situation can be structured and defined. The most successful applications have been to the processing industries where well established material-balance and capacity-constraint equations form the basis of the model and the objective is to minimise material costs, which are easily measured. In this field many millions of pounds have been saved, justifying the considerable resources of computers and computing staffs that have been established by companies to run the models.

Nearly as successful have been other models of physical processes, buying materials, building up stocks, movement of vehicles or workpieces in a factory. Here basic material-balance and continuity considerations can also be used, and allocation or sequencing rules can be based on the observed behaviour of schedulers or foremen in standard decision situations. Appropriate variable costs can usually be ascertained.

When we come to models of consumer behaviour, however, relationships cannot be based on such well-established principles and the validity of the approach is more open to question. Nevertheless many useful results have been obtained.

All the above decision situations, however, are reasonably well structured. The range of management choice is fairly well defined, and the objectives are given. Models can therefore be set up to calculate what tactics to employ each time the decision situation arises. In other words, the models are used as tactical decision-making tools. In this role they can be of considerable assistance to the responsible management. For higher management decisions, concerning company policy and strategy, the modelling approach would appear to have limited application because of lack of structure in the problem situation and the small amount of relevant data available in a suitable form.

There is no doubt, however, that at the tactical level great benefits can be obtained from decisions made more accurately and rationally, using models. The case of the oil companies, who are saving several million pounds by linear programming, has already been quoted. There are many other instances where sizeable amounts of money are being regularly saved. The improvement that optimising models quite often produce is in the range 5 to 10 per cent. Although modest as a percentage, such a saving may add up to a very worth-while figure if the operation being optimised is on a large enough scale.

The potential for improvements is greatest where current 'manual' methods are furthest from optimal. When conditions and parameters are changing rapidly, manual methods often lag behind. The computer is not influenced by previous experience, but recalculates the optimum each time on the latest information. It is more likely to produce good answers, sooner, than a manual 'learning' process.

Finally, a word must be said about the intangible benefits of model building.

A computer model gives an understanding of, and insight into, operations, which cannot be obtained in any other way. Factors can be varied at will, and consequences observed, without risk or cost, other than of computer running time. The effect on one aspect of an activity of changes in another, perhaps under different local management, can be noted. Knowledge of such inter-relationships may indicate situations which are optimal within local boundaries but less than optimal in an overall context.

The benefits of the extra understanding gained through the use of models cannot be readily quantified. It is, however, an important factor to be taken into account by management when deciding to employ this type of approach.

Further reading

E. M. L. Beale, *Mathematical Programming in Practice*, Pitman 1968.
G. Hadley, *Nonlinear and Dynamic Programming*, Addison-Wesley, 1964.
John Smith, *Computer Simulation Models*, Griffin 1968.
W. E. Norman, *The Impact of Computer Techniques on Transport Planning*, NCC, 1969.

18

Computers in Finance and Accounting

R. V. Fabian

Although finance and accounting are commonly linked together as related subjects, it is necessary to distinguish clearly between them before discussing the application of computers to these areas. Finance, used in the broad sense, means the determination of a policy related to the financial aspects of a business and the manipulation of resources, with emphasis placed on the best use of share capital and other sources of funds. Accounting relates to the principles and techniques used in establishing, maintaining and analysing the financial transactions of a business, and is therefore primarily concerned with devising recording methods, keeping accounts, maintaining internal control and reporting to management.

Development of accounting applications

Some pioneering work was done in the 1950s using early computers such as LEO I, but computers were first used effectively in commercial accounting in about 1960 and were used for the first time in finance a few years later. Most of the early users of computers for accounting procedures had previously been operating mechanised systems based on the use of punched-card tabulators, calculators and sorters. As a result, it is not surprising that the first procedures to be transferred to computer processing were the accounting procedures that had already been well defined for punched-card processing. Thus, the favourite procedures to be chosen were for payrolls, sales invoicing, simple sales accounting, and limited stock control.

It is tempting to say that this emphasis on accounting was because thoughtful men considered the computer to be more suited to the routine, repetitive tasks already defined for punched-card systems than to creative tasks requiring innovations in less well-defined areas. It is, however, more likely that repetitive tasks were chosen because the end of the road on repetitive work was easier to see, the road itself was easier to walk upon and the suppliers of computers found them easier to sell as replacements for punched-card equipment.

In any event, by current standards the early computers had limited storage and processing facilities, were not highly reliable and were poorly supported by programming aids and program libraries. During the early years, there were sadly more failures to achieve the desired results than there were successes, but all progress is based on the trials and misfortunes of early pioneers from whose errors subsequent successful operators learn their lessons.

Modern computers have developed significantly from the early machines in terms of power, reliability and versatility, but the fundamental characteristic, on which has been founded the wide acceptance of computers by business, remains basic computing power combined with comprehensive data-handling capabilities. The ability of modern computers to perform a million and more calculations a second, allied to their capacity for storing billions of characters and making them available at high speed for processing, provides management with a greatly improved capability for controlling and developing the accounting and financial aspects of a business.

The areas of accounting activity that are currently being processed by computers are those that deal with large volumes of data and that used to involve a large amount of clerical effort. The procedures that fall into this category are for sales accounting, purchases accounting, stock control, payrolls, financial accounting and cost accounting. A brief description of these comparatively simple systems for the average manufacturing or commercial business is given below under appropriate headings. All these procedures require that the computer should record details of accounting transactions, make various calculations on them, and, at regular intervals, print results and summaries of the data held in storage. The computers available at present are well-suited to these tasks, and also to exception reporting which requires the reporting of only those transactions that fall outside predetermined limits and which have the objective of reducing the volume of figures that management needs to consider to run the business efficiently.

Specialised financial sectors of commerce have developed their own accounting procedures which, nevertheless, have much in common with normal commercial accounting. For example, in the insurance industry, sales accounting is replaced by a renewals procedure, and, in banking, most forms of sales transaction are dealt with as entries in current or deposit accounts.

Sales accounting

Sales accounting involves receiving orders, checking creditworthiness, transferring goods from work-in-progress or stock, preparing invoices, posting to some form of ledger, preparing statements, receiving settlements and preparing statistics and analyses.

In the normal type of sales accounting system on a computer, the procedure begins when orders are received. The customer's creditworthiness is first checked, the stock availability is ascertained or the production capacity verified, and the appropriate information is coded and prepared in the form suitable for input to the computer on which a number of processes can then be carried out. Dispatch notes and invoices can be produced during the same run, the ledger file can be posted and an up-dated credit status report can be issued. Periodically, say monthly, statements can be produced, and subsequently cash settlements and credit for goods returned can be posted against the ledger accounts. When all this has been done, the monthly statistics can be produced, including sales statistics from the invoices and credits, and the ageing of debts from the statement run. The sales accounting procedure can often be integrated with the stock control procedure.

Stock control

Stock control includes keeping records for raw materials and components in addition to finished stocks. Basic information on orders and stock movements is obtained from purchase orders, goods received notes and stock requisitions which are coded and prepared in a form suitable for input to the computer. The operations that can be carried out on the computer include:

1   Posting stock movements to the appropriate stock ledger accounts
2   Evaluating requisitions
3   Raising orders to replenish stocks falling below the re-order level
4   Keeping records of stockholdings and movements
5   Preparing reports on the status of stock items, such as out-of-stock, slow-moving or delivery overdue
6   Analysing issues by nominal ledger or cost headings.

The stock records normally include figures for maximum and minimum holdings, lead times for delivery and economic order quantities. In the more advanced applications, both these figures and the stock prices are automatically recalculated in the light of current prices and transactions. Postings to individual accounts are made principally in daily batches of input, and at the end of any selected day's processing a print-out can be prepared showing the status of each item of stock with its current balance, goods on order, and unit price.

Integrated sales accounting and stock control

A limited amount of integration of procedures has taken place in sales accounting and stock control. Integration of two procedures requires that one procedure will supply the basic input for another. Thus, from the basic information used by the computer to produce the invoice/dispatch notes, the stores issue notes can be prepared, the goods can be earmarked, and the appropriate stock account can be debited. This approach can be developed throughout the joint procedures, thus reducing the computer input required for separate procedures and avoiding the reconciliation of their respective outputs.

Purchases accounting

Suppliers' accounts can be dealt with by a process similar to that used for customers' accounts, although rather fewer operations are involved and the integration that can be achieved with other procedures is usually limited to a linking with a nominal ledger, financial accounting or costing procedure. In a normal purchases accounting procedure, input information is coded and prepared from the invoices received, after they have been checked against purchase orders and good received notes. The information is then posted to the suppliers' accounts, cheques are drawn, remittance advices are prepared, the bought ledger is posted and the cash book is printed. If the original input is suitably coded, it can be processed further to produce detailed expense analyses, to report on price variances and to provide information for costing and management accounting purposes.

Payrolls

The preparation of payrolls normally requires the use of static information kept on file in the computer and of variable data that has to be produced week by week. The static data includes the employee's name, works number, rate of pay, tax code number and standard pay deductions. The variable data necessarily contains the works number as a link and includes such items as hours worked, output bonus earned, and variable deductions. Payroll systems usually provide pay slips prepared on the computer, coin analyses for making up pay, the basic information for the costing system and for management accounting, any

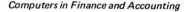

required statistics on manpower utilisation and statutory returns for income tax and National Insurance purposes.

Costing

Several types of costing systems are employed in industry and commerce, including job, batch, process and standard costing. For job, batch and process costing, the costs are collected and analysed under appropriate headings, direct costs are allocated to the job, batch or process, and indirect costs are allocated on a predetermined basis. Computer procedures are used extensively on this type of work. Standard costing is more complex, as it requires the work done to be valued at predetermined or standard rates.

In a standard costing system operated on a computer, it is preferable for records of the standard cost of units to be held on a magnetic tape or disk file, which is then used to evaluate the measured units of the work done to produce standard costs. These are compared with the actual costs that have been accumulated from stores issues, purchases and payroll data. The differences between actual and standard costs are analysed, and control reports are prepared showing the variances under appropriate headings. In more advanced applications exception reporting techniques are used, giving only those variances outside specified limits of tolerance.

Financial applications

Despite the later development in this field, the financial work that is now processed on computers covers an extensive range of procedures. These fall broadly into the two categories of supplying information for planning and supplying information for control.

Planning information

Computers are used in this area to provide data to assist in planning the effective utilisation of funds. The most advanced way in which this is being achieved is through the use of business models for corporate planning purposes. The models are designed to enable the significance of external and internal conditions on the company's future growth and profitability to be assessed, and to provide management with the opportunity of assessing the consequence of alternative courses of action. Work of this nature is in its early stages and few organisations can yet show an effective working model of the whole business.

Although as yet there has been little achievement in constructing comprehensive company financial models, computers are being used more generally to evaluate the effects and implications of individual decisions that call for alternative uses of funds. For example, a computer can rapidly calculate the cash flow that would be required for investing in capital projects by a variety of financing methods, each of which might involve different rates of interest and different timings for making payments. The computer can also be used to compare the effects in terms of income over a number of years that would probably arise as a result of investing in alternative capital projects.

Working capital is tied up in stocks, work-in-progress and debtors. Where the number of separate items is large, it can be a difficult and lengthy process to ensure that funds are being used efficiently. Clerical record keeping can absorb so much manpower that it is not practicable to analyse the records to highlight key matters, such as excesses or deficiencies in stocks. The speed of a computer makes it possible to carry out this type of analysis in a short period by providing exception reports on those items that are tying up more capital than is justified by performance. For planning purposes, the computer can indicate, for example, the effect on customer service if the capital invested in stocks were to be reduced by a given amount for all items of stock or for selected items such as those turning over a given number of times in the year. Conversely, the computer can calculate the impact on working capital of a change in the level of service to customers in meeting orders from stock or from production.

Where the amounts owed by debtors or the volume of capital projects is considerable, the computer can be used to provide data for forecasting cash flows by analysing the debtors data to assess the likely dates and amounts of receipts and by analysing projects data to determine the likely dates of and amounts for payment.

Control information

Recently, data processing systems have begun to be designed specifically to provide information to management for the control of the business. Although these systems are usually based largely on accounting data, their purpose is in the financial field, while they also provide information and trends to management on most aspects of the business to indicate the effectiveness with which the resources are being utilised. To provide this data, the computer holds a 'bank' or 'data base' of information about the company and its activities, including data for marketing, production, and research and development, in addition to that for accounting and finance.

Computers are used in this area to provide data to assist in controlling the effective use of funds. One of the most widely used of these procedures is for budgetary control, where the actual results of trading are compared with predetermined targets, and any variances between the two are reported. Some budgetary control systems have now reached an advanced stage of development where variances are reported under a variety of headings, against which the accountant provides appropriate explanations to enable management to assess the conditions that led to them and the urgency with which they should be corrected.

Computers are also being used to indicate whether funds are being used in the most appropriate priorities. To achieve this, inter-firm comparisons between associated companies in large groups are made and the performance of competitors is assessed where sufficient information is available. Appropriate adjustments are made to the various figures to ensure that the results are on the same basis for comparison purposes.

Other uses of computers for financial control include the analysis of current situations and past results, and the calculation of key ratios, for example, covering the comparison of earnings to share prices, and the establishment of the return on capital employed.

Packages for finance and accounting

Some of the accounting procedures described earlier in this chapter require the use of common formulas and techniques, while most of the routines in the procedures need to be carried out in some form or other by most computer users and can readily be dealt with in a similar manner with only a small adjustment to the resultant output. Computer bureaux and service organisations have developed packaged programs that have general application on a large range of common problems. These have been used to a considerable extent in such areas as payrolls, sales accounting and purchases accounting.

Regrettably, the standard packages cannot be written to suit the requirements of every computer user because the requirements of different companies, even in the same industry, can vary considerably. As the cost of developing computer systems is extremely high, however, the use of packages is worth consideration for they enable computer projects to be implemented sooner and at a lower development cost than where the user prepares his own programs. Before the full value of packages can be achieved, the software houses must give greater thought to achieving maximum flexibility (and thus maximum spread of use), while the financial executives and accountants must become more accommodating in adjusting their requirements to suit the packages available if their companies are to reap the full rewards of realising the high potential of modern computers.

Real-time processing

Conventionally, finance and accounting applications have been regarded as requiring batch processing, where transactions are collected for a period (say, every day) and input to a computer for processing at the end of the period. This method is acceptable because in most cases inquiries regarding accounting data are not so critical that it is unrealistic to wait until the next processing run for the answers. With the introduction of immediate response and real-time processing systems, such as for airline and hotel reservations, the accounting procedures become an integral part of the system design, with the accounts up-dated and continuously available for interrogation. It is only when the finance and accounting applications are part of a main system operating in real time, however, that this method of processing is likely to be found.

Technological changes

The main technological obstacles to using the full data-handling capabilities of computers for finance and accounting have been the inaccessibility to users of individual computer records and the delay in up-dating the records when a transaction has been made. In many cases, a non-routine request by a computer user for an item of accounting information held on a computer has taken several hours to be serviced, and therefore users have frequently retained their visible records, possibly duplicating information already held on computer files. In some cases, these visible records are maintained on small visible record computers in user departments. Visible record computers possess calculating capabilities similar to, but less powerful than, those of larger computers, although for storage of information they often rely on magnetic striped ledger cards which are capable of being read and understood by both men and machines.

Localised files of information based on visible record computers are, however, frequently not available either to other departments or to other systems in operation within a company and thus may hinder the development of an integrated finance and accounting system. In order to preserve the advantages of the visual presentation of information offered by visible record computers, while providing the ability to maintain a file of information common to all sections of an organisation, on-line systems offering immediate response are used. A user of an on-line computer system may communicate directly with a central computer by using terminal devices linked to the computer by cable, telephone line or even by satellite. Information on the main computer files can be changed or accessed by a user and instructions can be generated by the computer and communicated to other users, all within seconds. For example, terminal devices installed in branch depots can be used to input orders for goods to a central computer, and the invoice and delivery documentation can be printed by the terminal. The stocks and sales ledgers can be up-dated and re-order action can be initiated where necessary. Moreover, the status of any customer or item of stock can be available for instant inquiry either from head office or a branch.

The chief technical improvements that have affected or will shortly affect the uses of computers in finance and accounting arise as a result of:

1   Increased computer reliability through the introduction of integrated circuitry, better diagnostic techniques and internal controls
2   Larger and faster direct-access storage devices
3   New types of data input devices
4   The ability of computers to control the concurrent processing of several operations, including the work carried out by peripheral devices.

In addition, the data base concept has been developed to make composite information files available to separate systems, and software packages have been introduced to organise these files and to provide indexing, up-dating and interrogation facilities. Data can now be encoded directly to magnetic tape or disk, either off-line to the main computer or on-line by typewriters or by visual display devices. These latter methods of data input aid error detection and correction, as the computer can apply comprehensive validation checks at the moment of data capture and can report errors to the operator for immediate correction.

Immediate future developments

Recent developments in computer technology are causing senior financial people to consider the best ways of making use of the more advanced equipment. This will result in a requirement for more sophisticated methods of input and output to enable the accountants to have more immediate response to their demands for rapid and comprehensive information. In the unsophisticated world of the one-man business, these requirements are capable of being satisfied with little formality in accounting techniques, but the larger the company the greater is the task of storing and accessing accounting information, and the greater is the need for formality in data processing systems.

Immediate future developments described here relate to the type of company that is of sufficient size not only to warrant the use of a computer to store comprehensive information, but also to be running, or to be capable of running, in a batch-processing mode on a computer, all of the various accounting procedures outlined earlier in the chapter. The emphasis in these accounting procedures has been on recording historical facts and on using these facts to enable the company to collect its debts and to pay its way, and to assess the extent of its profit or loss in a particular trading period. The emphasis is, however, changing from accounting for past results to looking in a financial way at likely future performance.

The rate of change of this emphasis is increasing. Accounting records can therefore be expected henceforward to be used increasingly to determine future business trends and to influence future management decisions. The requirement will then be for greater speed in the production of information that is relevant to future planning. Input of accounting records to the computer, such as for sales and purchases, must get closer to the point at which the movements of goods originate. Data describing the movements of goods and money must be initiated by the original transaction (preferably as an automatic by-product) and communicated without delay to the computer. Information processing needs to become, in this way, similar to the flow-line production process that characterises manufacturing operations. This timing will need on-line processing and will also lead to fully integrated processing as the accounting function will be more closely linked than previously with the manufacturing and marketing functions. It is this integration of the various elements of business through processing that gives particular significance to the developments in the financial function referred to below.

On-line fast processing of data to up-date accounting records is of itself of little value unless these records can be accessed, analysed and manipulated with equal speed and convenience. Accountants will soon be requiring an on-line system of inquiring into records that will provide instant information to a large number of executives. The information so provided will essentially be selective, relevant and brief.

The existence of more up-to-date information regarding the results of past arrangements and efforts will enable company management to examine more closely the inter-relationships between the various aspects of company operations and to look for improved facilities for reviewing the likely results of future actions. In the short-term future, the effect on cash flow of various decisions regarding company operations is the most pertinent. Money is the most liquid of the resources available to a company, and therefore speed in providing accurate indications of the probable distribution of available funds (or the likely call on bank overdrafts) is of particular importance to management, if it is to take advantage of the most favourable interest rates.

In the long term, the calls on cash and capital are fundamental to the economics of business development. Essentially, management wishes to know the requirements for capital that would result from, say, various arrangements of production facilities and various levels of turnover. It might be possible to state accurately some of the requirements for capital because they result from existing arrangements or past decisions. Other requirements will, however, depend on the probability of events and will therefore have an in-built margin of error. In these cases, the facility will be required to test alternative theories and to produce figures that can be checked as soon as possible by comparison with actual results. This implies the introduction of some type of financial model of the business, which can be manipulated to provide indications of the likely results of various courses of financial action. A considerable increase can therefore be expected over the next decade in the number of companies that use computer models of their operations.

Developing an integrated finance and accounting system

Having described above the capabilities of modern computers and then the finance and accounting developments to be expected in the near future, it is now appropriate to consider how the developments can be achieved, using the known and expected capabilities of computers in hardware and software. Computer users are of many different types with different amounts of money at their disposal. Some managements, while demanding that the operation of procedures is economically justified in each case, nevertheless allow considerable financial freedom to the computer group in respect of development costs. A computer group that is in this position will feel that during the next decade its principal aims should be to build:

1   A model of the company's operations
2   An integrated finance and accounting system.

Much of the outlook, planning and organisation required in building a model is similar to that involved in preparing an integrated system. Some of the work is also similar to the extent that each requires investigation, systems analysis, programming and education. The development of models has been dealt with at length in Chapter 16 and the details that follow here are therefore concerned with a description of the methods to be adopted in developing an integrated finance and accounting system.

The main stages through which an organisation must proceed to develop the system are to:

1   Carry out a preliminary survey by investigating broadly but conscientiously the overall structure and procedures in force in the organisation's finance and accounting arrangements
2   Specify the objectives clearly to enable those working on the system to know precisely what it is expected to provide
3   Carry out a detailed system investigation, taking the work in stage 1 and proceeding to develop it in depth

4   Plan the work in stages, in a way that would enable each stage to be implemented separately, while itself contributing something specific to the overall objective

5   Implement each stage with care, check that it will fit in with the other stages, and carry out a review of its effectiveness before proceeding to the next stage

6   Appropriately educate everyone who will use the system (which must be, with such a system on such a subject, a large proportion of total staff).

These matters are elaborated upon below.

Preliminary survey

Before defining objectives, it is necessary to carry out a preliminary survey to determine the feasibility of the project in relation to the company's operations and to produce an overall assessment of the economics of developing and operating the system so that management can take a reasoned decision that the new system is or is not advantageous as compared with existing arrangements. For this assessment it is necessary to produce:

1   An outline of the system

2   A broad assessment of the development costs and the operating costs (to the nearest thousand pounds)

3   An estimate of the time for the development of the procedures to the point that the first procedures are successfully operating (with a margin of 50 per cent added to cover under-estimates).

Specifying objectives

In specifying the objectives, many considerations must be taken into account, some desirable ends must be discarded through impracticability or excessive cost, and the goals that survive to be included in the specified objectives must have been debated, investigated broadly for feasibility and justified economically, to the extent that this is possible at such an early stage. Although these matters will take considerable time and thought, they must not be skimped for it is on the achievability of the objectives in as economical a manner as possible that the success of such a development project depends. The main objective for an integrated finance and accounting system operating on an on-line basis would be developed from the initial concept that led to a preliminary survey. The many subsidiary objectives that would arise in so large a scheme would become apparent during the survey, and could be stated clearly and accurately upon its conclusion.

Systems investigation

In all cases where a computer system is intended to replace existing systems that completely or partially meet the specified objectives, the design of the new system must be preceded by a detailed analysis of existing arrangements so that the best of the present procedures can be retained, a new system can be developed and a comparison can be made of the cost-effectiveness of the proposed new system against the existing system. It is also necessary to determine the essential requirements for printing and displaying output for immediate and long-term use to define the elements of basic data from which the output is to be produced, and to ascertain the organisation structures in operation, the staff numbers involved and their distribution among the departments using the procedures. This investigation serves to collect the data on which the new system should be constructed to ensure that it provides for all the detailed requirements that should be incorporated in it.

Planning the work

The scheme will be complex, and it would therefore be unwise to introduce the whole system at one attempt as this could lead to failure. It would need to be developed in sections in a way that would enable each to be implemented separately, while fitting in with its associated sections. This method provides a reasonable prospect that each section could subsequently be successfully implemented and that some sections would be carried out in parallel.

An illustration of the sections under which such a system could be developed is given below for an integrated accounting system that lacks the additional complication of a finance system coordinated with it. The sections might be

1   Sales accounting
2   Stock control
3   Purchases accounting
4   Payrolls
5   Nominal ledger and trial balance
6   Budgets and comparison of actual costs with budgets
7   Operating summaries of costs and cost recoveries
8   Management information.

Implementing in sections

The ultimate strength of anything is determined by the strength of its weakest part, and this applies to computer systems. In the integrated finance and accounting system inaccuracies of either programs or data introduced in the early stages will perpetuate themselves right through the system. The effectiveness of the development work should, therefore, be closely checked to ensure that it is of the highest quality through each system and subsystem. No section should be implemented until thoroughly tested and found acceptable to those who are to make use of it.

The principal responsibilities for the scheme will devolve upon the financial executives and the accountants, although the output will affect most senior people, either directly or through their staff. Each of these senior personnel must be made aware of his responsibility in accepting the output from the system, and the methods employed in it, including the accuracy of basic data that is fed into the computer.

Educating those involved

The types of staff involved in the scheme are likely to include:
1   At the senior non-accounting, non-technical level:
    (a) Managing director
    (b) Other directors at head office and at subsidiary companies
    (c) Heads of departments that are affected (most departments) at head office, subsidiaries, works or branches
2   At the senior finance and accounting non-technical level:
    (a) Finance director and the financial controller
    (b) Chief accountant at head office, and the senior accountants at subsidiaries, works or branches
3   At the detailed technical level:
    (a) Systems analysts and programmers in the computer department during development
    (b) Accountants and clerical staff responsible for procedures in the departments during development
    (c) Systems analysts, maintenance programmers, operators, schedulers, and job controllers in the computer department during implementation
    (d) Accountants and clerical staff responsible for input in the departments during implementation
4   At the junior accounting, non-technical level: the accountants in charge of sections at head office, subsidiaries, works or branches
5   At the junior non-accounting, non-technical level: section heads in departments at head office, subsidiaries, works or branches who will be responsible for staff preparing input or for receiving output from the computer.

The education given to each of these groups must be appropriate to the relationship that the employee will have with the system, and should be in detail around the point where the system touches him, and in outline on the remainder. Thus the staff at the detailed technical level will need comprehensive computer training and also a thorough training in the objects and method of operation of the integrated finance and accounting system, while the personnel in the other groups will need less computer technical training, and different amounts of training in the detail of the system in accordance with the requirements of their ranks.

Role of financial executives

The impact of computers in the finance and accounting spheres is likely to change the role of the financial executive considerably. His work in the past has included a large element of controlling staff engaged on recording transactions and providing information. Many finance executives have been more concerned with the techniques and economics of recording and providing information from the books and records of the business than with interpreting the results of the past to provide guidance for the future. As computers make much more information readily available, the emphasis of the financial executive's work must turn to providing a more comprehensive management information service, including the analysis and presentation of information on an exception basis in a manner which will allow managers to use the selected information properly for control and for decision-making.

Many financial executives are facing the problem of understanding the impact which is being made by computers, and it is disturbing to find that many of the younger accountants are taking insufficiently detailed interest in them. If the younger accountants in industry wish to retain the pre-eminence that their predecessors have gained for them in the business world, they must very soon show a greater interest than at present in the ways in which a computer can be used to provide financial guidance for the future operations of a company. They must want integrated finance and accounting systems, and they must want to build models of the company's activities. If the accountants do not put the pressure on the board, the data processing men will, and there will then arise the possibility that by 1980 the finance director will have been replaced by a different type of man, called, perhaps, the financial services director, who will be a computer specialist with financial knowledge (rather than vice versa) and who will wield even greater power than the financial men do at present.

19

Computers in Production Management

D. Milner

The applications of computers in the field of production can loosely be broken down as follows:

1 Control functions
2 Planning
3 Analysis routines
4 Design Automation

Control functions

Production control and stock control

The use of the computer in the work of the production control department can ensure flexibility and economy in the volume of record and computation involved and can make an important contribution to efficiency by speeding up the feedback of information from the production line or manufacturing department. Besides this the computer can analyse the information and modify and amend the details of manufacturing orders.

Consider the function of the production control department. Its main aim is to make the most effective use of men, materials and machines. It is not responsible for the actual work but provides a service to the operating departments. To carry out its function of scheduling, loading and progress control, it must inevitably generate written instructions and must receive certain information from other departments. It must, at all times, be able to answer two basic and very simple questions:

Can a particular task be undertaken and if so when?
How far have the tasks in hand proceeded?

The accuracy of these answers will reflect the success or failure of the production control arrangements. The end-product of the system is instructions for the operators on the jobs they are required to do and assurance that the material required and the machine loading permits the achievement of stated delivery dates. Actual conditions are seldom ideal, so it is absolutely essential to be able to check the progress of the orders.

Figure 19:1 shows an outline of the function of the production control department.

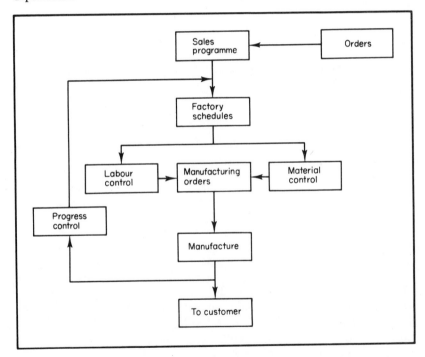

Figure 19:1　Functions of the production control department

Automated warehouse control

There are instances of automatic warehouses where the movement of goods is initiated by computer and where automatic control of stock is a by-product. Even the manual punching of cards or tapes has been avoided where mark-sensing is used. This is a system where, for example, the traveller or salesman marks a card for the required items with a special graphite pencil. The cards are then forwarded to the computer room where a special mark-sensing machine scans them and automatically punches the appropriate holes as with an ordinary punched card. The cards are then used to activate the mechanisms to extract the goods from the shelves and, subsequently, to take the goods on rollers to the loading bays. The same cards are then processed on the computer to produce invoices, statistics and stock control as for a normal routine. Close control over stocks can be achieved and re-ordering carried out when the stock level of any section reaches the minimum stockholding.

In warehousing applications the computer is able to play a decisive part in minimising warehouse stocks and associated transport changes.

Numerical control of production processes

The automatic control of production processes and particularly of machine tools does not in all cases require the use of a computer. However, with numerically controlled machine tools it is true that work involving continuous path forms can most effectively be carried out by using the computer to facilitate the preparation of the program tapes which control the machines.

There are a number of computer programs which, from specified data relating to the required product or component, will produce the operating tapes containing detailed instruction for operating the machine tools. One of the main languages available is called APT, which stands for Automatically Programmed Tools. APT is a language for describing the sequence of operations to be performed by numerically controlled (N/C) machines. The APT computer program is a long series of instructions for a computer. When the APT computer program is implemented on a general-purpose digital computer, the computer can accept a set of statements in the APT language, perform certain required computations, and produce a set of numerical commands. These commands are then punched into a control tape for an N/C machine. Figure 19:2 illustrates how the APT system fits into the manufacturing environment.

Integrated works control

Further development on these and similar lines leads to fully integrated works control, which is made possible by the use of the computer. It is necessary that recording centres should be dispersed throughout the plant, each connected on line to the computer.

As each job is tackled the operator keys in on a simple keyboard machine the

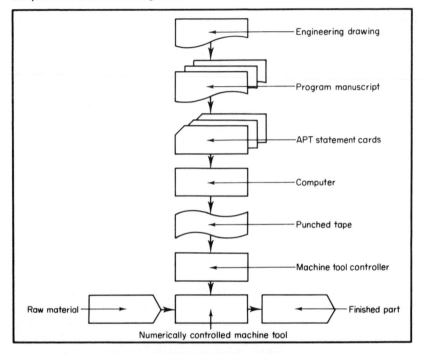

Figure 19:2 APT system flowchart

variable information required, such as the job number and time started. This information, coupled with the static information held in store, such as the machine number and works number, is processed by the computer to provide an up-to-the-minute record of job processing and machine loading. Provided that priorities are established in advance the computer is able to progress each job through. As new orders are received, the computer, from the details standing in its memory of the route required for a job and of plant loading, will be able to schedule the job on the appropriate machine.

Similarly, as each job is finished and the appropriate signal received from the recording centre, the computer will indicate to the operator which job to tackle next and will provide the appropriate requisitions and route cards. In a system such as the one described the main difficulty is in achieving the required speed of feedback and this is why it is necessary to have the dispersed recording centres.

Planning applications

Certain planning applications on computers are well-tried and tested. To take a simplified example, in any project which cannot be arranged as a straight flow line, one process proceeding directly to another, management has the problem of working out the correct sequence of activities. The modern way of doing this is by critical path analysis, that is by preparing a diagrammatic representation of the interdependencies of the activities on each other in a network. The computer cannot help here. Once the network is drawn, however, duration times for the activities are assessed, then, by a series of addition and subtractions, the earliest and latest times for the commencement and finish of the separate activities can be calculated within any limits set by the overall duration of the project or the times set by processes running concurrently. If the network is of any size, say more than about 200 activities, then it becomes worth while to have the analysis done on the computer.

Having analysed the network, a critical path will have emerged as the pathway through the activities which actually determines the duration of the whole project. No margins can be allowed in the start or finish times of the activities on this path. In most networks only a small proportion, say about 20 per cent, of the items, are on the critical path.

There now arises the problem of allocating the resources to carry out the plan as finalised in the critical path network. When the allocation is attempted it is frequently found that another critical condition has developed, in other words there is a critical path in terms of the resources available to meet the network demand. The computer is extremely useful in rescheduling the resources so as to make available the allocations required for uninterrupted progress along the critical path found through the network on the time basis. This is achieved by transferring resources from activities on non-critical paths to assist with activities which are indicated as critical.

As the project proceeds, feedback and control become vital. The speed with which the network can be updated by the computer is one of its advantages.

Line of balance is essentially the same kind of technique applied in those cases where there is no need for a network to show the inter-relationships, because they are strictly sequential, but where there is a quantitative problem of ensuring that what comes off each stage in the process is in balance with the requirement of subsequent stages.

Traffic prediction may be either a matter of determining long-term needs for say road or route planning, or of dealing with current control of traffic on a real-time basis. The latter involves the collection of current data on traffic flows and on conditions affecting the flow, and in a sufficiently short time to be effective, bringing about the operation of signals and of signs to secure optimised use of facilities.

Analysis routines

These include market survey, general survey, stock recording, factor analysis, multiple regression, forecasting and variance analysis.

Analysis of all kinds is most relevant to computers. Consider a production analysis which requires basic information, as recorded from the census of parts details, to be analysed over perhaps twenty different headings and simultaneously over several hundred headings of a different class. This is a relatively simple task for the computer. Further analysis can also be applied to the data to give more accurate measurement of trends, say as standard deviation or variances as desired by management.

Armed with this kind of information managements are in a much better position to make decisions on such matters as capital projects which have longterm implications for the future of the organisation.

Design automation

For several years, automatic machine tools have been used for manufacturing small components in large quantities. In this way, lathe and milling-machine operators may be transferred from repetitive jobs to do more exacting woi k. In a milling operation, the workpiece (metal to be machined) is moved up or down, left or right, or backwards or forwards under a tool, such as a rotating cutter. With manual working of these machines, an operator controls the movement of the workpiece clamped to the milling-machine 'bed' or table in such a way that the desired shape is machined.

In a digital computer control system, the table and workpiece are moved the required amounts by means of signals sent to vertical, horizontal, or transverse motors. These signals are pre-recorded on magnetic or punched tape, which can be rewound after one item is completed, ready for the next workpiece. There are several methods of achieving the control. One method uses optical equipment which generates an electrical pulse for each quarter-thousandth of an inch movement of the workpiece in the three planes. By electrically counting these pulses, the computer can issue signals to drive the workpiece to a given position. Another system works on an incremental principle, in which special drive motors move on a fixed amount every time a pulse is given. Three such motors are used.

To cut a straight line in a workpiece on the table, the longitudinal drive motor needs to receive pulses at a fixed rate to drive the work under the cutter at a fixed speed. The faster the pulses are, the faster is the cutter rate.

If both transverse and longitudinal drives are 'pulsed' at the same speed, an angled cut is made. And by varying the two drive-rates according to the correct mathematical relationship, a circular drive can be pulsed to vary the depth of the cut or to disengage the tool from the workpiece.

All the pulses for the three motors can be recorded on magnetic tape. The problem is how to get the right pulses, in the correct sequence and relationship to each other, onto the tape. To do this, use is made of the computer and a machine-tool control language.

The machine-tool control program also sets up the correct sequence of pulses for certain shapes and materials. For example, if a machine is to cut a straight line between two points, the instructions in the input language need only define the starting point and end point of the line and the computer program generates all the pulses required to move the workpiece between these two points. The speed of cutting is also given in the input language, which generates the corresponding pulses at the correct rate.

Such programming may take a long time and may have to be frequently tested on trial workpieces made of plastic. But once the program has been perfected, it can be used for mass production. In a fully automated system, the magnetic tape also controls the ejection of the finished component, clamping of the new workpiece, and rewinding of the tape.

Automatic drawing

Instead of a work table being moved under a tool, a pen may be made to move over the surface of a sheet of paper. Connected to a computer, such a device can trace curves and shapes using simple instructions in an input language.

Such systems are used for plotting large templates in sheet metal working, and for drawing cam profiles. Use has also been made of these drawing aids in the micro-electronics industry. Micro-circuits are used in most modern computers and are manufactured by etching out or diffusing materials into small pieces of silicon using various masks which outline the shape of the circuit. The masks are extremely small and must be made by optical reduction from very large master drawings to obtain the required accuracy. Computers can calculate the best layouts and draw the required masks.

Future developments

In the future, a computer system might completely design and manufacture components. The component to be made can be 'drawn' onto the surface of a cathode–ray tube display by means of a light-pen connected to a computer. The display scans the whole face of the tube under computer control, and when the light-pen is brought near to the surface of the tube it receives a small 'flash' of light as the scanning beam passes it. At this instant, a signal or 'interrupt' is sent from the light-pen to the computer which remembers the position on the screen which the beam scanned when the pen gave an interrupt. This procedure continues as the operator moves the pen over the screen, and eventually a complete trace of all the points is constructed. In this way, an operator can 'draw' the required component and then enter its dimensions into the system from a normal keyboard. The computer then constructs the trains of pulses required to machine the shape automatically.

This data is then put onto magnetic tape which can later be transferred to the machine-tool control equipment. There is no reason why many machines should not be programmed by the designs produced by one computer system, so reducing the time required for an operator to work out by hand all the required component dimensions.

20

Computers in Inventory Management

A. E. Parish

The justification for the use of a computer in inventory management is the tighter control of stocks made possible in day-to-day operations, the containing of inventory within limits suggested by the current availability of working capital, and the facility for smooth measured change when conditions demand it. The inventory is kept in better balance and the available cash is deployed to the best advantage.

Any consideration of inventory by management must start with its effect on liquidity. Business success depends upon making a profit, but unless there are idle funds available this in turn is materially influenced by the speed with which the available funds circulate round the business cycle.

Uncontrolled inventory slows down this rate of circulation to a serious degree. Excessive stocks absorb capital readily but release it only with reluctance: inadequate stocks inhibit either production or sales with equally serious results.

Inventory is the least liquid element of working capital and usually represents between 60 and 80 per cent (or even worse) of the working capital in a manufacturing business. Moreover, it may represent up to 40 per cent, or more, of capital employed with a probable average of about 20 per cent for manufacturing industry. Over UK industry as a whole, stocks add up to about £13 000 million, or nearly a third of the gross national product.

Stock recording by computer

A computer can maintain efficient and effective stock records. The details will vary from company to company but the following advantages are worth noting:

1   Delays in recording stock movements are part of the stock replenishment lead time. The discipline essential to computer data preparation shows up delays more easily and hence makes for more effective control of these. Automatic document reading and on-line terminals can further accelerate the feeding of data to the computer.
2   Pre-posting of stock movements, i.e. telling the system before telling the stores, is easier with a computer. Moreover the computer can summarise and rearrange data into a more useable form before passing it on to the stores, e.g. lists of requirements in walk round (bin location) sequence.
3   Available stock can be allocated automatically to incoming demands (subject to management override) and the stores asked to service only those demands which it is known they can satisfy. Stores personnel cannot then allocate stock in short supply on the random basis of which order was picked up first.
4   The computer can amplify and pass on information automatically to other computer-based systems, such as for costing and invoicing.
5   Monitoring of the situation can be carried to greater depth by the computer. For example, records may be built up for each supplier to show his delivery performance (average lateness) and quality performance (average rejects percentage). The incidence of stock run outs (stock outs) can be recorded in the same way to monitor control system performance.
6   Routine reporting is easier. For example, each stock updating run on the computer can produce a valuation of the issues, receipts, new supplies requested and the opening and closing inventory levels for management information.

In general, fuller records can be kept and fuller use made of the information by frequent analysis and reporting on an exception basis. Communication with other routines is easier and quicker. Since data need be submitted to the computer only once it is easier to ensure that all reporting is based on the same information.

Stock control by computer

Stock control methods change form slightly with circumstances, but there are only three basic methods in general use and even these are closely related to each other. They are:

1   Stock balancing for line production
2   Re-order point (minimum stock) control
3   Cyclic re-ordering (target stock or order-up-to system).

The first is subordinate to, and used only with, production control. The other two can stand alone. All require a forecast of future demand; a method of automatic forecasting by computer will be described later. Manually inserted forecasts can be used just as easily but are unlikely to give as consistently good results.

Stock balancing for line production

The capacity planning element of production control determines the total number of units to be made by each production line each week. If manufacture (of electric lamps, for example) is for stock, it is likely that not every model can be made each week. A selection must be made, and this can usefully be done by the stock control system.

In the situation described and assuming a manufacturing lead time of one week, an item does not need to be replenished if the existing stock is enough to cover the maximum expected demand in the next two weeks (the target stock). Any later requirements can be covered by manufacture in a later week.

If production and sales are roughly in step, those items with stock below target are the obvious choice and their stocks must clearly be brought above the target level if planned production capacity allows this. If it does not, an allocation of available capacity must be made.

It is a common feature of flow line production that if demand is seasonal, a constant rate of production will be attempted which will give rise to stockpiling during some periods of the year. At such times all stocks will be above target levels. Again, a system of allocation will be necessary to maintain balance of stocks.

A regular forecast of future sales is made for each model. The excess (or deficiency) of stock above (below) the target stock is divided by the forecast to express the difference in weeks of stock.

This puts a time scale on the stock cover. Production is then allocated to increase the stock, first of the item with the lowest cover, then the item with the next lowest cover, and so on, no item being left behind, until the available production capacity is exhausted.

The replenishment quantities may be chosen so that all selected items finish with the same stock cover in weeks, or batch sizes may be decided by some other rules. In the latter case enough items must be picked for their batch quantities just to exceed in total the planned capacity. The batch of the least urgent item must then overflow into the following week.

If stockpiling is done in the seasonal sales trough, items with high machine and labour hours and low material content will be preferred for manufacture in the early stages: this minimises the build-up of inventory investment. The computer can be told not to schedule excess manufacture for stock of certain items before a certain date or to restrict schedules to certain items until their stock reaches a preset maximum, provided that the stock cover of no item is allowed to drop below target stock level.

Re-order point control

With this system of control, a replenishment order is requisitioned (it is possible for the computer to print the orders for standard items) when the available stock (physical stock plus replenishment stock already on order) falls to a preset level known as the re-order point.

This system has been in use for a very long time under the name of minimum stock control. The name has been changed because minimum stock is now the name given to the warning level where stocks are dangerously low.

The re-order point is an estimate of the expected demand in the lead time, plus a safety stock component to guard against demands in excess of forecast. The size of the safety stock determines the level of customer service.

If stock levels are reviewed (i.e. checked against re-order points) only weekly or less frequently, the available stock may drop below re-order point just after a review, but no action will be taken until the next review, nearly a week later. To guard against this, the lead time needs to be increased by, strictly, half the review interval, but preferably by a full review interval. The latter will inflate stocks and cyclic re-ordering is likely to be a better system unless lead times are long.

A re-order point control system will work very well if stock levels are updated and reviewed daily or even more frequently.

Cyclic re-ordering

This system is used where physical conditions determine when replenishment orders may be placed, say, monthly, or where stocks can be reviewed only infrequently, say, at weekly intervals or longer.

A target stock is calculated. This is the expected demand in a period equal to the lead time plus the interval between successive orders (the order interval). This period is the time before the next subsequent replenishment order can be delivered. Current ordering action must, therefore, increase the available stock (physical stock plus quantity covered by outstanding previous replenishment orders) to the target stock quantity.

The target stock quantity is calculated as in a re-order point system and includes a safety stock component.

The computer can revise re-order points and target stock levels automatically on the basis of information given to it on lead times, order intervals, and level of customer service required. As a result stock levels can be adjusted continually in response to sustained changes in demand. Automatically the stock investment is progressively shifted from items with falling demand to items with rising demand. There is a considerably reduced risk of obsolete stock accumulating. However, large, abrupt changes in demand surprise even the computer which will require time to adjust unless management can give it warning.

The computer can also monitor continuously the lead time and adjust automatically to a forecast of lead time. However, it is generally better that this is done by a separate program and reviewed by management before being fed to the stock control system.

With any of these control systems the computer produces a list of new replenishment orders required. It normally assumes that all requested orders will be placed and needs to be told only of exceptions as a result of an overriding management decision.

Demand forecasting

A number of short-term forecasting systems are in regular use. The most widely known is exponential smoothing and a simple form of this will be described to illustrate the method.

A forecast is made regularly, say each week or month, for each item. Weekly forecasting is assumed in the following description.

The forecast is made for the coming week and is then compared with the actual demand one week later. If the actual demand exceeds the forecast, the latter is augmented by a fraction of the differences between the two: if the forecast is the greater it is reduced in a similar manner. The figure thus arrived at is the new forecast for the coming week. For example:

Forecast for week 10	= 120
Actual demand in week 10	= 150
Forecast error	= 150 − 120 = 30
Smoothing constant	= 0.2, say
Forecast for week 11	= 120 + 0.2 x 30
	= 126
Actual demand in week 11	= 100
Forecast error	= 100 − 126 = −26
Forecast for week 12	= 126 + 0.2 x (−26)
	= 126 − 5.2
	= 120.8

and so on.

The fraction (0.2 in the example) is known as the smoothing constant. If it is small (say 0.1), the forecasting system responds only slowly to real change in demand levels, but it ignores transient changes in an otherwise stable demand. Large values (say 0.4 to 0.5) have the opposite effect. The smoothing constant therefore needs to be chosen in the light of how the demand for the item is likely to vary. A good average figure to use is 0.2 until experience suggests otherwise.

More recent developments avoid the need for the smoothing constant to be decided by management: systems are now available which automatically vary the value of the smoothing constant in the light of the computer's own assessment of how the demand is varying.

From the one-week forecast, a forecast of demand in the lead time is projected, taking account of known seasonality. Hence an estimate of expected demand in the lead time is derived. The safety stock element is calculated separately in the manner described later. (For a cyclic re-ordering system, read lead time plus order interval in place of lead time.)

Safety stock

The forecasting system tries only to estimate the most likely demand: this is equivalent to the average of static data. It follows that the actual demand may be higher or lower than the forecast. Stock control is most often concerned only with cases when the demand exceeds the forecast.

The forecast error (difference between actual demand and forecast) is used in the calculation of the new forecast as already outlined. It is also analysed statistically. From this a statement may be derived in the form: there is only a 10 per cent risk that a larger forecast error than x will be encountered. In other words, there is 90 per cent confidence that the error will not be greater than x. The 90 per cent instanced here is one measure of customer service. If the safety stock element in a re-order point system is based on x, then there is 90 per cent confidence that the new delivery will be received before stock fails to meet demand. Therefore, a stock-out will occur only once in ten deliveries on average. The actual percentage to be used is chosen by management.

This idea of customer service is often measured by the percentage of demand which will be met immediately on request. This calculation takes account of the order interval. The 90 per cent figure used in the above context would lead to more than 90 per cent of the demand being satisfied on request. In this case management specifies a percentage of demand to be met ex-stock and the computer performs the rest of the calculation.

Note that the larger the order size, the better the customer service for the same safety stock. 100 per cent is impossible all the time although it may be achieved for long periods if a high service is requested. The cost in terms of safety stock will be high.

Choosing the batch size

A re-order point shows only when a new batch should be requisitioned to replenish stock. The system must also decide how many to order.

The cyclic re-ordering system decides how many to order. When to order is imposed on the system by management, or external circumstances.

In the re-order point control system, it is important that the re-order quantity responds to changes in demand as well as the re-order point. Too large an order will delay re-ordering of the next batch a long time while the excessive stock is consumed. Meanwhile, the system can take no further action. Too small an order quantity will achieve low stocks but also will give rise to frequent replenishment orders which may be expensive.

Small orders will also demand larger safety stocks to maintain the same level of customer service.

Batch sizes may be fixed quantities, they may be based on time or they may be based on the well-known economic order quantity formula.

All of these methods and especially the last named are dealt with in the textbooks on stock control. They will not be discussed here as it is not possible to recommend one method in favour of another unless the circumstances are known.

Whatever the method chosen, it is important to remember that changing the batch size can have a most profound effect on stock levels: the average inventory will approximate to the sum of (for all items) safety stock and half the average batch size. Moreover, the frequency of ordering can have considerable influence on purchasing or machine set-up costs and factory capacity, and on quantity discounts on purchased items.

Application packages for inventory control

The design of a computer-based inventory control system which exploits the modern techniques available requires considerable expertise which many companies cannot justify employing. Nevertheless, if they wish to develop their own system they can use a firm of consultants or one of the software houses to do this for them.

When experienced staff are available the cost of developing one's own system is not likely to be less than about £10 000 and might be considerably more. Expenditure of such sums must be examined critically especially when the company management are strange to computer-based inventory control. At that stage they cannot fully specify to the systems analysts what they require of the system, although this is no problem if an outside firm of specialists is retained to advise. All of the leading computer manufacturers can offer one or more systems of inventory control supported by proven programs, which they maintain, and usually a wealth of literature and training courses as well for both computer staff and management.

Most of the leading computer bureaux also offer the use of inventory control systems to their clients.

It is far easier to make use of some of these facilities at least initially. When they become inadequate for needs, it is time to design one's own system.

Each of the manufacturers' application packages has its own approach to inventory control based on practical experience in specific application areas. Consequently they will not all place the same emphasis on the various problem areas discussed in this chapter.

Generally speaking, all include a forecasting program and facilities for recalculating order sizes and re-order points (and target stock levels). Most include stock updating programmes which vary widely in facilities offered. The largest area of difference is in the type and scope of analysis programs offered.

Similar considerations apply to suites of programs used by service bureaux, some of whom have developed systems for specific trades and industries.

At first sight it seems unlikely that a generalised set of programs would fit anyone's needs exactly, but the computer industry has learnt how to build in flexibility without an untoward increase in complexity that is visible to the user. They continue to improve their skill in this direction and a number of exciting developments are currently under way in this field.

Using a set of properly documented, proven programs not only saves the cost of developing one's own, at least initially, but it makes it possible to bring the computer to bear on inventory control perhaps a year earlier. This could be worth more than the saving in system and programming cost because of the earlier reduction in stock levels.

Until recently, the argument was for or against application packages. Now the argument is over the relative merits of different systems. The demand for more packages is growing.

21

Computers in Marketing

M. Christopher

Success in the markets of the future will be based on the ability of management to identify, relate and interpret the multiplicity of pressures and influences that make the consumer purchase their products. Even the most unsophisticated attempts at charting the nature of consumer response quickly become complex, especially when quantitiative analysis is applied, as it must if measurement and thus prediction are to be attempted. In the past, the marketing executive may have known what he needed to achieve if he was to make some sense out of the mass of marketing data that was available or potentially available. The problem has been that he lacked the technology to perform these operations; technology in the sense of relevant quantitative techniques and computing power.

Over the last ten years, the quantitative revolution in marketing has reached remarkable proportions. Now the sophistication of the techniques is tending to outstrip the quality of the data available as input. Tremendous reliance is coming to be placed on the results of such operations and often without regard to the data on which the solutions are based. It is thus a crucial requirement that the limitations of both the data and the techniques are understood before any use is made of either. This caveat should be constantly in mind as the developments outlined in this chapter are discussed.

Hand in hand with the growth of the analytical technology has been the rise of the computer as a viable means of processing large sets of data, performing complex procedures and then communicating its output in a readily understandable form. Of particular importance has been the recent development of time-sharing computer facilities making use of conversational, or near-conversational, languages. This latter development has enabled the manager to communicate directly with the computer and has widened considerably the scope of man-machine interaction. Many of the applications of the computer in marketing discussed in this chapter are greatly enhanced by this ability that enables the manager to alter the parameters of the situation being studied and to receive almost instantaneous indication of the effect of that change.

Considerable attention is currently being placed on the possibilities opened up by the computer era for the construction and operation of 'marketing information systems'. The idea behind the marketing information system is that it provides an up-to-date picture of what is happening in the marketplace and how this is affecting current performance. It thus provides a basis for adjustments to marketing programmes. Here the computer is performing three specific roles; in the first place it is acting as a 'librarian': information relating to the marketing programme and its performance is stored, and its retrieval made simple. Second the computer acts as an 'analyst' through its ability to determine statistical relationships, thus the marketing manager is able to ask for specific statistical relationships to be produced by the computer. Finally, in the most sophisticated cases, the computer can act as a 'model bank' providing predictions and even decisions.

The degree to which the computerised information system is integrated into the operational and strategic framework of the marketing activity will depend on the degree to which speedy reaction to marketing information is crucial. In many industries the highly sophisticated real-time type of information system is unnecessary and inappropriate. In many cases too, the input data will be at too low a level for the more sophisticated analytical and predictive operations,

The purpose of this short examination of the computer's place in marketing, therefore, is to explore what is possible now and within the scope of the typical company with typical computing facilities. Some of the major current applications are described and then finally some recent developments are explored with a view to the future.

Media analysis

It is often surprising to the layman to discover the extent to which the business of advertising a brand is based on hard quantitative analysis. The 'creative' aspect of advertising manifested in the television commercial or the newspaper advertisement is merely the end product of what can be a highly sophisticated process. Just deciding which vehicles should be used to carry the advertisement, with what frequency and on what occasions, can involve the use of complex computerised media selection models.

Media selection models come in various forms, ranging from a relatively simple linear-programming allocation solution to an advanced simulation model. Underlying all the various approaches, however, are a number of common features requiring specific information inputs.

The first requirement is a definition of the target audience at whom the campaign is to be directed. This in itself will normally reduce the number of vehicles available as some media will obviously be more appropriate in terms of reaching the target and will be weighted accordingly. The second input is cost data. This determines the cost-effectiveness of a particular media schedule; often it can be expressed in terms of the cost per thousand of the target group reached.

So far the problem is straightforward, and if the analysis was limited to these dimensions, the computer would be superfluous. However, not every reader or viewer of a selected vehicle will be aware of the advert and, even if exposed to it, it may make no impact. In order to overcome these problems, approaches have been developed with are 'probabilistic' or 'stochastic' in nature. In other words, each factor in the media selection model is described in terms of the probability of its occurrence.

Thus, the probability of an exposure to an advertisement in a vehicle can be related to its relative impact which in turn is related to the awareness of that advertisement. Because of the considerable computational problems that such an approach entails, simulation is used to provide a profile of the effectiveness of a given media schedule in terms of meeting the stated objectives within some overall cost constraint. In this way alternative schedules may be compared and, through interaction with the computer, a satisfactory (rather than an optimum) schedule selected.

The major failing of computerised methods of media scheduling is that they are not able to take into account the all-important *qualitative* variables in media decisions. Broadbent and Segnit ('Factors Influencing Media Selection') have listed some factors which are crucial to such decisions, but which the computer is not always capable of taking into account:

FACTORS NOT USED	FACTORS PARTLY USED	FACTORS USED
Marketing objectives	Brand information	Media budget
Creative objectives	Creative approach	Media costs
Test/research	Media objectives	Reading/viewing
Trade advertising	Regionality	by target group
Availability and	Ad exposure	
timing	Selectivity	
Proven effectiveness	Reading/viewing	
Competition	predictions	
Exposure occasions		
Environment		
Non-media support		

Clearly there is some way to go before a realistic fully computerised model for media decisions is viable. Until that time the role of the computer in such decisions must be confined to a secondary, though important, position as a means of identifying the impact of the analyst's assumptions on these decisions.

Survey analysis

Market research is an essential basis for marketing decisions and its use by UK industry over the last decade has increased tremendously in line with the wider acceptance of the marketing concept. A good deal of consumer market research generates considerable data—a typical survey might cover 2000 respondents who are asked twenty-five questions and whose answers to these questions need to be analysed according to specific classificatory requirements. It is this latter feature that is particularly susceptible to computer handling. If, for example, it was desired to know what proportion of those 2000 respondents were over 25 but under 35, married, with an income of over £2500 and bought the product in question more than six times a year, then this would clearly be a tedious task to perform manually. Using only simple data processing equipment, however, it is possible to perform cross-tabulations such as these in a matter of minutes. For many market research survey analyses it is sufficient to extend the analysis no further than simple cross tabulations of this type and frequency counts.

More and more, however, the trend in market research is towards the use of more complex and sophisticated procedures to bring to light relationships and underlying characteristics in survey data. A prime consideration of market research is to discern 'groupings' amongst respondents—be they consumers, television viewers, readers or whatever. These groupings, when identified, can often provide creative leads for marketing management by suggesting a basis for market segmentation. Thus, it may be found from the survey data given in the previous example that the market for this product in terms of heavy consumption lay in three major groups: the young unmarried group, the middle-aged high-income group with no children, and young married couples with no children. Knowledge of the existence of such segments could clearly be of some value to the marketing strategist.

Statistical methods for identifying such groupings have been in existence for some time, but the advent of the computer has been the key to their wider usage. One frequently used method is that of *cluster analysis,* which, as the name suggests, looks at an array of data, such as the scores on a number of attitude scales of a group of consumers, and then compares each individual's scores to identify those consumers who are similar to each other in terms of their responses but who are more dissimilar in their scores to all other

286

individuals. Thus, the aim of cluster analysis is to minimise within-group variance while maximising between-group variance.

Figure 21:1 demonstrates the type of groupings that can emerge from this kind of analysis. In Figure 21:1 *(a)* the twelve respondents are scored according to the possession of five attributes (A,B,C,D, and E). A cluster analysis has been performed, and the respondents are placed in 'clusters' (groups) in Figure 21:1 *(b)* according to their similarity to other group members in terms of their scores. The marketing analyst wishing to pinpoint market segments now has the task of seeing in what ways these groups are distinct. It may be that group 1, for example, comprises in the main ladies between 25 and 35, but they are not heavy consumers of the product. The respondents in cluster 3, however, are heavy consumers and they are well educated and married, and so on.

One further aid to this interpretation of market groupings is *factor analysis*. Factor analysis is a means of reducing large sets of overlapping data into a smaller set of meaningful 'factors'. Thus we may ask consumers a large number

(a)

Respondents	A	B	C	D	E
1	●	●	●	●	●
2	●	●			●
3	●		●	●	●
4		●	●	●	
5			●		●
6	●		●	●	●
7		●	●	●	
8	●	●			
9		●	●	●	●
10	●	●	●		
11		●	●		●
12			●		●

(b)

Respondents	A	B	C	D	E	Group
1	●	●	●	●	●	Group 1
3	●		●	●	●	
6	●		●	●	●	
2	●	●				Group 2
8	●	●				
10	●	●	●			
4		●	●	●		Group 3
7		●	●	●		
9		●	●	●	●	
5			●		●	Group 4
11		●	●		●	
12			●		●	

Figure 21:1   Cluster analysis
     (a)   Scores on five attributes
     (b)   Respondents grouped according to scores

of questions about how they perceive a brand in relation to its competitors, and reduce this mass of data, by the use of factor analysis, to just, say, two or three dimensions relevant to the sonsumers' perception.

These techniques are just two of many procedures that are available to the contemporary marketing researcher. They owe their viability, however, to the computer which, through its capacity to store data and perform lengthy operations in a matter of moments, reduces otherwise near-impossible procedures to manageable proportions.

New product decisions

New products are the lifeblood of the modern company. In some areas of the UK grocery business, for example, over 80 per cent of the total sales are accounted for by products that were not in existence ten years ago. Accompanying this high level of innovation is a correspondingly high level of new product failures. Estimates vary, but is seems likely that in the fast-moving consumer goods industries, between 10 and 40 per cent of new product launches are not successful, and are withdrawn. Clearly a considerable risk is undertaken in launching a new product if no hard information is available about its likely impact in the marketplace. As a result of these inherent risks, the screening and testing of new product proposals has become an established part of the product development sequence.

To enable the uncertainty surrounding new product introduction to be converted into measurable risk, a body of techniques has grown up under a generic title of 'venture analysis'. Venture analysis may be defined as a 'systematic and quantitative discipline for organising and processing inform-ation to guide business decisions'. Central to the idea of venture analysis is the determination of the probability that a particular couse of action will result in a particular outcome. By using the methods of decision theory the product manager is able to put his finger on the areas of uncertainty and to determine the odds of success or failure.

A number of steps may be specified in the process, the purpose of these steps being to accumulate information and to make at each of these stages one of three decisions: to launch the product now, to scrap the product, or to continue the evaluation sequence. Figure 21: 2 shows the stages in the evaluation process.

After each of these evaluatory steps, the information received is used to update the current expectations about the product's chances of succeeding in a national launch. Only when a stage is reached in this testing sequence where the probability of success is greater than a certain value would a launch be considered.

Not surprisingly, the quantification of this evaluatory information poses problems. Venture analysis requires the computation of probability distributions that describe the likelihood of occurrence of the events being examined. Thus, for example, after the product test, it is necessary to determine how the results of the test affect management's estimates of the probability of the product bringing an acceptable return on investment (ROI) if launched now.

A simplified example of the approach required is given below, where management has ascribed probabilities to the occurrence of specific ROIs. It will be seen that these probabilities add up to 1. All possible ROIs have been specified and therefore one of them must occur. To calculate the 'expected value' of the ROI (i.e. the mean of the ROIs weighted by the likelihood of their occurrence) the individual values of ROI are multiplied by their corresponding probability and these values summed. In this case, the expected value is 11.5 per cent, which may or may not be in excess of the required minimum ROI.

Possible ROI	Probability of occurrence	Expected value of ROI
5%	0.2	1.0
10%	0.4	4.0
15%	0.3	4.5
20%	0.1	2.0
		11.5

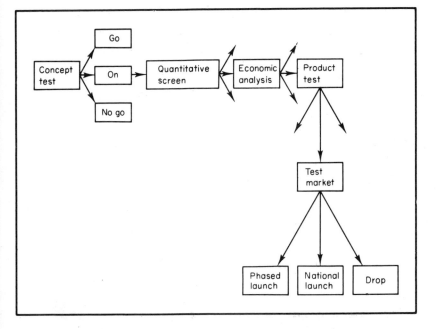

Figure 21:2   Stages in the evaluation of new products

Because of the large number of different information inputs that need to be evaluated at each stage in the venture analysis process, a number of computer methods have been developed to handle the data manipulations. Two of the earliest methods which have become models for further developments were DEMON and SPRINTER. These computerised models enable information relating to a large number of relevant variables to be evaluated in a probabilistic framework; for example, the product manager's own estimates of risk, the investment and payoff implications, likely demand levels, and response functions describing the reaction of demand to changes in marketing inputs may all be taken into account in the final output, taking the form of a 'risk profile'.

Models of market response

'Models' have become something of a fashion item in marketing management and most companies with any pretensions to sophistication would claim to have at least one. In fact, depending on how broadly one cares to define a 'model' it could be said that every operating rule is a model—for example, if present marketing policy is to increase promotional spending at a rate directly proportional to our major competitor's expenditure, then this is a model of our competitive response! It may be unsophisticated when expressed mathematically but in its marketing context it is probably highly appropriate.

Quite often, extremely complex models of marketing systems are constructed, usually at great cost, only for it to be discovered that changes in the basic parameters occur after the model has been in existence only a few months. Other models, because of their complexity, never actually reach the stage of aiding management decision—their builders or their superiors despairing of achieving success.

This is not to dismiss all attempts at model building as unproductive, but rather to start by insisting on a rigorous cost—benefit framework for model-building. The procedure here is to answer the following questions:

1   What are the areas of uncertainty that the model is supposed to describe?
2   Is the model to aid decision-making?
3   Is the model to have predictive accuracy?
4   What are the benefits accruing through achieving features 1, 2 and 3 above?
5   What are the costs of construction?

Generally models of market processes which are designed to aid management decision will be of a type which allow for executive interpretation of the output of the model and for the readjustment of the model in the light of this output. However, developments in model building are leading to the possibility of servo-mechanism type models being constructed which can perform self-adjusting activities in the light of market response. The distinction is made here between an 'open loop' (see Figure 21:3) and a 'closed loop' (Figure 21:4). The open-loop configuration requires a specific response from the executive to the output of the model in the light of its performance against predetermined objectives. Closed-loop systems, on the other hand, once they have been set in

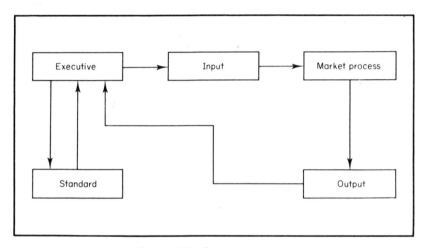

Figure 21:3   Open-loop system

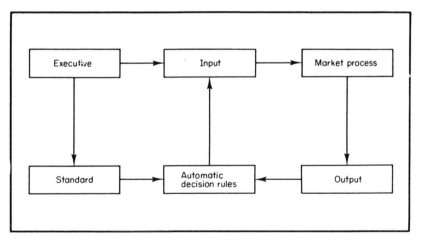

Figure 21:4   Closed-loop system

motion, control themselves, and respond to specific situations in the light of stated decision rules. Thus a computerised system of inventory control can maintain stock levels, determine order requirements, and so on, without human intervention once the model and its operating rules have been specified. Closed-loop, or self-regulating systems, however, are currently only appropriate for the fairly routine aspects of marketing control and are obviously of little use in decisions requiring creative judgement.

The computer, although it makes effective managerial use of marketing models possible, is not in itself a sufficient development to ensure viable marketing models. The model is only going to be as good as the structure we give it. If in structuring our representation of reality we oversimplify, or we fail to recognise, existing marketing relationships then the finished model will be poorer and will lack descriptive validity and predictive power. Although we may overcome the possibility of missing important variables out of the model by including all those variables that we could possibly conceive of as affecting the dependent variable this could only be achieved at the expense of ease of construction of the model, and indeed would probably be almost impossible. Somewhere there has to be a trade-off between completeness and complexity.

Simulation

In the same way that a traffic engineer would be loath to construct a flyover at a road intersection without first simulating the situation and testing the design and any alternatives under various traffic conditions, so too should the marketing manager be wary of jumping into the marketplace with, say, a revised marketing strategy without first ensuring that no alternative strategy would produce superior results.

The problem has been that to test such a strategy requires a reproduction, in the form of a model, of the marketing environment and the construction of response functions relating changes in demand to variations in marketing inputs. To increase the realism it is further necessary to examine the impact of the proposed strategy under different levels of competitive activity. These are the basic requirements for the simulation of marketing strategies and clearly to attain any degree of realism, thus introducing many variables, the complexity may be considerable. One of the most frequently used methods is the Monte Carlo method of simulation described in Chapter 17.

Marketing information systems

Over the next twenty-five years or so, it is likely that some quite remarkable developments in computer technology, and our ability to utilise it, will revolutionise the role of the computer in marketing.

Mention was made earlier in the chapter of the growth of the marketing information system concept. The central feature here is that a computer-based data bank, which is updated constantly, is available to aid in the evaluation of marketing decisions. The essence of the system as a management tool is that it provides for interaction between man and machine, producing a more or less instantaneous response to complex questions.

With the development of visual display as a means of input and output, this conversational ability will be greatly enhanced. A major advantage of this is the greater scope for graphical portrayal of information so that it can be more easily understood. The technology involved in these preducures is available—the major constraint is managers' meagre understanding of their potential.

Figure 21:5 suggests the nature of the interactive marketing information system.

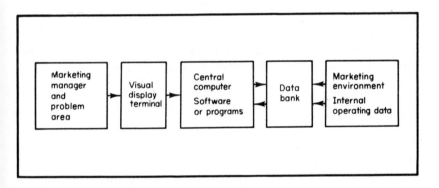

Figure 21:5   Marketing information system

With a system of this type, the marketing manager can evaluate the likely effects of a change in marketing strategy at the touch of a key or lightpen. For example, the manager could request the computer to display the current advertising-sales response curve and then feed in changed values for, say, media weights, and sit back and watch the resulting change in the nature of the response function. Similarly, a price change might be contemplated, now the manager can view the price-demand relationship that the computer has extracted from the. data bank and again evaluate a change in a basic parameter—or perhaps a change in price policy across a product line is contemplated, how important are cross-elasticities and/or substitution effects? The possibilities are enormous.

In terms, too, of understanding better the processes of buyer behaviour the computer is likely to have considerable impact. Some of the most recent attempts at modelling buyer behaviour have relied on computer simulation of customer activity—both at the micro-level of the individual consumer and in a macro, market-wide level. The developments outlined earlier in the discussion on survey analysis have enabled underlying behavioural constructs to be isolated and measured—a necessary prerequisite for a fuller understanding of consumer processes.

Some commentators have forecast a day when the majority of marketing decisions will be taken out of the province of the manager and entrusted solely to the computer. Although this may be feasible for certain routine closed-loop type operations, it is unlikely to become a general rule as long as the creative interpretation of data and consequent decision-making is a necessary part of the business activity. The computer can be an unparalleled aid in decision-making, it can present alternatives and their implications, it can produce risk profiles and sensitivity analyses—but it cannot make the decision about the kind of business the company should be in, what the missions of the company are and how they would be best achieved.

Until the computer can rival its human counterpart in its ability to make qualitative decisions—an eventuality which cannot be ruled out—there will continue to be a necessary symbiosis between man and machine.

Further reading

W. Alderson and S.J. Shapiro, *Marketing and the Computer,* Prentice-Hall, 1963.
R.G. Murdick, *Mathematical Models in Marketing,* Intext Educational Publishers, 1971.
D.B. Montgomery and G.L. Urban, *Management Science in Marketing,* Prentice-Hall, 1969.
E. Pessemier, *New Product Decisions,* McGraw-Hill, 1966.
R. Buzzell, *Mathematical Models and Marketing Management,* Harvard University Press, 1964.

22

Computers and Information:

Data Bases and Integrated Systems

G. P. Jacobs

Nowadays one has only to look through the job advertisements in the computer press to find that a large number of organisations are developing 'data bases'. Unfortunately the terminology has become rather ill-used and is a source of confusion rather than enlightenment even between professional computer specialists.

In order to be as catholic as possible, this chapter considers a data base as the store of data an organisation has collected concerning its own activities, those of its competitors and those of the marketplace. One further fact that a data base implies is that the data stored should be ordered in some way so that information can be extracted as simply as possible. Before discussing how data is stored in computer systems to facilitate both the demands for processing commercial transactions, such as sales orders, and also for efficient information retrieval, it will be useful to consider clerical filing systems to see what parallels may be found.

Simple files

Whether or not it has a computer almost every organisation stores its data in files. Even the one-man business whose owner hates paperwork usually gathers his bills together in a more or less tidy form. The larger an organisation becomes, the less possible is it for any one person to rely on his memory, and files are set up both for reasons of tidiness and for speed of communication between people.

Consider a file of customers' details held on ordinary record cards. This will frequently consist of one or more trays of cards stored in alphabetical order of customer name. Very often special header cards are used to mark the start of the section for each letter of the alphabet so that the search for any particular customer's card can be speeded up. Such a file is 'updated' for three reasons. When an existing customer orders some goods his card is extracted and altered appropriately after finding it in the alphabetically ordered list. However, when a new customer is encountered for whom no card exists a record card has to be established and then inserted into the file in the appropriate place. Finally regular and systematic pruning is carried out of records for customers who no longer do business. This merely consists of finding the record cards from the alphabetic sequence and tearing them up.

More complex files

Commonly in business one finds files like the one which has been described and there are many of them. Customer details, stock records of finished goods and raw materials, orders received, purchase orders, goods receipts and invoices are all filed in alphabetical sequence or date sequence or perhaps in a numerical code sequence. The common factor with all these files is that everything that the enquirer requires may be found in the files themselves. Joe Blogg's customer details card is in the customer details file, his order copy in the order file and so on.

But in different environments, such as libraries, one may not find the object of the search in the files themselves. One does not find a book in a library index: one finds where the book is stored. Library indices are particularly useful as models of more complex computer files because they provide for situations where the searcher does not know precisely what he wants in advance. The simplest case is an index in alphabetical title sequence. This enables the searcher with a firm requirement for a book to find it. But libraries often have indices in title and subject matter sequence as well, in order to satisfy less well-defined requirements for a particular book.

In a business environment, the same situation arises when the sales manager asks, 'Tell me which customers have spent less than £5000 on our products in the last financial year'. Without some form of indexing system this would mean examining the record of every customer and extracting the relevant ones. Indexing of customers in purchase value sequence could provide the answer to this question. In all fairness, the particular question cited could be just one of a host of similar questions which can arise spontaneously in commerce and which often cannot be anticipated long in advance. It would be quite impractical to maintain indices to cater for *every* likely question. The design of computer filing systems or data bases with, at best, the ability to handle ad hoc information requests is discussed later in this chapter.

Differences between clerical and computer files

Files in computer systems differ from those in purely clerical systems in the following respects.

1 With the exception of 'visible record' computers with magnetic ledger cards, computer system files are not so easily visible nor therefore accessible to the person or department for whose benefit they have been established.
2 The computer filing method to be chosen depends on the number and type of storage devices available in a particular installation. The availability of magnetic tapes, punched cards and the so-called random access devices like magnetic disks, magnetic drums or magnetic cards determine the options open to the file designer.
3 Computer files are usually stored in a numerical sequence rather than an alphabetical one: coding systems and computer files go hand in hand. Computers themselves lack discrimination and there is greater scope for variability in alphabetical data. A clerk would recognise that John Smith, J. Smith, J.A. Smith, Smith J.A. are one and the same person; a computer program generally will not, except at inordinate cost.
4 Because of the nature of random access devices it is possible to build and maintain far more complex file structures than is possibly convenient in clerical systems. These will be discussed in due course.

Terminology of computer filing systems

Record   A file consists of a number of independent 'records'. This terminology is consistent with the customer record cards or stock records in clerical filing systems.

Fields   A field is a constituent part of a record and every record consists of a number of fields. Typical fields on a stock record might be stock code number, item name, quantity in stock and re-order level.

The key field   This is the name given to the field by which a particular record may be identified. The key field of records on a customer file will usually be a customer's unique number, on stock item file records it will normally be the stock item number, for a file of invoice records it may be the invoice number or possibly a combination of invoice number and invoice date.

File-handling software　This is a general name given to software facilities provided normally by the computer manufacturer which gives programmers facilities to organise files, records and fields in particular ways, to update such files and to locate data held on the files. The facilities provided usually consist of offering generalised programming instructions for identifying the type of file and the functions to be performed on it. Often these instructions are identical irrespective of the hardware device on which the file is stored. This software simply saves programming time.

File updating　Updating of files consists of three independent activities. These are *insertion* (placing a new record in the correct place on a file) *amendment* (altering an existing record on a file) and *deletion* (removal from a file of a record no longer required).

Methods of computer file design

For most organisations today a data base consists of a series of independent files which, when used together, start to form an integrated control system. Although it is felt that the term 'data base' should really be limited to environments where the term 'file' has almost ceased to exist, one cannot ignore a large majority. Consequently this section is devoted to discussing the way in which computer files are commonly organised and what benefits accrue from the alternative methods.

The first five methods discussed are in common use, and are supported by software facilities from every major computer manufacturer. It is always possible for an organisation's programmers to write their own file-handling software where the manufacturer's provisions are inadequate. Nevertheless one should be wary of the computer department that insists it needs to spend a lot of time and effort in providing its own file handling facilities.

The first of the file structures to be discussed is the *only one suitable for magnetic tape or punched card storage.* All subsequent methods discussed require random access devices, such as disks, drums or magnetic cards, as the storage media. It is important that this point gets home. It is virtually impossible to build a flexible data base with swift access to comprehensive information without the computer having random access devices attached. Needless to say these devices are considerably more expensive than magnetic tape units and the tapes themselves.

Serial or sequential

These are files where records are arranged in strict serial number sequence of the key field: for example, a customer file in customer number sequence. New records have to be inserted in the correct place.

This method sounds like the equivalent of the clerical file of customers in alphabetical order but in fact it is more limited. To find customer number 470325 all records with lower customer numbers (keys) will have to be examined and discarded. To insert a new customer whose serial number is higher than any others on the file, all existing records have to be examined first to identify the precise place to slot in this new record.

Clearly this method has inefficiencies but it is the *only structure possible* for files stored on punched cards or magnetic tape. However for very large files with millions of records the expense of using random access devices may be so great that serial files on magnetic tape is the only economic option. Serial files may be used with random access devices like disks and drums.

Serial files and sorting of data go together. Insertions, amendments, and deletions all have to be sorted to the same sequence as the main file before updating. The main file itself often requires sorting into different sequences to produce management reports. A serial file is most useful where there is a high level of activity, that is, where most records are changed during updating.

Index sequential

As its name implies this method makes use both of storing records in sequential order of the key field, and of an index which makes the location of a particular record easier. The index, which the file-handling software will establish for the programmer, effectively splits the file into sub-groups of records by indicating where the first record in a group may be found. The file-handling software usually establishes a further index, which in fact is an index to the index already mentioned, in order that a particular record may be found as quickly as possible.

This filing method may be likened to a library system where books are stored on shelves in alphabetical order of author's name and title with an index which tells the name and author of the first book on each shelf. The second index may be likened to the tray cards on the front of each tray of index cards indicating (say) that that particular tray has cards for all authors between A-G. When the librarian has a new book to insert he has to find from his index cards on which shelf to store the book. Having found the right shelf he inserts the new book in the correct alphabetical sequence, moving all existing books on that shelf along to allow room for the new one.

When a reader comes along searching for a particular book a quick look at the index tray cards, the index cards themselves and the books on the appropriate shelf enables him to find his choice with short delay.

The programmer is allowed similar facilities by using index sequential file-handling software. However the enquiring mind soon says 'What happens when a shelf becomes full. If all the books have to be moved, all the index cards get out of date.' Continuing with the library analogy, index sequential file software says that the librarian is aware of the likelihood of this happening from the start, and allows extra shelves for this 'overflow' condition to avoid having to move books and change the shelf references on many of his index cards. When one more book than a shelf can hold arrives, the librarian stores it in his 'overflow' shelves and inserts in the original shelf an index card telling a potential enquirer that this book is on a particular overflow shelf.

This works adequately provided there are not too many books needing to be stored in 'overflow' shelves in which case it becomes exceedingly cumbersome both to insert new books or to find a book. Every so often when too many books are on 'overflow' shelves the librarian will have to reorganise his library and his index cards to speed up the whole process again. Reorganisation is obviously something to be avoided. In computer terms it is extremely time consuming.

Obviously it is important that the librarian, bearing in mind the average size of books, chooses shelves of such a size that he does not have to reorganise too often, nor yet have too much expensive unfilled shelf (or magnetic disk) space.

Index sequential software; including software to handle file and index reorganisation, is suitable for a wide range of batch-processing tasks and for file enquiry systems provided that the rate of insertion of new records is not high. It is not the ideal for real-time applications where the rate of receiving new records is frequently too high.

Random

Random files are useful where it is important to retrieve data with the utmost speed while having no interest in precisely how the data is sequenced. Realtime systems, where data to update or retrieve from files is often initiated from remote visual display units or teleprinters communicating over telephone lines, frequently use random files.

The records are completely unsequenced on the file. The place where the data is to be stored on the random access device is generated by a calculation, based perhaps on the key field. Normally the function of random file-handling

300

software is to provide such calculation facilities without the application programmer needing to concern himself about how it is done.

However, the 'overflow' problem of index sequential files arises here but for a different reason. It is because it is virtually impossible to perform such calculations without getting duplicates, that is, the same result yielded from two or more different key fields from different records. This 'virtually impossible' really means commercially impossible. It is possible to avoid duplicates only at the expense of allocating far more disk space to a file than can possibly be needed.

It is difficult to find a close parallel in a commercial environment to a random file, but the following imaginary situation might shed some light on the process and the problems encountered. A housing authority decides to build an estate where each of the 100 houses is of a different design yet they sell for the same price. Each potential buyer has his own 'mental formula' for selecting his house and if only ten buyers come forward it is unlikely that any two will want the same house. The nearer the number of buyers approaches the number of houses available the more likely it becomes that more than one buyer wants the same house. The authority has to decide what to do with duplicate requests and obviously first-come-first-served is one solution, the second requester having to look elsewhere. However this is handled, it may take several selections by a buyer to find a house he can have.

In the computer file the number of records (buyers) is normally known but the space to be allocated (houses to be built) is a variable to be chosen by the systems analyst (housing authority). It is equally expensive in space on backing storage as it would be to have some houses empty, in order to avoid duplicate requests.

Random file-handling software usually caters for 'overflow' situations once again without the programmer needing to concern himself with the method employed. Suffice it to say that the trade-off between waste disk space and the slow-downs caused by overflow has to be carefully considered by the systems analyst.

However, few systems can be justified without producing summary information reports for management. Random file structures are suitable for individual enquiries but not particularly suitable for reports where all, or at least a large number of, records need to be examined. It will almost invariably be necessary to spend time in sorting records from a random file into a reporting sequence, a factor which may be obviated when using other filing methods.

Direct

This is really a special case of a random file where the structure of the key field enables it to be interpreted directly as an address on a random access device without the need of a calculation and, by implication, without the possibility of duplicates arising. If an organisation is marketing 750 product lines and uses a 3 digit product code, by using a direct file with 999 product positions, considerable efficiency would be gained without wasting too much space on the random access device. On such a file, product code 325 would be stored in the 325th position, and if code 963 did not exist then the 963rd position would be wasted.

The software provided for handling such a file structure is similar, for the programmer, to that provided for random files, and most of the advantages and disadvantages of using random files apply to direct files too.

A direct file does, however, allow records to be processed sequentially as the product code example above may illustrate.

This type of organisation should be used when *existing* coding structures permit. Since changing coding structures is both a costly business and gives rise to real control problems even in clerical systems, one ought not to enter into such activities merely to get the benefits of direct file organisations.

Indexed random

This is a variation on both index sequential and random that minimises the potential wastage of disk space inherent in the random file organisation yet permits both easy file interrogation and the facility to select data sequentially.

As in index sequential, an index is maintained of key fields, but instead of indicating the start of a group, an entry in the index points directly to the area where the record is to be found. The key fields in the index are in serial order and so, by examining each key in the index in turn, and retrieving the associated record, the file may be read sequentially. Data records are scattered over the random access storage device in the order they arrive in the system, and all that is necessary to insert a new record is to determine the next available space for a record, and to insert its key in the index.

This can be compared with a librarian who decides to minimise the total shelf space for his book collection. Starting from scratch with empty shelves he puts his first purchase in the first position on his first shelf, makes out an index card with author's name, title, shelf number and shelf position, and inserts it into his index. Each new book goes alongside the last, except when the shelf becomes full then he starts a new one, but as he makes out the new index cards he files them in author's name sequence.

There are never any gaps on his shelves and so his collection minimises shelf space yet his index tells him how to find any book quickly. Clearly this is fine if a customer is looking for just one book: the index tells him precisely where to look. But if he wants ten books by the same author which the library has purchased at different times, examination of the index tells him that he has to walk to and fro across the library to find them all.

This extra effort of walking is similar to the extra activity imposed on disk reading mechanisms when indexed random files are used. They economise on space, but at the expense of time. Indexed random filing is best where files are relatively small but the time factor can easily become critical for files with a high rate of searching activity.

Getting away from files

The file structures discussed above are, for the most part, comparable to, or extensions of, files used in clerical or library systems and most computer manufacturers provide software assistance to enable programmers to handle these file structures as simply as possible. Nevertheless even with this software assistance available, a systems analyst has the function of choosing which file structure will suit his applications in the light of information requirements known at the time and guessed at for the future. There will always be some information requests in the future which cannot easily be satisfied with the file structures as designed. It is all rather inflexible. Yet this near clerical concept of filing, which has been a major factor in computer systems development in the past, still dominates the minds of many data processing managers and systems analysts today.

Clearly this is a limitation. Files are merely a means to an end—that of producing information accurately and speedily in response to requests for such information. Frequently the conventional filing structures as outlined inhibit this end as often as they satisfy it.

After all when you buy a new car you are not normally interested in the manufacturer's considerations concerning the precise thickness of the camshaft. You merely want the car to look right and give a satisfactory performance. Equally the line manager who urgently needs a report, is not desperately concerned about the gyrations the systems analysts and programmers have to go through to extract the information.

Data bases have been influenced by recent developments in hardware. First there is the ability to obtain much greater random access storage capacity much more cheaply than in the past. Second there are the advances concerned with linking computers with telecommunications equipment and the development of interactive systems where response time to enquiries is crucial. These hardware factors have not only made it possible and somewhat more economic for organisations to have their complete data bases stored on one physical storage device, but also have meant that there is a greater need to maintain data privacy and to recover quickly and safely from the occasional situations where the hardware goes haywire.

The response to these challenges is the new concept of 'data base management software'. The main purpose of this software is to remove from the data processing team the problems concerned with how and where data is stored, and to enable the data base to be changed without needing to change all programs which refer to it. The importance of this last point cannot be overemphasised. Changing conventional file contents and the programs which use these files, a fairly frequent occurrence in most installations, is a very time-consuming and thus expensive programming activity. Under the new approach programs may also be written more speedily to extract the information required. In such a context 'files' do not need to exist.

Some examples of this software such as IBM's GIS, CDC's Mark VI and Informatics Mark IV marketed by the Informatics Corporation and available for IBM 360 and 370 series, almost obviate the need for programmers altogether. They provide self-contained programming languages suitable for managers' use. In some cases, programs may be entered to a computer directly via a remote teleprinter or visual display unit. To take an example using IBM's GIS, if a sales manager wanted to know the name and address of each customer whose purchases in January 1971 were between £1000 and £2000 he could write a program as easily as the following steps indicate.

```
QUERY CUSTOMERS
WHEN VALUE BT '1000', '2000'
AND DATE BT '010171', '310171'
LIST NAME, ADDRESS
END PROCEDURE
```

Other manufacturers' software such as IBM's IMS, Honeywell-GE's IDS, ICL's DBMS and Burroughs' Disk Forte provide services to the programmer rather than immediately to the end user. Although, on the surface, this approach seems less satisfactory than that described above, greater flexibility in information handling and reporting is possible when programmers have data base languages to work with than when management-oriented language software is offered. The programmer's productivity is still much improved compared to the environment where he has to concern himself with files.

New data structures

I have said rather glibly that files do not need to exist under the new concept of data base management software. As far as the programmer and the recipient of information is concerned this is true, but clearly data has still to be structured in an ordered way to enable information to be obtained quickly. Some data base management software still makes use of the file structures discussed earlier but the use of these files is 'transparent' to the programmer. In other words the programmer can refer to data stored on several files as if it were all held on one large comprehensive 'file'. This is a major selling point of ICL's DBMS and Burroughs' Disk Forte.

Nevertheless several of the data base software packages mentioned in the previous section do store data in physically different ways and this section describes, for the more enquiring reader some of the techniques used. The main feature of conventional files is that records are completely independent. The data base software packages frequently make use of interlinked records and list structures.

Inter-linked records

There are three types of inter-linking of records commonly in use and these are known as *chains, rings* and *trees* or *hierarchies.* The common feature of each of these methods is that a record contains, as integral fields, links to other records which are either dependent on it, or which it is dependent on, or both. These link fields are commonly known as *pointers.*

Figure 22:1 shows how all sales orders for a given customer may be linked together. The 'P' in the bottom right corner of the boxes represents the pointer field from one record to another. The 'E' in the last order indicates that this is the end record in the chain.

Note that the customer record, the master record of the chain, may have two pointers both to the first and to the last record. This facility may be advantageous for updating the chain when new orders are received. If the customer record has a pointer to the last order, then a new record may be inserted after finding first the customer record, then the last order, and changing the 'E' in the last record to a 'P' pointing to where the newest order is to be held. Deletion of a record is achieved by altering the pointer of the preceding record to bypass the record which is to be deleted. At the discretion of the data base package user the sequence of the orders in the chain may be specified, for example in date of requirement sequence. This clearly has implications on updating procedures but the software handles these problems without the programmer having to think them out.

Figure 22: 2 is an example of a two-way chain where not only is the customer record linked to both the first and last order, but each order is linked both to the next and to the preceding order. This gives the facility to examine the chain both 'forwards' and 'backwards'. This allows a particular order to be found by

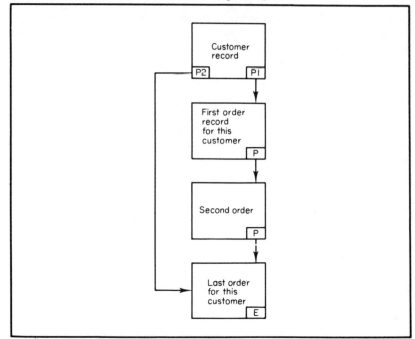

Figure 22:1   Sales order chain (one way)

which ever route happens to be the quickest way to find it, clearly important in time-critical systems.

Figure 22:3 illustrates a ring structure, in which it may be seen that up to three pointers are permitted, but once again the software normally allows its users the discretion to use only those that are required. The two main differences between rings and chains are that the ring never has an 'end', the last record always points back to the master again; and also there is the facility for every 'slave' record to point back to the master if required. The advantage to be obtained by these extra pointers is purely that of increased speed, because fewer steps are involved, in getting between one record and another. In this diagram the P1 pointers represent the 'forward' direction, the P2 pointers the backward direction and P3 pointers link each order record to its master customer record.

Figure 22:4 begins to show how these structures are really used. (To avoid too much confusion the pointers have been left out of this diagram.) Order 1 is not only linked to a customer on one ring structure, but also to two products ring structure, in other words, the order from a particular customer is for two products. One has only to let the mind dwell on this a little further to see, for example, that customer records may be linked to salesman records, to customer classification records, to accounts receivable records; product records may be

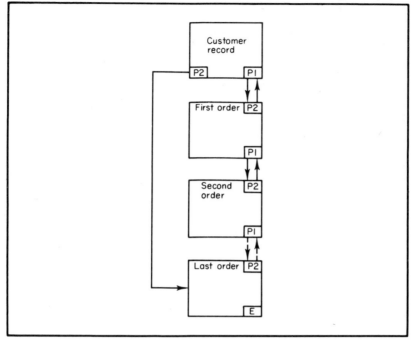

Figure 22:2 Sales order chain (two way)

linked to material records and so on. This is how these types of data structures allow information systems using them to be integrated. The data structures become reflections of an organisation's commercial activities.

Let us take a look at one common business problem in the manufacturing area which is most efficiently handled with a tree structure. This is the bill of materials problem. Finished products are often made from several levels of subassembly, and it is very common for a purchased material to be used in the production of many different products. The production process can be represented graphically to show an inverted tree structure. In Figure 22:5 the Fs represent finished products, the Ss subassemblies and the Ms materials. The numbers serve only to distinguish different items at each level.

It can be seen from these examples that even within the same finished product, one material may be used many times at different levels of assembly. For example M2 is a component of S1, S4 and S5 within product F1. The organisation manufacturing F1 and F2 will need specifications for each of F1, S1, S2, S3, S4, S5 and F2 which identify the components and the quantity of each. Counting the number of ingredients in F1 and F2 as they would appear on the specifications one needs to count each element shown on the diagram. F1 thus contains 20 ingredients and F2, 5 ingredients. But, overall, these 2 products

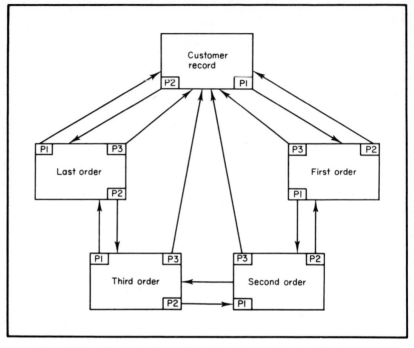

Figure 22.3   Sales order ring   with pointers forward, backward and to master

are manufactured from only 7 basic ingredients which are made up into only 5 subassemblies.

For the purpose of stock control of finished goods, subassemblies and basic materials, only 14 (=2+5+7) records are needed and probably each record would contain static and semi-static details like codes, descriptions, standard costs, economic batch size, safety stock level as well as current balances. The bill of material specifications only need pointers to the whereabouts of the ingredient records. Each record needs a further pointer which points back up the tree from ingredient to subassembly. This data structure not only permits the calculation of summary material requirements from a sales forecast but can also be used to answer questions like 'If M2 cost 10 per cent more, what would be the effect on company profit given current planned sales?'

List structures

A further data structure used in data base systems is the list structure, and usage of this method is commonly known as 'list processing'. This method involves the setup and maintenance of lists of records for selected characteristics of the data base. The entry in a list is not, however, a record itself but merely a pointer to it.

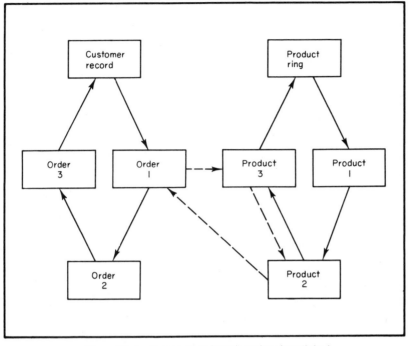

Figure 22:4   Customer and product rings interlinked

One list for example might contain pointers to all orders taken by salesman number 15, a second list might be used for all products which contain sulphuric acid and so on.

Lists may be better understood by considering a book as a data base, and its own summary index as the lists. Each separate topic or keywork in the index is equivalent to a list, and each mention of a topic is an item in the list for that topic. In a book index the list items 'point' to their data by mentioning the page numbers on which the topic occurs.

Just as in a book index, the data base list compiler has to decide precisely which lists or references should be included at the time a system is to be implemented. All lists excluded then cannot too easily be provided later, just as a book index cannot be extended after publication without a reprint.

List processing is of primary benefit for retrieving information and allows fast access to *only required data* without needing to examine the total data base. Given existing lists of (say) customers in Yorkshire, all supermarkets, all buyers of Brand X and all customers who bought in April, it is possible to extract quickly details of all supermarkets in Yorkshire who purchased Brand X in April and to summarise these details as required.

Data base software using list processing offers this facility to satisfy often

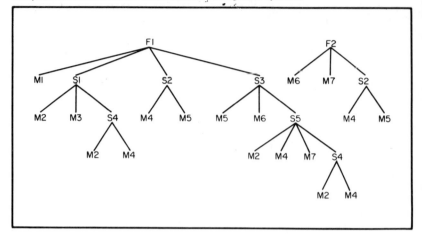

Figure 22:5 Production as a tree

complicated and ad hoc information requests quickly. The problem still remains of how many and which lists to store. The larger the number of lists, the more flexible the information requirements which may be satisfied, but the amount of disk storage required, and thus the cost, escalates rapidly. Clearly the decision on which lists should be stored is as much one for senior management as for the data processing department. The value of information has to be measured against its cost.

Using data base software today

The data base management software packages, of which several have been mentioned, offer in general the following facilities.

1 They offer 'data transparency'. Programs using the data base do not require changing when the data base structure is changed.
2 They can minimise data redundancy by using pointers. Not every record has to contain a customer number (say) if a pointer to the main customer record is used instead. Reducing redundancy can have a very significant effect in reducing the amount of disk space, and thus cost, of holding a data base.
3 They offer facilities for making selected parts of the data base available to nominated users only.
4 They have built-in facilities, or at least procedures, for reconstituting the data base in the event of corruption caused by hardware breakdowns.
5 They may allow several different users to get at and to update the data base simultaneously.

310

6 Some of the packages, notably Informatics Mark IV, reduce the necessity for employing costly programming staff.

Nevertheless in offering considerable flexibility someone has to make a decision about which facilities to use and this function usually devolves upon the data processing department which has no history of infallibility. It is vitally important for senior management to share this role.

In some cases, the flexibility is such that even the data base software designers are not aware of the potential or of the best way to use the tool they have provided. One company using Honeywell-GE's IDS in a stock-control environment found a fantastic difference in job run-time caused by what seemed like a minor decision. When they ordered a ring structure in the normal ascending stock code sequence, updating took seven hours. Reversing the sequence reduced the run time to 35 minutes. There was no information in any manual provided to indicate that this would happen. Clearly the designers had not thought of it, yet an analyst's ingenuity got the best from the software.

Lest the reader should go away believing that data base management software is a must for his organisation, now is the time to present the caveats. In many cases this software sits in the main memory of the computer while programs using the data base are being run. Such packages are frequently greedy for memory, notably IBM's IMS, and so the user will often require a much larger main memory than he would otherwise have needed for approaching his data processing in the conventional manner, Main memory is a very expensive component of a computer, though the price is decreasing with time.

Second, a considerable amount of space on disk or other random access device is necessary to store a comprehensive data base, even one where data redundancy has been minimised. Normally this puts such data packages only within the reach of the largest and most wealthy organisations.

Third, once having made the decision to install your manufacturer's data base software, do not change computer manufacturers. In the current state of the art there is not a whit of standardisation between the different packages offered.

Fourth, as virtually every package provider recommends, you must expect a further arm of your organisation to come into being, the data base management department, though this is likely to come under the general aegis of the data processing function. This new function is required to set up and maintain standards for all those using the data base. Since analysts and programmers will normally only be interested in parts of the total base at a time, someone has to be responsible for maintaining the whole structure. Although this new function may be a vital pre-requisite of the new technology, extra staff undoubtedly means extra cost.

Finally there are very few organisations in the UK who have taken the plunge into data base systems. Those that have claim to be generally happy after extensive teething problems.

Glossary

Backing store. Any device for storing data other than the computer's main memory. May be punched cards, punched paper tape, magnetic tape and all random access devices.

Batch. A collection of similar transactions in the form of source documents, punched cards or other input, or a group of records on a magnetic storage device.

Batch processing. The handling of customers' work in lots at pre-arranged times.

Batch processing applications. Suites of programs designed such that one program is run after another in order to complete a particular function.

Bit. Abbreviation of *bi*nary digi*t*. One of two digits (0 and 1) used in binary notation.

Central processing unit. The part normally regarded as 'the computer', i.e. the arithmetic unit, high-speed store and control unit as opposed to such peripheral equipment as magnetic tapes and disks, punched-card readers and printers.

Computer bureau. An organisation providing computer processing facilities, for hire, usually charged for on the basis of time used. Some computer bureaux also provide package programs, and systems and programming assistance.

Concurrent processing. Operating two or more programs on a computer simultaneously.

Control unit. The part of the central processing unit that takes instructions from the memory, interprets them and initiates appropriate action.

Data. Information consisting of numbers, alphabetical characters or symbols to be operated on by a computer program.

Data base. A file of data so structured that its contents can be used to provide input to several systems with the object of holding each basic item of data once only on file.

Data preparation. The conversion of data into a form which a computer can read automatically, as when girls read documents and operate keyboards to punch information into cards.

Data processing. Commonly refers to the use of computers for commercial or managerial—as opposed to scientific—purposes.

Dedicated A dedicated machine is one which is installed to carry out a single task, rather than for general computing purposes. Dedicated machines are often used in defence and aerospace projects. They are also used for process control, message switching and other applications.

Device. An item of equipment attached to the computer which handles input, output or the storage of data, such as a card reader, a line printer or a disk file.

Diagnostics. Programs used by computer engineers to locate faults and to test the computing equipment, or specially designed programs used to assist programmers during test runs to detect errors in their program logic.

Direct access. The ability to find data held in core storage, on magnetic disks, or on magnetic drums by using an indexing technique without the need to scan the complete data file.

Disk. A peripheral device consisting of flat circular plates coated with a magnetised material from which data can be read and to which it can be written by means of read-write heads.

Facilities management. The provision, operation and management of all activities necessary to establish a computer-based service for a customer.

File. A collection of data held on a peripheral device, such as a magnetic tape or a magnetic disk. Also data held in core storage on punched cards or on paper tape.

Front-end computer (processor). An auxiliary computer in an on-line (q.v.) system which handles the input and output of data to the main central processing unit (q.v.). The front-end processor may be local or operate as a remote terminal station.

Hardware. The electrical and mechanical equipment of a computer system.

High-level language. Statements written by a programmer are translated by a compiler into machine instructions. A high-level language consists of statements which might represent as many as 12 machine instructions. (Examples of high-level languages are COBOL, FORTRAN, PL/1.)

Indexing. A technique to determine the location of information on a disk file or in core storage.

Input. The data fed into a computer, which might be in the form of punched cards, magnetic tape, punched paper tape, or marks, letters and figures on source socuments to be read by a document reader.

Instruction set. The repertoire of operations that the central processing unit can perform given only one instruction in machine code.

Integrated system. Where several computer systems are designed to interact and work together as one system, with the subsystems dovetailed to achieve, as far as possible, continuous and automatic processing and the elimination of unnecessary duplication.

Interrogation. An enquiry into data held on computer files, usually through an on-line typewriter or a visual display unit.

Job. One execution of a program or group of programs.

Libraries. Collections of programs or computer data stored on tape or disk.

Low-level language. Statements in a low-level language generally only represent one machine instruction. (Example of a low-level language is ASSEMBLER.)

Machine code. This is the language directly understandable by the computer. All programs executed must be in machine code.

Magnetic disk store. A piece of equipment used to store data by recording it on magnetic coatings applied to the flat surfaces of a continuously rotating metal disk.

Magnetic stripe ledger card A conventional accounting machine ledger card with a strip of material attached, which can be magnetised to hold data in a similar form to magnetic tape. The data can be read from and written to the magnetic stripe by the device handling it, usually a visible record computer.

Magnetic tape. A continuous strip of plastic material, coated with a magnetic oxide on which data can be recorded as a series of magnetised spots. It is read from and written to be a magnetic tape unit which passes the tape at high speed under its read-write head. Because of its physical characteristics, data is usually written to, or read from, the magnetic tape in a logical sequence, such as in numerical order: this is termed serial processing.

Maintenance programming. The process of keeping operational computer programs up to date by making necessary minor modifications and corrections.

Memory. The part of the central processing unit that stores data and instructions. It is a type of *store.*

Model A representation of a system, problem or process in a mathematical form in which equations are used to simulate the behavior of the system, problem or process under varying conditions.

Mode. The method of operation.

Multi-processing. Simultaneous use of two or more associated processors.

Multi-programming. Sharing one processor between two or more programs on a time basis.

Off-line. (a) *of a piece of peripheral equipment:* not directly linked to a computer.

(b) *of a process:* executed by batch-processing (q.v.).

Off-lining. Transcription of input or output to intermediate temporary storage, usually disk or magnetic tape.

On-line. (a) *of a piece of peripheral equipment:* directly linked to a computer. (b) *of a process:* executed in response to data as they arrive—often over telephone or radio links.

Output. Data produced by computer processing in the form of printed stationery, magnetic disk or tape files, punched cards, punched paper tape or visual display.

Package. A program or system written to be used with little or no alteration by different organisations.

Peripheral device. An item of equipment operated under the control of the central processing unit, such as a magnetic tape unit, a disk unit, a printer or a card reader.

Print-out. Printer computer output.

Program. A list of instructions used to control a computer in the execution of a given task.

Program maintenance. A continual process of modification designed to remove errors, to introduce improvements and to adapt programs to changed requirements.

Random access device. A backing store device, which allows programmers the facility to locate and extract *any* record in a fraction of a second. The most common are magnetic drums: Magnetic card files (not punched cards) also come into this category.

Real-time. A system in which the processing of input to a procedure takes place simultaneously with the event that generates the data.

Record. A unit of data representing a single transaction; or the basic element of a file.

Register. A special store location having specific properties for use during arithmetic operations.

Remote devices. Input/output devices, such as teleprinters, which are not located in the computer room. They may be only yards away or several hundred miles away.

Remote testing. Testing of programs carried out by the computer operators, following instructions given by the programmers. In this way programs can be tested in batches, thus easing the problem of scheduling work on the computer. Also the computer operator will process work through a computer faster than the programmer. If the programmer tests his own programs it is called 'hands on' testing.

Run. A computer process in which a program is operated or several programs are operated in a predetermined sequence.

Software. Standard programs provided by the computer manufacturer to control the execution of its work, and to perform certain standard tasks, e.g. sorting data.

Software house. A service organisation which provides computer programs, either as packages or specially written, and which also provides programmers to work under the direction of a client.

Software package. The name given to a suite of programs aimed to provide an answer to a specific problem. It implies that the suite of programs may be used in any computer installation which has a similar computer to that on which the programs have been written, and which has a similar problem to solve.

Static data. Information which changes infrequently or is the same on every record in a file.

Store. Any device or medium which is capable of receiving information and retaining it, and which allows the information to be retrieved and used when required.

Store location. Any part of a computer store that is capable of holding a unit of information.

Stream. Succession of jobs.

Suite. A number of interrelated programs.

Symbolic language. A programmer writes his program in a symbolic language (e.g. COBOL, FORTRAN) as a series of statements. These statements represent instructions which, when processed by a program compiler, are translated into machine code.

System. A set of computer programs designed and written to carry out a process or procedure (such as payroll or sales accounting); also used to describe a hardware configuration.

Systems analysis. The work of analysing problems and procedures and of reviewing methods used with the object of designing computer processes to solve, replace or supplement them.

System generation. Generation of an operating system to incorporate only those facilities provided by the manufacturer that are specifically required by that user.

Tape. Magnetic or punched paper tape used for holding data in a form acceptable to a computer.

Teleprocessing. The transfer of computer data between locations via a telephone network.

Terminal. A peripheral device, similar to a typewriter, which is normally adapted to enable it to communicate data and receive output data.

Updating. The process of keeping data up to date.

User programs. Programs writtem by the computer user to solve specific problems (e.g. payroll program).

Utility programs. Programs provided usually by computer manufacturers to perform basic functions, e.g. listing cards, printing out the contents of tapes, disks etc.

Variable data. Information which is frequently changed or differs from record to record.

Visual display. A device that displays a set of information, usually on a cathcode ray tube, in the form of characters, figures, graphs or drawings.

Visual record computer. A small computer which is able to print on ledger cards.

Word. A basic unit of data in a computer memory. The unit consists of a predetermined number of characters or bits to be processed as a whole.

Index